International's Series in

ECONOMICS

Regional
Economic Growth:
Theory and Policy

Regional Economic Growth:
Theory and Policy

HORST SIEBERT

Assistant Professor of Economics
Texas A & M University

INTERNATIONAL TEXTBOOK COMPANY
Scranton, Pennsylvania

Standard Book Number 7002 2231 6

To Christa

Preface

In the past twenty years the theory of development has become a core field of economics. This is illustrated both by the immense literature on the problems of underdevelopment and by the construction of a series of growth models by Domar, Duesenberry, Joan Robinson, Solow, Kaldor, and Arrow. However, all these models, with skilled use of the tradition of mathematical sophistication, yield solutions for point economies and ignore the spatial aspect of economic growth. Yet growth occurs in space; it is influenced by the spatial structure and it has a feedback upon the economic landscape. It is the aim of this book to introduce the space dimension into growth theory and to analyze how spatial subunits of national economies behave over time, to study the determinants of their expansion and to explain the interaction between the growth processes in the regions of a national economy.

The problems of regional economic growth are equally relevant to developed economies as well as to underdeveloped nations. In developed countries, depressed areas exist which lag behind the national growth rate. These regions are of concern to the policy maker due to their low income, lack of capital, shortage of skilled labor, and scarcity of entrepreneurial quality. Concomitantly, developed countries experience the phenomenon of overagglomeration requiring government interference. In developing nations the spatial aspect of growth is also of utmost importance. How to allocate the scarce resources among different regions, which strategy to follow for economic development, and how to prevent a spatially dual economy are some of the problems with which the regional planner is faced. In all these cases the policy maker has to take action relying only too often on a rule of thumb. It is the modest object of this study to increase the insight into the process of regional economic development and to provide some information for the policy maker.

Chapters 3 and 5 are a revised form of my publication *Zur Theorie des regionalen Wirtschaftswachstums*, J. C. B. Mohr (Paul Siebeck), Tübingen, 1967. Some of the concepts in Chapters 4, 6, and 7 are also based on this publication. I am grateful to the publisher for releasing this material. I am indebted to Professor Hans K. Schneider for arousing my interest in regional science and for his criticism of an earlier draft, as well as to Professor Walther G. Hoffmann for helpful comments. Also I would like to express my sincere thanks to John Friedmann for his encouragement during the preparation of this book. Finally, I am grateful to my graduate students at Texas A & M University whose response, criticism, and discussion have improved the manuscript.

                                                                                    H. S.

March 1969

Contents

chapter 1   Introduction . . . 1

    A. The Problem of Regional Economics
    B. Regional Economic Growth
    C. Approach of the Study

**PART I   GROWTH IN A CLOSED REGION: THE INTERNAL
            DETERMINANTS**

chapter 2   The Region as an Element of Spatial Structure . . . 11

    A. The Spatial Distribution of Economic Activities
    B. The Delineation of Regions
       Problems

chapter 3   Analysis of Internal Growth Determinants . . . 24

    A. Determinants of Potential Output: The Supply Side
    B. Determinants of Actual Regional Output: The Demand Side
       Problems

**PART II   GROWTH IN AN OPEN REGION: THE EXTERNAL
            DETERMINANTS**

chapter 4   Expansion Effects of Interregional Factor Movements . . . 49

    A. The Relevance of External Determinants for Regional
       Growth Analysis
    B. Mobility of Labor
    C. Mobility of Capital
    D. Mobility of Technical Knowledge

E. Mobility of Consumption Goods as a Substitute for Factor Mobility
    Problems

chapter 5   Expansion Effects of Interregional Commodity
              Movements . . . 84

A. Allocation Gains Through Reductions of Interregional
    Trade Barriers
B. Expansion Effects of Increases in Interregional Demand
C. Expansion Effects Through Variations in the Interregional Terms
    of Trade
D. Review of Interregional Interactions and Their Expansion
    Effects
    Problems

PART III   THE COMBINATION OF INTERNAL AND EXTERNAL GROWTH
           DETERMINANTS

chapter 6   Formal Structure of the Model . . . 119

A. A General System of Equations
B. The Treatment of External Economies
C. A Specific Two-Region Model
    Problems

chapter 7   Implications of the Model: Theorems on Regional Growth
              Differentials . . . 132

A. The Relation Between Interregional Income Differences and Growth
    Differentials
B. Implications on Growth Differentials: The Specific Model
C. Implications on Growth Differentials: The General Framework
D. Further Implications on Growth Differentials: Leveling Effects
E. Open Questions
    Problems

PART IV   REGIONAL GROWTH POLICY

chapter 8   Goal Relations of Regional and National Growth
              Policy . . . 159

A. The Decision Structure of a Policy Problem
B. Possible Relations Between Goals
C. Goal Relations Between the Growth Policies of
    Different Regions

D. Compatability and Conflict Between Regional and
National Growth Policies
E. Preventing Widely Divergent Interregional Income
Differences
Problems

chapter 9   Instruments for Regional Growth Policy . . . 176

A. Explication Models and Decision Models for Instrument Selection
B. Decision Criteria and Strategies
C. A Survey of the Instrument Variables
Problems

Selected Bibliography . . . 203

Glossary of Most Frequently Used Symbols . . . 207

Index   . . . 209

chapter **1**

Introduction

A. THE PROBLEM OF REGIONAL ECONOMICS

Regional economics is the study of man's economic behavior in space. It analyzes economic processes in a spatial setting and inquires into the structure of the economic landscape. Traditional theory has long ignored this spatial aspect of economic behavior. The classical models and the reasoning behind them were based on the assumption of "one-point" economies without any spatial dimension. The core questions of economic analysis—what to produce, how to produce, for whom to produce—were analyzed for a world in which no distance, no transportation costs, and no other friction of space existed. It is the challenge of regional economics that our knowledge about economic phenomena can be substantially increased if space is introduced as an additional variable into the framework of economic theory. The explicit consideration of the dimension of space leads to the following five main problem areas of regional economics.

The first branch is concerned with the determination of the economic landscape, i.e., the distribution of economic activities over space.[1] Which factors influence the location of individual activities? How can we explain the distribution of agricultural production over a plane? Which hypotheses are relevant to determine the location of a specific firm, an industry, the industrial and tertiary sector? Which models are able to diagnose the spatial behavior of residential location? In addition to the consideration of partial models of micro location theory, regional economics explores the macro aspect of location analysis. It seeks to find the overall result of a numerous series of individual location decisions. What structure of the economic landscape is generated by partial models? How can partial location theories be integrated into a general system? How can we account for the fact that an economy is characterized by agricultural and

---

[1]On location theory: H. O. Nourse, *Regional Economics,* McGraw-Hill, New York, 1968, Chaps. 3–5; W. Isard, *Location and Space Economy,* M.I.T. Press, Cambridge, Mass., 1956; M. L. Greenhut, *Plant Location in Theory and Practise,* U. of North Carolina Press, Chapel Hill, 1956; E. M. Hoover, *The Location of Economic Activity,* McGraw-Hill, New York, 1956.

industrial belts and agglomerations of population? What is the interdependence between individual location decisions? Are there any regularities in the systems of cities of an economy? How can we explain these regularities? All these questions relate to the first main problem of regional economics, namely, the determination of the economic landscape.

A second major issue of regional economics emerges from the introduction of a new category into theoretical analysis—the concept of the region. The region here is defined as a spatial subsystem of the national economy. The introduction of this new concept leads to the delineation of spatial subsystems and the measurement of their economic activities. What criteria have been developed to delimit a region? What type of accounting systems[2] do we have to use to record the transactions between the different sectors of the regional economy? Are regional accounting systems a blueprint of already existing national accounting frameworks? Should we use aggregated systems including such sectors as households, business, government, and the external account? Or is it more fruitful to disaggregate the business sector in the form of an input-output table? All these questions relate either to the definitional problem of delimiting the region or to accounting identities as an instrument for a systematic collection of information on the performance of a regional system. At no stage of the discussion are hypotheses introduced. A hypothesis tries to explain reality, but neither the definition of the region nor the measurement of its activity have the characteristics of explanation. Consequently neither question is part of regional theory— if theory is interpreted in the strict sense as a system of testable hypotheses—yet each represents an important prerequisite for regional theory.

Once the region has been defined and its activity has been measured, the third problem of regional economics is to analyze the interaction between regions. Two basic forms of interregional interaction may be distinguished: the movement of factors of production and the exchange of commodities. The explanation of why these movements of factors and commodities occur and how they affect the economic activity of a region is central to the study of regional economic problems. Here the following questions are asked: What are the reasons for a factor of production to move to another area? What determinants influence the interregional mobility of factors of production? This phase also seeks to find under what conditions an exchange of commodities between regions takes place, and explores analogies to international trade that can be used to explain this interregional commodity exchange. Other questions include: Which models other than international trade theory are available to explain the interaction between regions? Can input-output models determine the interregional commodity exchange? How does a business cycle in the national economy affect the different subunits of the nation? If there is an economic expansion in one area,

---

[2]W. Z. Hirsch (ed.), *Elements of Regional Accounts,* Johns Hopkins Press, Baltimore, Md., 1964; W. Z. Hirsch (ed.), *Regional Accounts for Policy Decisions,* Johns Hopkins Press, Baltimore, Md., 1966; W. Hochwald (ed.), *Design of Regional Accounts,* Johns Hopkins Press, Baltimore, Md., 1961.

what effects will this have on the economic activities of another region? Can we explain the economic activity of a national economy as the result of inter-acting regional systems?

All these aspects lead into the fourth branch of regional economics which is interregional optimum or equilibrium analysis. Models of this type try to determine some sort of an optimum for an economic system in a spatial setting.[3] Since an optimum is always defined with respect to an objective, optimum analysis requires the introduction of at least one goal into the analysis. Once a goal, such as the pareto-optimal allocation of resources or the minimization of a factor input is given, the following questions are put forward: What are the optimal transport flows between different points in space? What are the optimal locations for different economic activities? What are the optimal production levels of different activities at different points in space? What is the optimal specialization of regional production, and what is the optimal exchange of commodities between regions? How can we determine a pareto optimum in a spatial setting? Which optimizing methods are available to specify these optimum conditions? As can be seen from these questions, interregional equilibrium analysis is related to the study of the economic landscape and of interregional interaction. It differs from these problems in that it does not attempt to explain reality but to specify optimal patterns of production, location, and trade. Moreover, it represents an integration of location analysis and the study of interregional exchange. Finally, optimum analysis may be regarded as the discussion of the implications of certain goals. It is therefore a link to the fifth problem of regional economics, namely, regional policy.

Whereas regional theory is the explanation of economic behavior in space, regional economic policy may be defined as the set of those activities which attempt to influence economic behavior in a spatial setting. Regional economic policy controls economic processes and structures in subsystems of the national economy. Here the following questions arise: What are the objectives of regional policy? How are these objectives determined? How are they interrelated to national policy goals? What is the optimal mix of policy instruments if a specific goal is to be reached? What decision models are available that make possible the choice of the best instruments with respect to specific goals?

B. REGIONAL ECONOMIC GROWTH

Regional economic growth is the sustained increase in the volume of an economic variable of a spatial subsystem of a nation.[4] The term will be used inter-

---

[3] L. N. Moses, "A General Equilibrium Model of Production, Interregional Trade and the Location of Industry," *Review of Economics and Statistics,* Vol. 42 (1960), pp. 373–399; L. Lefeber, *Allocation in Space: Production, Transport and Industrial Location,* North Holland, Amsterdam, 1958.

[4] S. Kuznets, "On Comparative Study of Economic Structure and Growth of Nations," *The Comparative Study of Economic Growth and Structure,* National Bureau of Economic Research, New York, 1959, p. 162.

changeably with development and expansion. The following variables may be chosen as indicators of economic growth.

Growth may be defined as an increase in the welfare of a region.[5] This definition presupposes that a concept of total welfare can be meaningfully defined.[6] Because the problem of measuring total welfare by interpersonal comparison has not yet been solved, and because intertemporal comparisons of welfare situations are inconclusive due to changes in the preference patterns, this approach to the definition of growth cannot be followed.

Growth is here understood as an increase in the output of a region. The term may refer either to the productive capacity or to the actual volume of production[7] in the region. This concept emphasizes the increase in output which is produced by the factors of production that are employed in an area. This means that for the measurement of output, the area concept[8] of income estimation is applied. All the final commodities produced by the factors of production available in the region will be included in regional output, even if some factors may be owned by residents of other areas. A related approach could view growth as the change in income accruing to the residents of an area. This definition is based on the residents concept[9] where factor payments made to other areas are substracted from regional product and incoming factor payments are added. Thus wages for out-commuting labor are included and wages paid for in-commuting labor are excluded. Similarly, received dividends and interest payments are a component of regional income, whereas outgoing dividends and interest payments are not included. In our abstract model, however, no commuters exist and interregional payments for the use of external capital will only be introduced at a later stage.

Economic growth may also be defined as the increase in the set of final commodities which are available to the region.[10] This concept takes into account the effects of trade on the availability of commodities as the supply of final goods may be increased through the exchange between regions. This definition will also be used.

All five problem areas of regional economics closely relate to the study of regional economic growth. Regional growth theory, which analyzes how growth occurs in a spatial setting, uses the region as its basic category. Consequently,

[5]M. Abramovitz, "The Welfare Interpretation of Secular Trends in National Income and Product," in M. Abramovitz (ed.), *The Allocation of Economic Resources, Essays in Honor of B. F. Haley,* Stanford U. P., Stanford, Calif., 1959.

[6]Compare G. W. Nutter, "On Measuring Economic Growth," *Journal of Political Economy,* Vol. 65 (1957), pp. 51–53.

[7]G. Jaszi, "The Measurement of Aggregate Economic Growth," *Review of Economics and Statistics,* Vol. 63 (1961), pp. 317–332.

[8]R. Ruggles and N. D. Ruggles, "Regional Breakdowns of National Economic Accounts," in W. Hochwald, (ed.), *Design of Regional Accounts,* Johns Hopkins Press, Baltimore, Md., 1961, pp. 135–136.

[9]*Ibid.*

[10]Nutter, *op. cit.*

the delineation of the subsystems of the national economy is a prerequisite for regional development theory. Also the problem of how to measure the increase in the economic activity of the region has to be solved. More important, regional growth theory has to analyze the region as an open economic system, being interrelated to other areas via the movement of factors of production and exchange of commodities. Therefore the following questions have to be answered: In which way does the economic expansion of an area influence growth in another region? Does development in one region increase export demand for the other region and thus induce development there, or does the economic expansion of one area withdraw factors of production from other regions, thus reducing the level of economic activity in the other area? What are the interrelations between regional and national growth? These problems show that a regional growth theory must also be a study of interregional interactions.

Regional expansion is also connected with changes in the economic landscape. In the process of economic growth shifts in demand occur, new resources are discovered, the transportation system is improved, production costs are reduced, and factor intensities change due to new production possibilities and different growth rates of the factors of production. All these events force the individual entrepreneur to reconsider his location and may very well lead to a relocation of resources in space. Thus the economic landscape is the result of economic growth. On the other hand, it is also one of the important determinants of economic development. The growth rate of a region depends on the allocation of resources in space at a certain moment of time, and it is therefore strongly influenced by the individual location decisions. Consequently regional growth theory has to take into account the analysis of the economic landscape.

Finally the study of regional growth is linked to optimum analysis and regional policy: The conditions of the pareto optimum in space may be interpreted as a goal system of regional policy, and optimum analysis can be used to determine optimal regional growth paths over time. The policy aspect of regional growth relates to such problems as: What instrument or which combination of policy measures should be used to increase the rate of growth of a region or a system of regions? What alternative strategies are available for regional growth policy? Which government measures should be used to induce expansion of underdeveloped areas in a developed national economy? Which measures can be undertaken to prevent overagglomeration?

C. APPROACH OF THE STUDY

Regional growth theory requires the explicit introduction of two fundamental dimensions—time and space. The time dimension was successfully brought into economic theory with the release of Keynes' assumption of a constant production capacity. Model building in the field of growth theory of national economies continues to achieve high levels of theoretical sophistication, including the empirical application of rather abstract models.[11] Independent of these striking developments in dynamic analysis was the introduction of the spatial dimension, mainly through the work of Walter Isard[12] in the late 1950's. These two theoretical innovations, however, failed to be integrated. Growth theory formulated its models for a wonderland of no spatial dimension,[13] and regional science did not bother to introduce the time dimension. The present study tries to draw upon both approaches.

In this endeavor we are confronted with a basic dilemma. On the one hand, regional economics has not yet produced satisfactory macroconcepts of the static structure of space—not to mention a dynamic analysis of the spatial dimension—so that only an attempt can be made to combine the space dimension with a dynamic analysis. On the other hand, we still do not have a theory of expansion of a simplified point economy which has been sufficiently tested empirically. Therefore our study is to be understood as a contribution to model building without any attempts to empirically test the relationships involved. It is intended as a possibility analysis—as a first step in the direction of explaining a phenomenon of reality. Similarly, just as a detective starts out with a list of the possible culprits in a murder case and analyzes each suspect carefully, we construct a framework of conceivable growth determinants and postulate hypotheses on their behavior and their effects on regional output. The resulting model, defined by a set of hypotheses and identity equations, will be useful for the explanation of regional economic growth.

The study is organized in four distinct parts. The first three parts relate to regional growth theory. They explain regional development without any government activity. The last part deals with the policy aspect and explicitly takes government activity and its influence on regional growth into account. In Part I a concept of the economic landscape is developed as a starting point for regional growth analysis. The region, as a unit of the structure of space, is introduced and the criteria used for its delineation discussed. We also analyze the expansion possibilities of a closed region and study the internal determinants of economic growth and their effects on regional output and the spatial structure.

In Part II the assumption of a closed region is released and the external determinants of regional development considered. The basic theme of this part is the interaction between two regions in the form of interregional factor and commodity movements. The interregional mobility of labor, capital, and technical knowledge is discussed. We also examine what expansion effects may be caused by the interregional exchange of commodities.

[11]Compare, for instance, the discussion of the embodiment effect of technical knowledge, R. B. Nelson, "Aggregate Production Functions and Medium-Range Growth Projections," *American Economic Review,* Vol. 54 (1964), pp. 575–606.

[12]W. Isard, *Location and Space-Economy,* W. Isard, *Methods of Regional Analysis: An Introduction to Regional Science,* M. I. T. Press, Cambridge, Mass, 1966.

[13]W. Isard, *Location and Space-Economy,* p. 25.

Part III combines the analysis of internal and external determinants of growth and organizes the hypotheses from the first two parts into a general framework. With the help of this framework and a specific two-region model, the problem of regional growth differentials is analyzed and conditions for the existence of differences in the regional growth rates are derived. The discussion of these conditions yields implications for regional policy.

Finally, Part IV introduces government activity and analyzes the policy aspect of regional growth. In this part we discuss the goal system of regional policy and the interrelation of the goals of the growth policies for regions and the nation. We also investigate the strategies to be followed and the instruments to be used if the objectives of regional policy are to be attained.

part I

GROWTH IN A CLOSED REGION: THE INTERNAL DETERMINANTS

chapter **2**

The Region as an Element
of Spatial Structure

Economic activities take place not only in periods of time but also in a spatial setting, so that a model of regional growth must introduce not only the time dimension but also the concept of space. All variables of the growth model have to be characterized by an indicator of space as well as a time index. Such a spatial characterization of the variables becomes necessary if we wish to answer the problem of how the spatial structure influences regional economic growth and how growth affects the economic landscape. We, therefore, need concepts of the structure of the economic landscape—namely, the distribution of economic activities in space.

A. THE SPATIAL DISTRIBUTION OF ECONOMIC ACTIVITIES

1. The area of an economy may be thought of as consisting of a finite number of spatial points. Each spatial point represents a unit of spatial extension—for instance, a square mile. The spatial points may also be defined as location units. In order to be able to use this second approach we must introduce three simplifying assumptions. First, all economic activities are of the same spatial size. Thus we assume that agricultural, industrial, tertiary, and residential activities all require the same amount of space. This assumption becomes more realistic if we interpret an industrial or household unit as consisting of a set of industries or households. Second, capital in our economy cannot be used as a substitute for land. This implies that the supply of all types of land, such as land used for office space or industrial production, cannot be increased by using capital for building into the air or going underground. Only one-story buildings are considered. Third, the land requirements for the transportation sector are negligible. This implies that we do not have to quibble about the location of the transport activities. With these three assumptions, the spatial points of the economy are identical to the location units for the different economic activities. They represent a unit measure of spatial extension which denotes the average spatial re-

11

quirement of all activities. This average spatial requirement may of course be greater or less than a square mile.

A given two-dimensional Euclidean space can be broken down into a set of location units by superimposing a grid system on the geographic area, as shown in Fig. 2-1.

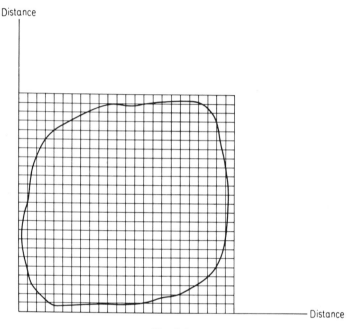

Fig. 2-1

Each element a of the grid system, which is an area in reality, represents a spatial point. The spatial points may be treated as having no distance. However, distance between different elements of the grid system is taken into account.

Using the first subscript to indicate the rows and the second subscript to denote the columns, all elements a with the first subscript 1 represent spatial points in the first row—the northern part of the economy. If there are n spatial points in each row and in each column and if each element of the grid system is matched by a spatial point in reality, the economy consists of n^2 spatial points. It is defined by the finite set A.

$$A = \left\{ a/a_{11}, \ldots, a_{1n}; a_{21}, \ldots, a_{2n}; \ldots; a_{n1}, \ldots, a_{nn} \right\} \quad (2\text{-}1)$$

The subscripts indicate the geographic position or neighborhood of individual elements. Different types of economic activities take place in the space defined by set A. We may distinguish production and consumption activities. Consumption activities consist of using space for residential purposes. Production activities can be divided into the agricultural, industrial, and tertiary sectors. The distribution of all these types of activities over all the elements of set A yields the economic landscape. Because we assume that each spatial point will have only one type of activity[1] with each unit of different activities requiring the same amount of space, it follows that only as many units of activities are possible as spatial points are available.

2. Set A in Eq. 2-1 is the possibility set for the location of economic activities. Each activity has to choose one element of set A as its locational point. This decision can be represented as the intersection of two sets.[2] Let set Q denote all the locational characteristics $(r_1, r_2, \ldots, r_m)$ of all spatial points a_{11}, $\ldots, a_{nn}$. The subscripts $a_{11}, \ldots, a_{nn}$ indicate the spatial points where the characteristics are given. Then set Q is defined as

$$Q = \left\{(r_1, r_2, \ldots, r_m)_{a_{11}} \cdots (r_1, r_2, \ldots, r_m)_{a_{nn}}\right\} \qquad (2\text{-}2)$$

Let there be an activity u_1 which has to make a location decision. The spatial point chosen as the location point must meet the locational requirements of activity u_1. These locational requirements $r_1^*, r_2^*, \ldots, r_m^*$ represent the minimum values of spatial characteristics which must be met for a firm to locate at a spatial point. They are defined by set

$$R_{u_1} = (r_1^*, r_2^*, \ldots, r_m^*)_{u_1} \qquad (2\text{-}3)$$

The intersection of sets R and Q yields set L which represents the spatial point chosen as a location by activity u_1.

$$R_{u_1} \cap Q = L_{u_1} \qquad (2\text{-}4)$$

---

[1] Let the area of a spatial point be large enough to comprise exactly one agricultural firm of average size. Let a household and a business unit consist of a set of individual households or business firms also requiring the area of one spatial point. Then a spatial point may actually be occupied by more than one type of activity. In this case, similar problems arise as in the sectoring of an economy. The spatial point should be attributed to that activity which in terms of some criterion is the main activity. The smaller we choose the area of the spatial point, the easier it is to attribute economic activities to the spatial points.

[2] On set theory: P. Suppes, *Axiomatic Set Theory*, Van Nostrand, Princeton, N. J., 1965; B. Rotman and B. T. Keebone, *The Theory of Sets and Transfinite Numbers*, Oldbourne, London, 1966. Compare H. Siebert, "Die Anwendung der Mengentheorie für die Abgrenzung von Regionen," *Jahrbuch für Sozialwissenschaft*, Vol. 18 (1967), pp. 215–222.

The procedure may also be presented in matrix notation: Compare H. K. Schneider, "Über einige Probleme und Methoden regionaler Analyse und Prognose," *Regionalplanung, Beiträge und Untersuchungen*, Institut für Siedlungs-und Wohnungswesen, Bd. 63, Münster 1966, p. 10. According to Schneider, let Q represent a matrix of locational characteristics, where the columns indicate the m characteristics and the rows denote r spatial points. A "1" element indicates that certain locational characteristics are given at a spatial point. "0" elements denote the lack of these characteristics. Let R represent the requirement matrix of n firms for m locational characteristics. "1" elements indicate the demand for locational requirements by specific firms. The multiplication of the two sets leads to a set L which gives the locations of all firms:

$$Q_{(rm)} R_{(mn)} = L_{(rn)}$$

The subscripts indicate the dimensions of the matrices.

From the definition of intersection and from the fact that the locational requirements will normally not be fulfilled at all spatial points, it follows that L_{u_1} is a subset of A. If the locational requirements are stated in a very loose fashion, L will represent a possibility set, having more than one element, for the location of the activity u_1. Some elements of this possibility set will be eliminated if we specify the requirements in a more rigorous fashion. If the solution set L_{u_1} has more than one element after the specification of all locational requirements, additional information is necessary to determine the actual location.

3. The requirement set may refer not only to one activity but to all firms of an industry, to all industries, or to all k economic activities. From the condition that at a spatial point only one economic activity can take place, it follows that $k \leqslant n^2$. The inequality sign indicates the case in which some spatial points have no economic activity. If $k > n^2$, we would have more activities than could be operated in the given space.

If there are k activities, the locational requirements for these k activities must be specified. Thus we need a greater amount of information than in the case of a single firm. For the k activities the requirement set reads

$$R_{u_1 \ldots k} = \left\{ (r_1^*, \ldots, r_m^*)_{u_1} \ldots (r_1^*, \ldots, r_m^*)_{u_k} \right\} \qquad (2\text{-}5)$$

The intersection of sets 2-2 and 2-5 yields set $L_{u_1 \ldots k}$ which—in the case of one solution for each activity—represents the spatial distribution of all activities

$$R_{u_1 \ldots k} \cap Q = L_{u_1 \ldots k} \qquad (2\text{-}6)$$

4. Operation 2-6 is only a starting point for the determination of the economic landscape. The problem is that the elements of set Q are not independent of the operation of intersection. The locational characteristics of set Q change as soon as activity u_1 has made a location decision. Nearness to firm u_1 may, for instance, be a prerequisite for firm 2. Or the existence of a firm u_1 at a spatial point may prevent another firm from locating near this spatial point.

A model has to be used to specify the interdependence between the locational characteristics of any spatial point and the location decision of activities. One approach to the solution of this problem is to use a simulation model[3] which takes into account the effects of the location decision of any firm on the set of locational characteristics.

The basic structure of such a model is shown in Fig. 2-2 in which only four activities are assumed. The figure illustrates the interdependence of location decisions; the locational choice of activity 2 may have a feedback effect on the

---

[3] On simulation: G. P. E. Clarkson and H. A. Simon, "Simulation of Individual and Group Behavior," *American Economic Review,* Vol. 50 (1960), pp. 920–932; E. P. Holland, *Experiments on a Simulated Underdeveloped Economy,* M. I. T. Press, Cambridge, Mass., 1963; G. H. Orcutt, "Simulation of Economic Systems," *American Economic Review,* Vol. 50 (1960), pp. 893–907; R. L. Morrill, "The Development of Towns in Sweden: The Historical-Predictive Approach," in J. Friedman and W. Alonso (eds.), *Regional Development and Planning—A Reader* M. I. T. Press, Cambridge, Mass., 1964, pp. 173–186.

situs of activity 1. Similarly, the location of each previously determined activity has to be changed because of these feedback effects.

The four different activities of Fig. 2-2 may be understood as agricultural, industrial, and tertiary production, and residential activities. In this interpretation Fig. 2-2 outlines the problems of integrating existing partial-location theories into a general framework for the explanation of the economic landscape.

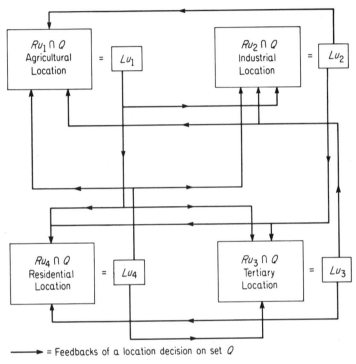

$\longrightarrow$ = Feedbacks of a location decision on set Q

Fig. 2-2. Interdependence of location decisions.

Let the first box represent agricultural-location decisions. Neglect all other types of activities. A von Thünen[4] model can be used to determine the distribution of agricultural activities over set A. According to von Boeventer,[5] "a system of Thünen rings will develop around the population centers." Crops with a lower yield per acre and a lower price in the market will be cultivated farther away from the center. Given the distribution of agricultural activities, a maxi-

[4] E. S. Dunn, *The Location of Agricultural Production*. U. of Florida Press, Gainesville, 1954; B. H. Stevens, "Location Theory and Programming Models: The von Thünen Case," *Papers and Proceedings of the Regional Science Association* (forthcoming).
[5] E. von Boeventer, "Towards a United Theory of Spatial Economic Structure," *Papers and Proceedings of the Regional Science Association,* Vol. 10 (1962), pp. 163–187.

mum-profit approach[6] may be used to determine the location of the industrial sector. The spatial distribution of the industrial sector depends on revenue and cost aspects and thus on the distribution of demand, of factors of production over space, and the magnitude of production and transportation costs for different spatial points.

The tertiary sector services the primary and secondary sectors. Consequently its location depends on the spatial distribution of the primary and secondary activities. As a final step, the distribution of residential activities is determined yielding a hierarchical order of central places.[7]

The economic landscape which is generated by these four partial models of location is inconsistent within itself because the feedback effects of a locational choice on the previous decisions are not taken into consideration. For instance, the distribution of residential activities influences the location of the other sectors via the demand side. The location of industry will have a feedback on agricultural location. Thus in the second round the feedback effects will lead to a revision of the original partial-location decisions. A simulation model would include these feedback effects and generate the economic landscape from a set of partial theories after a series of runs. The result of such an integration of partial-location theories is to partition set A into subsets which contain the spatial distribution of agricultural (u_1), industrial (u_2), tertiary (u_3), and residential activities (u_4).

$$A = \left\{ L_{u_1}, L_{u_2}, L_{u_3}, L_{u_4} \right\} \tag{2-7}$$

B. THE DELINEATION OF REGIONS

1. The subsets of Eq. 2-7 denote the spatial distribution of a specific activity over the total economy defined by set A. The spatial points included in these subsets are not necessarily geographically contiguous. Consequently other subsets of A may be constructed which are characterized by geographically adjoining spatial points. These subsets are called *regions*. The concept of a region is an intermediate category between an aggregate economy with no spatial dimension and a highly disaggregated economic system defined as a set of spatial points. The region is not as disaggregated as a set of spatial points and therefore allows a simplification in the analysis of spatial structure and of economic processes in space. On the other hand, it is not as aggregated as a national point economy without any spatial dimension. The new concept is an in-between category similar to the sector, which makes possible some aggregation of the

---

[6]M. L. Greenhut, *Plant Location in Theory and Practise*, U. of North Carolina Press, Chapel Hill, 1956; W. Isard, *Location and Space Economy*, M. I. T. Press, Cambridge, Mass., 1956.

[7]B. J. L. Berry and A. Pred, *Central Place Studies: A Bibliography of Theories* and *Applications*, Regional Science Research Institute, Bibliography Series No. 1, Philadelphia, Pa., 1961.

multitude of individual firms without requiring a complete aggregation into a national economic system.

2. The delineation of regions is identical to the definition of subsets of the universe A. The subsets of set A are constructed by the axiom scheme of separation. For subset I we have

$$\underset{I\,a}{\vee\wedge}\ (a \in I \longleftrightarrow a \in A \wedge f(a)) \tag{2-8}$$

This axiom scheme is to be read[8] as follows: There is a subset I, so that for all spatial points a: a is an element of the subset I, if and only if a is an element of A and if a is a bound variable. The axiom scheme of separation "permits us to separate off the elements of a given set which satisfy some property and form the set consisting of just these elements."[9]

If we want to delimit region I, we have to specify the property which distinguishes some elements of A from other elements of A. We can designate the subset I by substituting a definite formula for $f(a)$. Thus we have to find a function which relates each element a to another variable or a constant.

In order to simplify the presentation, let the economy A consist of two regions only. The two regions I and II are subsets of A.

$$A \supset \text{I} \qquad A \supset \text{II} \tag{2-9}$$

The union of the two subsets I and II yields A.

$$\text{I} \cup \text{II} = A \tag{2-10}$$

The regions must be delineated in such a way that each spatial point is a member of only one subset. No spatial point should be an element of both subsets. Hence the formula $f(a)$ must be chosen in such a way that

$$\text{I} \cap \text{II} = \phi \tag{2-11}$$

where ϕ denotes an empty set.

A delimitation of the form shown in Fig. 2-3 is not allowed. In this case the intersection of I and II will not yield an empty set—implying that certain

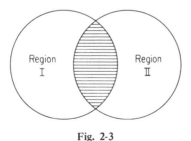

Fig. 2-3

spatial points are elements of both subsets. If condition 2-11 is fulfilled, I and II are disjoint sets,

$$I = \{a/a_{11}, \ldots, a_k\} \tag{2-12}$$

$$II = \{a/a_{k+1}, \ldots, a_{nn}\} \tag{2-13}$$

Another condition which has to be satisfied is that the elements of each subset are geographically contiguous. If we introduce a function F, "is a neighbor to," then for any spatial point a_{ik} to be an element of subset I, the number of neighbor relations N_I of a_{ik} with all points of I must be greater than the number of neighbor relations to II, N_{II},[10]

$$a_{ik} \in I \longleftrightarrow N_I > N_{II} \tag{2-14}$$

We assume that this condition is fulfilled for the following analysis.

3. One approach to delimit a region is to use the criterion of distance. We suppose that some spatial point, e.g., a_{11}, is an element of region I and that another spatial point a_{nn} is an element of region II. We can choose a_{11} and a_{nn} intuitively, e.g., they can stand for big towns. Then the axiom scheme of separation[11] reads as follows. Under the assumption $a_{11} \in I$ and $a_{nn} \in II$,

$$a \in I \longleftrightarrow a \in A \wedge m_{aa_{11}} \leqslant m_{aa_{nn}} \tag{2-15}$$

$$a \in II \longleftrightarrow a \in A \wedge m_{aa_{11}} > m_{aa_{nn}} \tag{2-16}$$

$m_{aa_{11}}$ represents the distance of any a to a_{11}, likewise for $m_{aa_{nn}}$. Distances can be read off from a distance matrix.

4. Another possible criterion for the delimitation of regions is the criterion of homogeneity.[12] If this criterion is used, the region is defined as a set of spatial points which have an operationally defined and sufficient uniformity with respect to certain variables.

The criterion of homogeneity has been expressed in terms of geographic, social, and economic characteristics. A delineation along purely geographic lines is not too meaningful for economic analysis as the resulting geographic area does not necessarily shed light on economic processes. The same problem arises if an

---

[10] Equation 2-14 assumes that the two subsets are rectangular. If this assumption is not made, 2-14 has to be reformulated.

[11] If in Eqs. 2-15 and 2-16 we use only the inequality sign, we have no condition for those spatial points, for which $m_{aa_{11}} = m_{aa_{nn}}$.

[12] On the criteria for the delineation of regions: J. R. Meyer, "Regional Economics: A Survey," *American Economic Review*, Vol. 53 (1963), pp. 19–54; H. O. Nourse, *Regional Economics*, McGraw-Hill, New York, 1968, pp. 129–136; J. R. Boudeville, "L'économie régionale–Espace operationnel," *Cahiers de l'Institut de Science Économique Appliquée*, Série L No. 3, Paris, 1958; J. R. Boudeville, *Les Espaces Economiques*, Paris, 1961; W. Isard, "Regional Science, The Concept of Region and Regional Structure," *Papers and Proceedings of the Regional Science Association*, Vol. 2 (1956), p. 17; M. B. Ullman and R. C. Klove, "The Geographic Area in Regional Economic Research," *Regional Income, Studies in Income and Wealth*, Vol. 21, Conference on Research in Income and Wealth, Report of the National Bureau of Economic Research, Princeton, N. J. 1957, pp. 87–94.

area is delineated with respect to uniformities in the social system (common historical background, institutional-administrative uniformity). Economic homogeneity relates to such variables as production activities, skill levels of the labor force, and per capita income. A region is then defined as a number of adjoining spatial points having similar production activities or the same level of per capita income. Thus we may distinguish agrarian and industrial areas, or regions with a heavy concentration of the tertiary sector, or we may differentiate between low-income and high-income regions.

Let the necessary characteristics of uniformity be $\bar{x}$ and $\bar{y}$ respectively and let the actual characteristics of a point a be x_a and y_a.[13] Then the axiom scheme of separation is

$$a \in I \longleftrightarrow a \in A \wedge x_a \geqslant \bar{x} \qquad (2\text{-}17)$$

$$a \in II \longleftrightarrow a \in A \wedge y_a \geqslant \bar{y} \qquad (2\text{-}18)$$

A delimitation along Eqs. 2-17 and 2-18 under condition 2-11 is possible only if $\bar{x}$ and $\bar{y}$ do not overlap, so that the condition for nonoverlapping regions I and II is

$$\bar{x} \wedge \bar{y} = \phi \qquad (2\text{-}19)$$

If $\bar{x}$ and $\bar{y}$ overlap, so that

$$\bar{x} \wedge \bar{y} = z \qquad (2\text{-}20)$$

all a's for which $x_a, y_a \in z$ will be included in both sets.

5. Regions can be delimited with the criterion of interdependence. In this interpretation a region is to be regarded as a spatially bound system. A system is defined as a set of variables which are interrelated to each other more strongly than to other variables. Using this criterion we do not concentrate on a one-sided interdependence on the supply side (supply area of a demand center), or on the demand side only (demand area of a supply center). We are concerned with interdependencies on both the demand and supply sides and consequently with an exchange or trade region.[14]

The definition includes nodal regions which are characterized by a central place, or a pole, and the surrounding hinterland with corresponding market nets.[15] The concept also contains a polarized region, which is defined by Boudeville as an area for which, at each spatial point, the intensity of internal commodity and service flows is greater than the intensity of external flows.[16]

In order to use this criterion of interdependence, we have to specify the

[13] Instead of a single criterion a mixed index can be used.
[14] H. C. Binswanger, "Das intra-regionale Gleichgewicht Zur Integration von Standort-theorie und Theorie des internationalen Handels," *Schweizerische Zeitschrift für Volkswirtschaft und Statistik*, Vol. 97 (1961), p. 144.
[15] A. Lösch, *The Location of Economic Activity*, Yale U. P., New Haven, Conn., 1960, p. 124.
[16] J. R. Boudeville, "L'économie régionale—Espace operationnel," p. 7; Boudeville's definition presupposes a distinction between internal and external flows. This distinction, however, can be made only after the region has been defined.

formula $f(a)$ in such a way that it represents the interdependence of the spatial points a. All elements of A have to be separated into two subsets.

The interdependence of spatial points can be represented by a graph.[17] A graph $G = [A, F]$ is defined as the set A and the function F which associates all members of A (domain of F) to all members of A (range of F), The graph can also be written as $G = [a_j^i]$, with i and j standing for all spatial points. Spatial points represent the nodes of the graph. As shown in Fig. 2-4, an interdepen-

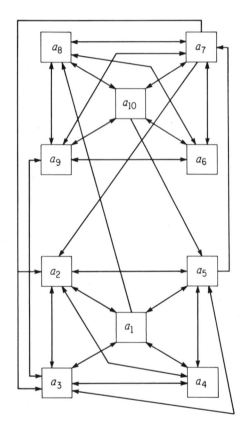

Fig. 2-4. Interaction between spatial points.

dence, e.g., a forward or backward linkage (in the vertical structure of production) of two spatial points, is represented by a directed arc. If the interdependence runs both ways the arc is undirected.

[17] On graph theory: G. Avondo Bodino, *Economic Applications of the Theory of Graphs,* Gordon and Breach, New York, 1962; C. Berge, *The Theory of Graphs and its Applications,* Wiley, New York, 1962; D. König, *Theorie der endlichen und unendlichen Graphen,* Akademische Verlagsanstalt, Leipzig, Germany, 1936.

This graph can also be represented by a matrix, in which blank elements indicate no linkages, and elements with "1" denote interdependences, as shown in Fig. 2-5.

	a_1	a_2	a_3	a_4	a_5	a_6	a_7	a_8	a_9	a_{10}
a_1	–	1	1	1	1			1		
a_2	1	–	1	1	1					
a_3	1	1	–	1	1				1	
a_4	1	1	1	–	1					
a_5	1	1	1	1	–		1			
a_6						–	1	1	1	1
a_7		1	1			1	–	1	1	1
a_8						1	1	–	1	1
a_9		1				1	1	1	–	1
a_{10}						1	1	1	1	–

Fig. 2-5

We have to find a formula which specifies which spatial points are most strongly interdependent among each other. The following algorithm may be used. Some spatial points are chosen as a preliminary region. Then we test to determine whether other spatial points can be added to the preliminary region. The condition for this operation is that the ratio of the number of linkages of the spatial point under discussion be stronger in reference to the preliminary region than to all other points.

We choose a_1, a_2, a_3 as a preliminary region. For a_4 the number of linkages with the preliminary region is 6; the number of linkages with a_5, . . ., a_{10} is 2. a_4 is to be added to the preliminary region. For a_5 the number of linkages with the new preliminary region $\{a_1, a_2, a_3, a_4\}$ is 8; the number of linkages with $\{a_6, a_7, a_8, a_9, a_{10}\}$ is 2. The spatial point a_5 is also to be added to the preliminary region. Similarly, spatial points a_6, . . ., a_{10} have to be tested with respect to the preliminary region $\{a_1, . . ., a_5\}$. The process of delimitation starts anew if we construct a new preliminary region consisting of at least two spatial points which lie outside the preliminary region $\{a_1, . . ., a_5\}$ = I. Then the procedure described above is repeated.

If we denote the number of linkages of a spatial point a with a preliminary region by N_p, and the number of linkages of a spatial point a with those elements of A not contained in the preliminary area with N_r, the axiom scheme of separation for region I reads

$$a \in I \longleftrightarrow a \in A \wedge N_p > N_r \qquad (2\text{-}21)$$

This rather simple algorithm, which may not lead to a definitive solution, has to be improved considerably. First, the formal structure of the algorithm has to be changed so that the solution does not depend on the initial choice of spatial points as a preliminary region. Second, the arcs of the graph should also indicate the weights of the movement of goods between spatial points.

6. Besides the criteria of homogeneity and functionality, another variable used to delineate regions is the uniformity of intensity with which the government plans to effect a set of spatial points. This definition leads to a planning region which is an area delineated by political actors.[18] As the delineation of regions by political authorities is not an arbitrary decision, the delimitation of a planning region presupposes yardsticks which may be identical to those already discussed (homogeneity, interdependence).

It is well established that the choice of the criterion for delineation depends on the purpose of the study. We may use a different delineation for agricultural studies than for the analysis of intergovernmental fiscal relations or the effects of changes in the transportation facilities on the economic landscape. In the present study it is assumed that the problem of delineating the regions has been solved. The two regions I and II are given.

It is also assumed that the two regions are subsystems of a nation. The magnitude of the region is not specified. Thus the question is left open as to whether the national economy in which the region is located has a small or a large area. Also it is unspecified whether the national economy is broken down into many small or fewer big regions. Our assumption of two regions is made for simplifying purposes and does not allow any conclusions on the size of the region in question. However, the region is supposed to be larger than a metropolitan area. Regions of this size are neglected in the analysis. International regions are used for comparative purposes only.

In the process of growth, the characteristics of spatial points and the interdependence among these points are likely to be affected. Consequently, the delineation of the region changes in the process of growth. For simplicity we ignore this effect and assume that the delineation of our two regions is constant over time.

In this chapter we have constructed the basis for the analysis in the following chapter. The structure of space, described in terms of set theory and differentiated into two subunits I and II, must now be integrated into a dynamic analysis. For this purpose the possible growth determinants have to be evaluated and their effects analyzed.

[18] J. Friedmann, "The Concept of a Planning Region–The Evolution of an Idea in the U.S.," in W. Alonso and J. Friedmann (eds.), *Regional Development and Planning–A Reader*, M.I.T. Press, Cambridge, Mass., 1964.

PROBLEMS

1. Further conceptual and mathematical problems will still need to be solved before a full synthesis of the partial-location theories can be achieved."[19] Discuss this statement.

2. Evaluate the application of a simulation model to the problem of integrating partial-location theories.

3. Discuss the statistical methods used for the delineation of regions.

4. Compare the criteria and methods used in the definition of sectors with those applied to the delimitation of regions.

5. Assume the matrix represented in Fig. 2.5 indicates quantities shipped between different spatial points. Find an algorithm for the functional delineation of areas starting out from this matrix. Compare the matrix with an input-output table.

6. Discuss the delineation of planning regions in France.[20]

[19] B. J. Stevens and C. A. Brackett, *Industrial Location, A Review and Annotated Bibliography of Theoretical, Empirical and Case Studies*, Regional Science Research Institute, Bibliography Series No. 3, Philadelphia, Pa., 1967, p. 7.

[20] J. R. Boudeville, *Problems of Regional Economic Planning*, Edinburgh U. P., Edinburgh, Scotland, 1966, pp. 4-5.

chapter 3

Analysis of Internal
Growth Determinants

Growth theory uses two alternative approaches for the analysis of growth determinants. Following the Keynesian tradition, one approach stresses the increase in aggregate demand by formulating multiplier-accelerator models.[1] The other more recent approach is supply-oriented and analyzes the increase of the productive capacity of an economic system.[2] These two approaches, however, are not complete alternatives in the sense that one excludes the other. An increase in both demand and supply represents changes in important factors of economic expansion and has to be taken into consideration by any theory of economic development. For simplifying purposes the demand side will first be neglected. Thus the variable to be explained becomes the variation of the potential volume of production. In a second step the demand side will be introduced.

It is assumed throughout this chapter that we have only one region, and that this region is closed. Commodities are neither exported nor imported, and factors of production do not move across the regional border. Consequently the increase in potential output cannot be influenced by other regions, but is due to factors inside the region only. These factors are called *internal determinants of growth.*

A. DETERMINANTS OF POTENTIAL OUTPUT: THE SUPPLY SIDE

I. A Production Function as a Basis for the Analysis

1. The potential volume of regional output is a function of the inputs available in the area. The relation between the potential regional output and

---

[1] J. S. Duesenberry, *Business Cycles and Economic Growth*, McGraw-Hill, New York, 1958.
[2] R. M. Solow, "A Contribution to the Theory of Economic Growth," *Quarterly Journal of Economics*, Vol. 70 (1956), pp. 65–94; N. Kaldor, "A Model of Economic Growth," *Economic Journal*, Vol. 67 (1957), pp. 585–624; J. E. Meade, *A Neo-Classical Theory of Economic Growth*, Allen and Unwin, London, 1962.

these internal inputs is expressed in a general-production function of the form:

$$O = f(K, L, Q, Tr, T, So) \tag{3-1}$$

In this aggregated analysis the potential regional output O is a function of the available resources of capital K, labor L, land Q, the transport resources Tr, technical knowledge T, and the social system So. The last two determinants influence the combination of the four preceding growth factors. The inputs are more or less arbitrarily built constructs and represent complex aggregates which are supposed to be the most important determinants of regional output and its variations. They have become so familiar through convention that their existence is taken for granted. One problem that can only be indicated here is that the definition of these inputs depends on the concept of the production function, and the concept of the production function in turn depends on the definition of the inputs.[3] Another problem that will be ignored in our analysis is that these inputs consist of heterogeneous types of commodities and can best be defined as a set of different types of machinery, or variable qualities of land and quantities of labor with different skill.[4] For simplicity we assume homogeneous inputs. It is also assumed that capital is of the directly productive type and does not include infrastructure outlays.

Transport inputs Tr are the quantity of resources used for the movement of commodities and persons (labor) over space. They are not an original but a derived factor of production.[5] A transport output is realized if, for a given state of technical knowledge and a given social system, services of land and of capital goods are combined with services of labor. Consequently transport inputs may be understood as a set of different resources including transport capital Tr_K, transport labor Tr_L, and transport land Tr_Q. These transport resources, which are not included in the regional supply of the internal factors K, L, and Q, may be substituted for Tr in 3-1. We then have

$$O = f(K, L, Q, \{Tr_K, Tr_L, Tr_Q\}, T, So) \tag{3-2}$$

Technical knowledge T and the social system So are rather vaguely conceived factors of production and are not operationally defined. Technical knowledge is understood as information on production processes at a moment of time. The social system is supposed to denote the social structure, institutional setting, behavioral patterns, and attitudes of the members of a regional economy. With

---

[3]The capital input is normally defined as a commodity which is used for the production of another good. Consequently, the definition of the input presupposes some notion of a production function. The production function is defined as a relation between output and input. It requires a definition of the inputs.

[4]I. Adelman, *Theories of Economic Growth and Development*, Stanford U. P., Stanford, Calif., 1961, p. 11. On the problem of homogenous inputs: P. A. Samuelson, "Parable and Realism in Capital Theory: The Surrogate Production Function," *Review of Economic Studies*, Vol. 29 (1962), pp. 193–206.

[5]A different definition is used by W. Isard, *Location and Space Economy*, M.I.T. Press, Cambridge, Mass., 1956, p. 79.

respect to technical knowledge, two important questions remain unanswered. First, how can the technical knowledge of an individual economic unit, such as a firm or a spatial point, be measured? Second, once the technical knowledge of individual units is clearly defined, what do we understand by the macro concept of the technical knowledge of a region? Does this second concept refer to the aggregation of the varying sets of technical knowledge from all spatial points of the region (union of the information sets of all spatial points), or is it to be understood as some minimum level of information which is common to all spatial points (intersection of information sets)? Or measured by unique levels of information which are only available at specific points with other points not having the same knowledge[6] (union minus the intersection of information sets)?

2. Relation 3-2 cannot be used for a dynamic analysis unless the variables are dated unequivocally. Characterizing the variables by time indices makes clear that relation 3·2 includes both flow and stock variables. Stock variables are measured at a moment of time. Flow variables are related to a time period. Stock magnitudes are time-point variables and have to be characterized by a time-point index. Capital, labor, and land are such time-point variables which need to be denoted as K_t, L_{t-1}, or Q_{t-2}. Flow magnitudes refer to time periods and are consequently described by a time-period index. As a time period is limited by two time points, a flow variable is described by two subscripts, indicating respectively the first and the last time point of a period. Potential regional output is such a time-period variable, where $_{t-1}O_t$ specifies that the output is produced in the time period $t - 1$ to t.

As the transport resource consists of capital, labor, and land, it is a stock variable. Technical knowledge may be regarded as a time-point variable. The social system cannot be incorporated into these variables at this time.

Using the aforementioned method of dating variables, the output of the time period $t - 1$ to t is a function of the stock variables which are given at the starting point of the period.

$$_{t-1}O_t = f(K_{t-1}, L_{t-1}, Q_{t-1}, Tr_{t-1}, T_{t-1}) \tag{3-3}$$

As shown in Fig. 3-1, at the end of the period we have the new levels of the stock variables K_t, L_t, Q_t, T_t, Tr_t. For example, the new capital stock K_t is given by the identity

$$K_t \equiv K_{t-1} + {_{t-1}dK_t} \tag{3-4}$$

The variation in the capital stock dK is a time-period variable. We assume that this flow variable will not have a capacity effect in the same period. We envisage the increase in capital as being added to the stock at the end of the period. Similar assumptions are made for all other stock variables. Labor, land, transport resources, and technical knowledge are only changed at the end of the

---

[6]A similar problem is raised by F. Machlup, *The Production and Distribution of Knowledge in the United States*, Princeton U. P., Princeton, N. J. 1962, p. 28.

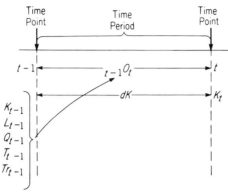

Fig. 3-1

period. For reasons of simplification it is also assumed that the time period is the same for the variation of all variables.

3. The static relation 3-3 between output and different aggregates of inputs is changed into a dynamic relation if the variables which are measured in terms of an absolute level are interpreted as changes over time. Then the absolute increase in the level of potential production dO is a function of the increase in the aggregate inputs. The term dTr indicates the increase in resources available for transportation—namely, in transport capital, transport land, and transport labor. The term dT denotes the nonquantifiable change in technical knowledge. It also includes technical change in the transportation activities

$$dO = f(dK, dL, dQ, dT, dTr) \tag{3-5}$$

The variables of this function have to be dated also. For this purpose we elongate the time axis in Fig. 3-1 by one period and obtain Fig. 3-2.

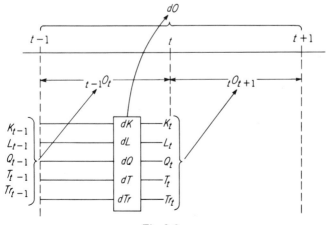

Fig. 3-2

As can be seen in Fig. 3-2, the stock variables at time point t produce the output of the period from t to $t + 1$. The variation of output is a change of a time-period variable over two periods. dO is defined as

$$_{t-1}dO_{t+1} = {_t}O_{t+1} - {_{t-1}}O_t \qquad (3\text{-}6)$$

Under the assumptions made, the change in output depends on the change in the stock variables in the period $t - 1$ to t, as the variation of the stock variables from t to $t + 1$ will only be effective in period $t + 1$ to $t + 2$. Consequently our basic relation reads

$$_{t-1}dO_{t+1} = f(_{t-1}dK_t, {_{t-1}}dL_t, {_{t-1}}dQ_t, {_{t-1}}dTr_t, {_{t-1}}dT_t) \qquad (3\text{-}7)$$

4. The increase in the development potential of a closed region is determined if we succeed in specifying a production function for Eq. 3-7. The form of the function and the weights of the different factors have to be estimated empirically. Once the function is given, hypotheses on the variation of the determinants yield implications to the development of a region, including the forecasting of the regional development potential. Our analysis does not attempt to estimate function 3-7 empirically, but limits itself to an abstract study of regional economic growth.

In order to simplify the analysis, the following assumptions are made. The regional social system does not change over time. We also assume that the total supply of land is fixed such that $dQ = 0$. Finally, since we are not able to consider all determinants of economic growth simultaneously, we will make use of the *ceteris paribus* clause. The effects of variations in each growth determinant will be treated successively with the other determinants assumed constant.

The analysis of regional growth determinants should solve three basic problems. First, it must formulate empirically testable hypotheses which explain the variations in growth determinants. Second, it must specify the expansion effects caused by variations of determinants. Third, it should explain the changes in the spatial structure stemming from variations in the growth determinants.

II. Variations in the Capital Stock

1. *Capital accumulation.* The variation in the capital stock of a closed region depends on the supply S and the demand for investment funds J.

$$_{t-1}dK_t = f(_{t-1}J_t, {_{t-1}}S_t) \qquad (3\text{-}8)$$

(a) On the supply side, the volume of investment in a period is identical to the amount of savings in the same period. The total amount of regional savings S depends on regional income Y. A Robertson lag[7] is assumed.

$$_{t-1}S_t = f(_{t-2}Y_{t-1}) \qquad (3\text{-}9)$$

[7] A. H. Hansen, *A Guide to Keynes*, McGraw-Hill, New York, 1953, p. 48.

More realistic than such an aggregated savings function is a disaggregated relation which contains different groups of savers characterized by differing saving behaviors. Neglecting other factor returns, total savings are split up into savings out of profits P and savings out of wages W. Since

$$Y = P + W \tag{3-10}$$

we have

$$_{t-1}S_t = {}_{t-1}{}^P S_t + {}_{t-1}{}^W S_t \tag{3-11}$$

Savings of wage earners depend on the regional wage sum W:

$$_{t-1}{}^W S_t = f({}_{t-2}W_{t-1}) \tag{3-12}$$

Savings of profit earners are by analogy a function of profits P:

$$_{t-1}{}^P S_t = f({}_{t-2}P_{t-1}) \tag{3-13}$$

Profits include retained earnings which represent an important source of investment funds.[8] Profits and savings depend on the level of regional income Y and its distribution v. The distribution of income is assumed as given.

$$_{t-2}P_{t-1} = f({}_{t-2}Y_{t-1}, v) \tag{3-14}$$

$$_{t-2}W_{t-1} = f({}_{t-2}Y_{t-1}, v) \tag{3-15}$$

Thus regional income determines the sources of investment in the next period via the savings functions.

(b) Savings are only one of two determinants of investment behavior related to supply. The volume of investment also depends on demand conditions. We assume that the rate of return r is the relevant determinant for net investment. A high rate of return will lead to a large volume of investment. A low rate of return will induce a low level of investment.

$$_{t-1}J_t = f(r_{t-1}) \tag{3-16}$$

Since entrepreneurs know the rate of return for the past,[9] we assume that the profit rate r_{t-1} determines investment demand of the period from $t-1$ to t. This function need not be interpreted as a behavioral relationship oriented toward the past. It can be understood as a future-oriented behavior which due to lacking information is based on neutral expectations. In a more realistic analysis r_{t-1} can be multiplied by a coefficient of expectation. For optimistic expectations this coefficient is greater than unity, for pessimistic, smaller, and neutral expectations equal to unity.[10]

2. *Effects on regional output.* In order to determine the expansion effects of additional capital, we must determine by how much the level of output

---

[8]Duesenberry, *op. cit.,* p. 91.

[9]Rates of returns for new commodities are neglected since due to our *ceteris paribus* assumption technical knowledge does not change. New commodities are therefore excluded.

[10]C. E. Ferguson, "On Theories of Acceleration and Growth," *Quarterly Journal of Economics,* Vol. 74 (1960), p. 82.

changes if capital is increased assuming all other determinants are constant. Does output produced by the nth capital unit increase more or less or by the same amount as output being produced by the capital unit $n - 1$?

We postulate the hypothesis that output increases with an increase in capital but at a declining rate (see Fig. 3-3), for

$$O = f(K): \quad f(0) = 0, f' > 0, f'' < 0 \tag{3-17}$$

The physical marginal productivity of capital decreases. Let the monetary rate of return be defined as the marginal-value product as is the case in perfect

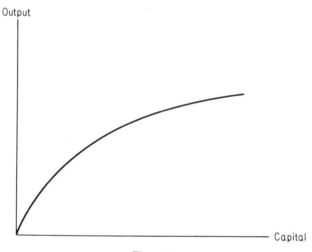

Output

Capital

Fig. 3-3

competition. Let p indicate the output price and r^M the monetary rate of return. Then the real rate of return r is given by

$$r = \frac{r_m}{p} \cdot \frac{\partial O}{\partial K}$$

Assume a constant output price. Then the real rate of return will behave with the same tendency as the marginal productivity of capital. The rate of return falls with an increase in the capital stock:

$$r_t = f(K_t) \tag{3-18}$$

Equations 3-18, 3-16, and 3-4 represent a simple model of capital accumulation. The system is closed by assuming the initial capital stock K_{t-1} as given. The relations are represented in Fig. 3-4.

Quadrant I illustrates the relationship between the rate of return and the capital stock. With an increase in the capital stock the rate of return decreases. The initial capital stock OA determines the rate of return OB in the first period.

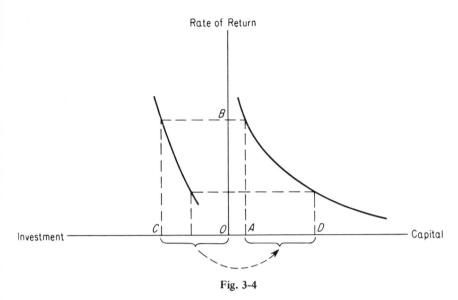

Fig. 3-4

The second quadrant demonstrates the dependence of the increase in the capital stock—namely, net investment—on the rate of return. The rate of return OB induces an investment demand of OC. This is the increase in the capital stock so that $OC = AD$. OD is the new capital stock. The sources of investment funds included in Eq. 3-8 may be thought of as representing a restraint on the realization of investment demand. This restraint, which will be different for each period, can be introduced as a vertical line into quadrant II of Fig. 3-4.

The new capital stock OD leads to a new, lower rate of return and to a reduced level of investment. As long as there is an increase in the capital stock, the rate of return declines. The region finally reaches a capital stock with a zero rate of return. As all other factors are assumed to be constant, the region moves toward a stationary state in which the rate of growth also becomes zero.

3. *Effects on the spatial structure.* An increase in the capital stock has effects not only on regional output but also on the spatial structure. In order to determine the spatial effects of a variation of growth determinants we need a dynamic theory of location which at the same time takes into consideration the necessities of growth theory. Such a theory is not available.[11] The following analysis can only be understood as the first step in the direction of analyzing the spatial effects of growth determinants.

[11] On a dynamic theory of location, see M. L. Greenhut, "A Theory of the Micro Equilibrium Path of the Firm in Economic Space," *South African Journal of Economics,* Vol. 34 (1967), pp. 230–243; E. M. Hoover, *The Location of Economic Activity*, McGraw-Hill, New York, 1948, Chaps. 9–10; E. von Boeventer, "Bemerkungen zur optimalen Standortpolitik der Einzelunternehmung," in H. Jürgensen (ed.), *Gestaltungsprobleme der Weltwirtschaft—Festschrift für A. Predöhl*, Göttingen, Germany, 1964, pp. 440–461.

Such an analysis has to make a distinction between the spatial origin and the spatial destination or incidence of the determinants. The spatial origin or "supply place" is defined as the spatial point where a variable originates. The destination or "use place" is defined as the spatial point where the variable will finally be located. The connection between the spatial origin and the spatial destination is the mobility of the variable. As we assume a closed region, only intraregional mobility can be involved.

The change in a growth determinant in a period can consist of a series of small changes in a large number of spatial points. In this case the origin of the increase in the variable is spread over many spatial points; it is spatially atomistic. In the opposite extreme, the change in the growth determinant may occur at one spatial point only—it is *totally* polarized. In an in-between case the determinant may change at some spatial points; the origin is *partially* polarized.

Information on the origin of a growth determinant is necessary only so far as the spatial origin allows conclusions on the spatial incidence of the variable. The spatial effects of the growth determinants may also be atomistic, partially, or totally polarized. These terms can be made operational by counting the number of spatial points of set A in Eq. 2-1 and specifying characteristic proportions of spatial points for the different terms. The definition depends on the degree of aggregation used in the delineation of spatial points.

Atomistic phenomena affect a great number of spatial points with relatively low intensity. Partially polarized determinants will have no effect for some spatial points and a stronger intensity for other points. Totally polarized determinants will have zero intensity for all but one spatial point. From these definitions the following tautological statement results: *The more polarized the incidence of a growth determinant, the stronger is the impact on the spatial structure; the more atomistic the spatial destination, the less severe will be the impact on the spatial structure.* This statement leads to a conclusion on the relevance of the intraregional mobility of the growth determinants.

Atomistic origin. The more immobile the determinant, the greater are the chances for an atomistic incidence. The inverse relation, however, does not hold. The more mobile the determinant the less atomistic the incidence, is not necessarily true since the mobility may not become effective.

Polarized origin. The more immobile the determinants, the greater are the chances for a polarized destination. With an increase in mobility an atomistic destination is a possible but not necessary result.

Theorems on the spatial effects of a determinant can only be deducted if the spatial origin is known or determined by hypotheses, and if relationships between the spatial origin and incidence are postulated. In a formal analysis, these relationships may be indicated by the graph $G = [a_j^i]$, where a_i is the set of spatial origins (possibly all elements of the region) and a_j denotes all points of destination, representing also all spatial points of the area.

The graph may be represented by a matrix with spatial points in the top and at the left. Let there be only three spatial points a_1, a_2, and a_3. Let the row represent the origin and the column denote the incidence. Then an arrow indicates the existence of a movement of a determinant from its supply place to its use place (See Fig. 3-5). The elements in the diagonal may also be filled if the determinant stays at the same spatial point.

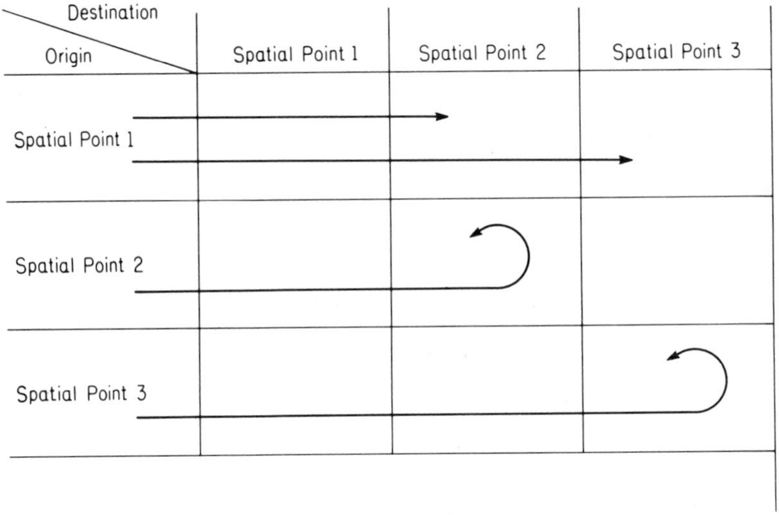

Destination Origin	Spatial Point 1	Spatial Point 2	Spatial Point 3
Spatial Point 1			
Spatial Point 2			
Spatial Point 3			

Fig. 3-5

In order to specify the graph G we have to postulate hypotheses relating to the origin and the incidence of the determinants. The following combinations are conceivable:

Origin	Incidence
Totally polarized	Totally polarized
Totally polarized	Partially polarized
Totally polarized	Atomistic
Partially polarized	Totally polarized
Partially polarized	Partially polarized
Partially polarized	Atomistic
Atomistic	Totally polarized
Atomistic	Partially polarized
Atomistic	Atomistic

The empirically relevant cases have to be chosen out of these conceivable combinations. This analysis will be undertaken for each growth determinant, as for each determinant different relations between origin and destination may hold. We will first turn to increases in the capital stock.

For simplicity we assume that the existing stocks are immobile. We consequently neglect the problem that the spatial structure may be changed by shifting the existing capital stock spatially.

The origin of a growth determinant depends on the given spatial structure and the typical behavior of this determinant. In the case of an increase in the capital stock, we can refer to the hypotheses already formulated. If the sources of investment increase from a rise in wage income, the origin or the supply place of the determinant depends on the spatial distribution of residential activities. As residential activities are normally organized in a hierarchical system of central places,[12] we have a partially polarized origin. Monetary capital in the form of wage savings being mobile, it can have atomistic or polarized effects on the structure of space. The incidence of this factor is indeterminate.

If the sources of investment are profits, the origin (supply place) of the increase in capital depends on the distribution of firms and profit situations in space. If there is a large number of firms in the region with equal size and equal profit situations, the origin of the increase in capital is atomistic. If there is only one large firm, we have a polarized origin.

The spatial incidence of the additional investment funds can be found by analyzing the investment flows in the region. If we assume that investment behavior is characterized by a pattern of rigidity in the sense that retained earnings of a firm are invested in the firm, we have a spatial ratchet effect which tends to preserve the given spatial structure,[13] for the probability of new locations arising just because of capital accumulation is negligible. If investment behavior depends on retained earnings, additional capital does not change the spatial structure. The following cases must be distinguished.

(1) If the profit chances of many firms are nearly similar at all spatial points, strong variations in the spatial structure from the accumulation of capital cannot be expected.

(2) If the region contains a small number of growing industries or expanding firms characterized by higher profit rates, a polarized accumulation may be the result under the retained-earning hypothesis. The change in the economic landscape is stronger than in case (1).

To summarize: If the profit situations are distributed evenly over the spatial points, no polarizing effect can be expected from an increase in the capital stock. The more differentiated the profit situations are among the spatial points the greater is the probability for polarization. As differing profit rates cannot be explained from additional capital with all other determinants not changing, capital accumulation cannot have very strong structure-changing

[12] B. J. L. Berry and A. Pred, *Central Place Studies: A Bibliography of Theories and Applications*, Regional Science Research Institute, Bibliography Series No. 1, Philadelphia, Pa., 1961.
[13] This statement implies one-plant firms.

effects. If the ratchet effect via retained earnings exists, capital accumulation may even have a structure-preserving function.

If, however, capital is mobile and pursues the spatial differences in rates of returns, and if we change the *ceteris paribus* assumption, then an immobile increase in technical knowledge or in the labor supply will attract the mobile capital. In this case the mobility of capital will reinforce the polarizing effect of another, immobile determinant.

With the additional capital being mobile or immobile, the *ceteris paribus* hypothesis of a declining profit rate with an increase in the capital stock leads to the result that the intensity of the effects of this determinant on the spatial structure decreases. The process of capital accumulation which leads to a stationary state in the dynamic analysis at the same time reaches a stationary spatial structure. As increases in the capital stock become smaller and smaller with a declining profit rate, the distribution of economic activities will be influenced less and less in each period, until finally the addition to the capital stock is zero and no changes in the structure of space occur in our *ceteris paribus* world.

III. Variations in the Labor Supply

Another internal determinant of a change in regional output is a variation of the labor supply. Increases and decreases of the labor force are basically sociological phenomena which can only be partly explained in terms of purely economic categories. In a simplified analysis the following factors influencing the supply of labor have to be distinguished.[14]

1. The long-run increase of the homogeneous labor supply depends on the number of workers. With a given wage and a given proportion of the work force to total population, the change in the labor supply depends on the increase in population (dB):

$$dL = f(dB) \tag{3-19}$$

Besides the change in population,[15] the wage is another factor influencing variations in the labor supply. Wage increases can represent incentives for the nonworking population to join the labor force and for those employed to increase their labor supply. Thus

$$_{t-1}dL_t = f(w_{t-1}) \tag{3-20}$$

This relation may hold only in the short run, as it is conceivable that a short period after the wage rise the supply and leisure behavior of the past breaks through and the labor supply is reduced to the original level. In this analysis we assume that the increase in the labor supply is determined by relation 3-19.

---

[14] On population growth: S. Enke, "Population and Development, A General Model," *Quarterly Journal of Economics*, Vol. 77 (1963), pp. 55–70; P. M. Hauser and O. D. Duncan, *The Study of Population*, U. of Chicago Press, Chicago, 1959.

[15] No effort is made to introduce time subscripts for *dB*.

2. Assuming constancy of all other determinants, it can be expected that an increase in the labor force will lead to declining marginal productivities, as the additional members of the labor force cannot be equipped with machines. The decrease in productivity is logically conclusive if machines have not been idle so far. Under these assumptions we have a similar function as for capital:

$$O = f(L), f' > O, f'' < O; K = \text{const.} \qquad (3\text{-}21)$$

Output increases with a declining rate. This process is possible only if K stays constant. This condition implies that the increase in output stemming from the increase in the labor supply is used for consumption only. If the additional output is used for capital accumulation, the condition for relation 3-22 is not fulfilled. Then *ceteris paribus* statements on the behavior of O and L are not possible.

3. The spatial origin of the additional labor supply depends on the distribution of the relevant population in space, namely, that part of the population which is about to join the labor force. Assuming identical birth rates for all spatial points of the regions, the increase in the labor force is partially polarized due to the hierarchical structure of residential activities.

It can be expected that, although obstacles to mobility exist, labor is very mobile intraregionally. As a result, the incidence of an increase in the labor supply is not linked to its origin. If in a *ceteris paribus* analysis labor is the only factor that changes, and if labor is mobile, we cannot expect polarizing effects from an increase in the labor supply, as it can be assumed that additional labor will follow the economic opportunities which, according to our *ceteris paribus* assumption, should be similar for all spatial points.

If labor is immobile it may create a situation in which the spatial points with a strong increase in labor supply have a locational advantage in terms of lower wages.   In this case the additional immobile labor supply may have a polarizing effect. This effect is reinforced if the other determinants are mobile and if the labor supply attracts these other growth factors to a specific location. On the other hand, if labor is mobile intraregionally, it can be polarized by another immobile determinant. Immobile technical knowledge at one spatial point may attract the mobile additional labor supply, and thus a mobile labor supply may intensify the polarizing effect of another variable.

IV. Technical Change

1. *Hypotheses on realized new technical knowledge.* Technical knowledge can be defined as the set of production processes known at a certain moment of time. Technical progress is the variation of this technical horizon—namely, the variation of realized production processes.   Both variables are used as non-operational concepts.

Technical progress is characterized by two elements, *inventions* and *inno-*

vations.[16]   An invention is the introduction of a new production process to the set of potential processes, i.e., those processes considered but not yet utilized. An innovation is the transformation of potential processes into actual processes. Inventions represent changes in the knowledge of society, whereas innovations are variations in existing production functions.

If technical progress is to be introduced as a growth determinant—namely, as a factor which causally influences the increase of regional output—hypotheses have to be formulated which explain inventions and innovations as well as the time lag between these two elements (see Fig. 3-6).

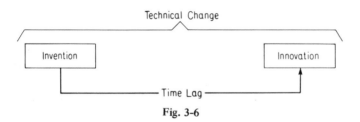

Fig. 3-6

To find a new process of production is an achievement that surpasses traditional procedures and requires some unknown insight. One approach to explaining inventions is seen in chance: "... The emergence of invention [is attributed] to the occasional genius who from time to time achieves a direct knowledge of essential truth through the exercise of intuition. ..."[17] As there may be some chance results of research, a certain part of all inventions may be given as an exogenous variable.

But autonomous inventions represent only part of the picture. Another set of inventions may be induced. Following Usher's[18] theory of invention we can distinguish four stages of a process of invention.

(1) *Recognition of the problem.* The traditional procedure has to be recognized as unsatisfactory in some way. Consequently the probability of an invention depends on the number of problems resistant to solutions by traditional means.[19] The dissatisfaction with the production procedure used so far and the desire to overcome this deficiency, lead to the second stage.

(2) *Surveying all known possibilities.* All data and all existing knowledge

[16] J. A. Schumpeter, *Business Cycles: A Theoretical, Historical and Statistical Analysis of the Capitalist Process,* McGraw-Hill, New York, 1939, p. 84.

[17] V. W. Ruttan, "Usher and Schumpeter on Invention, Innovation and Technological Change," *Quarterly Journal of Economics,* Vol. 78 (1959), p. 600.

[18] Ruttan, *op. cit.,* p. 601; A. P. Usher, *A History of Mechanical Inventions,* Harvard U.P., Cambridge, Mass., 1962, p. 56

[19] J. Friedmann, "A General Theory of Polarized Development," The Ford Foundation, Urban and Regional Advisory Program in Chile, Santiago, Chile, 1967 (mimeo), p. 11.

pertinent to the solution of the problem are collected. The probability of an invention, therefore, is a function of the information on existing solutions for a specific problem.

(3) *Act of insight.* After having surveyed all existing possibilities, an act of insight must occur which increases the available knowledge. This act depends (a) on the existing knowledge and (b) on the probability that two or more previously unconnected sets of information will coincide.[20]

(4) *Critical appraisal.* The new possibility is tested and revised in such a way that it can be commercially applied.

Because of stages (2) and (4), the development of new technical knowledge is a function of a systematic search effort which heavily depends on research expenditures. Consequently inventions in a region are a function of the amount of financial means available for those elements of the process of invention which are accessible to control. We therefore postulate the hypothesis that induced inventions are a function of research expenditures. Denoting the vague concept of an invention by E, we have

$$^iE = f(R) \tag{3-22}$$

The sum of regional inventions is thus split up into induced and autonomous inventions (^aE),

$$E = {}^iE + {}^aE \tag{3-23}$$

Expenditures for research can be regarded as depending on the absolute level of regional output.

$$R = f(O) \tag{3-24}$$

Inventions are a main determinant of innovations, or the realization of new technical knowledge, dT. But innovations are not explained by inventions alone. Financial means must be available to feed the innovation. As our analysis excludes monetary phenomena, these funds for innovations must arise from foregone consumption. Consequently the realization of new production processes also depends on the level of savings S.

Another source for innovation are those means which are obtained from current depreciation θ and which are intended for the replacement of existing machinery. Instead of a replacement investment, an innovation may be undertaken. Thus innovations in a region are determined by the following relation:

$$dT = f(E, S, \theta) \tag{3-25}$$

Depreciations may be regarded as a function of the capital stock or may be regarded as given.

Dating the variables by introducing a time axis means that research expenditures constitute a flow variable. If we disregard longer time lags, research

[20]*Ibid.*

expenditures during the period $t-2$ to $t-1$ determine the invention at the time point $t-1$. In turn this invention determines the flow-variable innovation from $t-1$ to t. The innovation, which by analogy to investment will only become effective at the end of the period, determines the flow-variable output in the period from t to $t+1$.

2. *Effects on regional output.* Realized new technical knowledge affects the regional production function, shifts the production possibility frontier outward, and increases regional output. The following types of technical change are distinguished for our purposes.

Process and organizational innovations lead to a cost-reducing production of given commodities. Product innovations enlarge or improve the available regional supply measured in real terms. Raw-material innovations, such as the discovery of new natural resources, make possible the use of new inputs and consequently also result in an enlargement of regional output. Transport innovations are variations in the realized technical knowledge of the transport sector. They can be process innovations (improved transport methods), organizational changes (more efficient use of existing capacity), and product innovations (new transport machines). All these cases are likely to lead to reductions in the transport rate.

Transportation costs, which like all costs are understood to be opportunity costs, mean that the frictions of space use up factors of production which cannot be employed for production proper. The smaller the transportation costs, the larger the volume of factors of production free for other use. New technical knowledge in the transportation sector reduces the amount of transport resources necessary to maintain a given level of transportation services and thus frees resources for other production purposes.

3. *Spatial effects of technical progress.*[21] An invention is likely to occur at one spatial point in a region. Its incidence differs, depending on whether the invention relates to the transport or the nontransport sectors.

In the case of process, product, and organizational inventions, the spatial incidence depends (1) on the time lag with which the invention is entered into the regional process of communication, and (2) the spatial distribution of the determinants for innovations.

If the information on new technical knowledge is immobile, a tendency for polarization exists. In this case new technical knowledge will be realized only at that spatial point where the invention occurred. It can be assumed to be realistic that inventors—usually firms—do not have a tendency to communicate their new inventions. Thus there is a pattern of persistence in the distribution of an invention which results from the communication animosity of inventors.

If inventions depend on research expenditures, a spatially unequal distribution of research expenditures leads to a partially or totally polarized origin, not

[21] Compare Hoover, *op. cit.,* Chap. 10.

only of a single invention but of a set of inventions. If the inventor succeeds in not disclosing inventions, a polarized incidence of the newly realized technical knowledge follows immediately.[22]

If information on new technical knowledge is mobile, we still cannot expect an atomistic distribution of innovations, since not all spatial points will fulfill the necessary requirements of an innovation. Also, the patent system may prevent widely spreading innovations. Thus we may expect a partially or a totally polarized incidence of new technical knowledge even if there is no information obstacle to the invention.[23]

The polarizing effect of technical progress continues to exist even if the information lag disappears over time. Basically the eventual disappearance of the information lag should make for an atomistic incidence of innovations. But this possible outcome may be prevented by the fact that during the period in which an information lag exists, the first users of the new method may have established themselves in the market, revised the original method, and financed new research from the temporarily increased profits. The information lag for such additional new knowledge keeps the original point of polarization one step ahead in a process of perpetuating the polarization tendency.

The polarizing incidence of technical progress at certain spatial points leads to a polarization of other determinants, if these are mobile. The realization of an invention needs more capital and/or labor. In order to induce a movement of these growth determinants to the spatial points of invention, the profit and/or the wage rates have to be increased. Thus polarized new technical knowledge will induce the polarization of other determinants.

This process of polarization is increased if we take into account the indivisibility of new capacities which lead to economics of scale. The existence of these internal and agglomeration economies will intensify the polarizing effects. To summarize: Process, product, and organizational innovations have a polarizing incidence. The more mobile capital and labor, the stronger are the polarizing effects which technical knowledge induces with respect to these determinants.

Innovations in raw materials very often polarize the spatial structure. This statement presupposes, however, that the resources cannot be transported technically or that the transportation costs are so high that resources are the decisive factor for location. This has certainly been true historically.

Transport innovations can have two different effects on polarization. A reduction of transport rates reduces economic distances in the region. Lower transport rates enlarge the possibility set of locations of economic activity because a given level of profit may now be reached at a greater number of spatial points. This is a depolarizing tendency. Transport innovations may also compensate for the polarizing effect of an unequal distribution of resources by

---

[22]We neglect the diffusion of an invention over space for multiplant firms.
[23]This problem of the mobility of technical knowledge will be analyzed more explicitly for the case of interregional interaction (Part II).

lowering the transportation costs of inputs and thus making resources more mobile.

On the other hand, transport innovations facilitate polarization by increasing the mobility of factors of production, the latter being a precondition for intensifying the polarizing effects of immobile process, product, and organizational changes. Changes in the transportation system also lower transportation costs of commodities, widen markets, and allow the full utilization of large capacities connected with internal economies.

A quantitative evaluation of the effects of technical progress on the spatial structure is not possible here. It is likely that technical progress has strong polarizing effects, as it is temporarily immobile spatially and influences other mobile growth determinants. Consequently new technical knowledge can be expected to have not a structure-preserving but a structure-changing function.

V. Complexes of Growth Determinants

Our analysis so far has assumed that the growth determinants can be analyzed in an isolated fashion. This *ceteris paribus* procedure is rather questionable, as can be easily shown in the case of technical progress.

New potential production processes can only be realized by adding new machines to the capital stock.[24] A new machine which increases the capital stock may represent net or replacement investment. Consequently the linking element between potential technical knowledge and actual processes is not, as in the traditional analysis, net investment but gross investment. The higher the rate of gross investment, the quicker the realization of inventions. Since the volume of gross investment depends on the magnitude of replacement investment, new processes are more rapidly realized as the depreciation rate increases. This relationship is indicated in Eq. 3-25.

The newly installed machine is the result both of a new process and of capital accumulation. Therefore a distinction between a movement along the production function (capital accumulation) and a shift of this function is not possible.[25] It is also impossible to talk about capital deepening and widening. The decisive variable is gross investment which, when embodying new technical knowledge, affects the time dimension of the capital stock (capital quickening).[26]

Technical progress likewise cannot be separated from an increase in the labor supply. An additional worker who joins the regional labor force not only increases the labor supply quantitatively but may also change the quality of the

---

[24] W. Salter, *Productivity and Technical Change,* Cambridge U.P., Cambridge, England, 1960, p. 65.

[25] N. Kaldor, "A Model of Economic Growth," *Economic Journal*; N. Kaldor and J. A. Mirrless, "A New Model of Economic Growth," *Review of Economic Studies*, Vol. 24 (1962), pp. 174–192; R. B. Nelson, "Aggregate Production Functions and Medium-Range Growth Projections," *American Economic Review*, Vol. 54 (1964), pp. 575–606.

[26] R. M. Solow, "Technical Progress, Capital Formation and Economic Growth," *American Economic Review, Papers and Proceedings*, Vol. 52 (1962), p. 84.

labor force. Or, capital accumulation not only is interrelated with the application of new technical knowledge as in the technical-progress function, but also may represent investment in human capital, or may go together with changes in social system.

Thus complexes of growth determinants affecting regional output exist which are agglomerates of interdependent and mutually conditioning and influencing single constructs. We may distinguish the complexes (dK, dT), (dT, dL), (dK, dS_0) as the most important ones. A more realistic analysis should not start from a single determinant, but from complexes of growth factors.

This approach of using complexes of growth determinants may shed some additional light on the spatial impact of growth determinants. Whereas the increase in capital does not have any polarizing effects in an isolated analysis, the complex (dK, dT) is polarizing, assuming dT does not represent transport innovations. These problems have already been discussed in the spatial analysis of new technical knowledge.

The aforementioned approach cannot be followed in this rather general possibility analysis. But the importance of these complexes of growth determinants reveals the simplifying assumptions which are necessary for our *ceteris paribus* procedure.

B. DETERMINANTS OF ACTUAL REGIONAL OUTPUT: THE DEMAND SIDE

I. Expansion Effects of an Increase in Demand

The growth of factors of the supply side determines the increase of regional productive capacity, namely, the potential growth of a region. The realization of this potential increase depends on the variation in regional aggregate demand.

1. The actual increase of regional income in real terms (constant prices) dY^a is a function of both the increase in potential output and also of demand dD, measured in constant prices:

$$dY^a = f(dO, dD) \qquad (3\text{-}26)$$

Equation 3-26 can be made more specific by the following logical procedure. Assume that originally we have an equilibrium situation in which potential output and actual output are equal. Then we have two constraints for the increase in real actual income. First, the increase in actual real income cannot exceed the increase in potential output.

$$dY^a \leqslant dO \qquad (3\text{-}27)$$

Second, the increase in actual real income cannot be greater than the increase in demand, measured in constant prices.

$$dY^a \leqslant dD \qquad (3\text{-}28)$$

dY^a is limited by either dO or dD, whatever constraint has the lowest value. Figure 3-7 illustrates the problem.

For a specific dO, all points above dO are excluded for dY^a. But dD may impose an additional restraint. If $dO > dD$, dD is the decisive restraint. If,

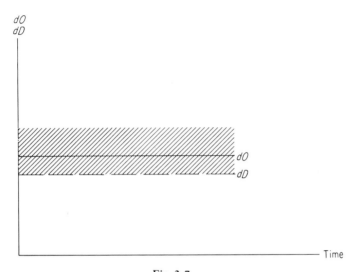

Fig. 3-7

however, $dD > dO$, dO is the relevant restraint. As the lowest value of dO and dD restrict dY^a, we can specify Eq. 3-26 as

$$dY^a = \min (dO, dD) \tag{3-29}$$

2. Since dO has already been analyzed, we still have to explain the increase in demand dD if we want to determine dY^a through Eq. 3-29.

The increase in aggregate demand for a closed region consists of the increase in consumption (dC) and investment demand (dJ).

$$_{t-1}dD_{t+1} = {}_{t-1}dC_{t+1} + {}_{t-1}dJ_{t+1} \tag{3-30}$$

By analogy to the disaggregated saving function 3-11, consumption of a period must be split up into the consumption out of wages and out of profits.

$$_{t-1}C_t = {}_{t-1}{}^P C_t + {}_{t-1}{}^W C_t \tag{3-31}$$

Consumption of wage earners depends on wages, consumption of profit earners depends on profits. We obtain similar relations as in Eqs. 3-12 and 3-13.

The change in investment demand dJ is defined as

$$_{t-1}dJ_{t+1} = {}_t J_{t+1} - {}_{t-1}J_t \tag{3-32}$$

J is determined by Eq. 3-16, and dC, dJ, and dD are differences of flow variables. Figure 3-8 demonstrates the time indices of the variables involved. It corre-

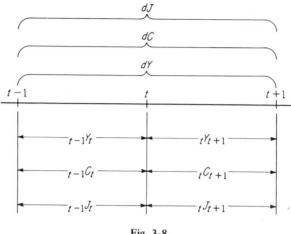

Fig. 3-8

sponds to Fig. 3-2, which deals with the same problem for the determinants of the supply side. The changes in flow variables relate to the same time periods in both diagrams.

II. Spatial Effects of an Increase in Demand

The study of the spatial effects of a variation in demand has to be undertaken in a similar fashion to the spatial-impact analysis of the other determinants, for the effects on the spatial structure depend again on the question of where the increase in demand originates and at which spatial points this demand becomes effective. The analysis differentiates between consumption and investment demand.

1. An additional consumption demand will display atomistic origins if growth is distributed evenly over the region and the increase in income occurs at all spatial points. A polarized origin of additional consumption prevails if the polarizing effects of the supply determinants create growth poles which represent centers of demand due to the increase in income. The relation between the origin and the incidence of additional consumption demand depends on the optimal size of firms in the production of consumption goods. Assume an atomistic origin. If the firm size in the consumption-goods industry is relatively small, an atomistic origin will be followed by an atomistic incidence. This conclusion stems from the fact that small-sized firms of the consumption industry tend to be spatially distributed according to the spatial occurrence of demand. The atomistic increase in demand will therefore affect many spatial points and thus have atomistic destination.

If relatively large firms prevail in the production of consumption goods, we have a partially polarized distribution of these firms over space. Additional demand with an atomistic origin will then be directed toward the spatial points where the large firms are located and will thus be partially or totally polarized. As a result, the larger the optimal size of firms the more polarized is the incidence of an increase in consumption demand.

If the increase in demand is not atomistic but partially or totally polarized at its origin, the incidence of increased demand for commodities produced by small-sized firms is characterized by partial polarization at the same spatial points where demand originates. In the case of goods produced by larger firms we also reach a polarization as the partially polarized origin leads to a partially or totally polarized incidence of the increase in demand.

2. Similar considerations have to be made for the spatial-impact analysis of increases in investment demand. Normally the increase in investment demand originates at some spatial points—namely, partially polarized points—due to the distribution of industry in space. An atomistic origin of an increase in investment demand is rather unlikely.

It can be assumed that the investment sector tends to be characterized by larger-sized firms. Under this assumption the increase in investment demand will affect only some spatial points and will thus be partially polarized. This effect can be expected if existing units have to increase their capacity in order to satisfy the additional demand. It also holds if new firms have to be established in case the existing capacity cannot be expanded.

A totally polarized increase in investment demand at the origin exists in the case of a "firme motrice"[27]—a strongly growing firm in the region. Very often if the firm's demand surpasses a certain level the supplying enterprises will locate near the "firm motrice." In this case strong backward linkages[28] intensify polarization.

PROBLEMS

1. Assume a Cobb-Douglas function with neutral technical change and express the development potential of a closed region as the total differential. Discuss the factors influencing the growth potential.

2. Follow the development of growth theory for national economies in the last twenty years. Compare the work of Domar, Duesenberry, Solow, Kaldor, Denison, and Nelson. (References are found in the text.)

3. Write down the basic equations of Solow's first neoclassical growth model[29] and derive the equilibrium growth rate.

4. Discuss how growth in a region is influenced by changes in its social

[27]F. Perroux, "La Firme Motrice dans la Région et la Région Motrice," *Théorie et Politique de l'Expansion Régionale,* Actes du Colloque International de l'Institut de Science Economique de l'Université de Liège, Brussels, Belgium, 1961, pp. 257–305.

[28]A. O. Hirschman, *The Strategy of Economic Development,* Yale U.P., New Haven, Conn., 1958, p. 100.

[29]R. M. Solow, "A Contribution to the Theory of Economic Growth." For an interpretation of the Solow model, compare G. C. Archibald and R. G. Lipsey, *"An Introduction to a Mathematical Treatment of Economics,"* Weidenfeld and Nicolson, London, 1967.

system. How do changes in the social system of region I affect the development of region II?

5. Discuss the impact of technological change on the economic landscape.

6. Assume that the technical knowledge of a spatial point is defined by the set $\{y_1, y_2, \ldots, y_n\}$ with y_i denoting a specific technical information. Define the concept of technical knowledge of a region, i.e., a finite set of spatial points as, (1) the union of the information sets of the spatial points, (2) the intersection of these information sets, or (3) the union minus the intersection. Discuss the meaning of these different definitions.

7. "... The body of scientific [technical] knowledge, in any given field at a given time, is definitively structured. Advance does not and cannot take place in random fashion in all directions at once, i.e. unselectively."[30] Discuss this statement.

[30] T. Parsons, *The Social System,* Free Press, 1951, p. 336.

part II

GROWTH IN AN OPEN REGION: THE EXTERNAL DETERMINANTS

chapter 4

Expansion Effects of Interregional Factor Movements

In the preceding chapter we have constructed a system of hypotheses which explains the internal increase of regional income. We will now analyze the expansion of an open area and see to what extent our model has to be modified in order to allow for interaction between regions. We have to study how a dynamic process which starts in one area spreads to other regions, and how it affects the economic activity of these areas. Consequently we have to determine the additional growth determinants which can arise in the case of an open region. Since these growth factors relate to an open area and do not originate within the region, we call them *external determinants*. Two basic forms of interregional interaction will be distinguished—the movement of factors of production and the exchange of commodities. In the present chapter we discuss the expansion effects of factor movements. In Chapter 5 the growth effects of interregional commodity exchange are analyzed.

A. THE RELEVANCE OF EXTERNAL DETERMINANTS FOR REGIONAL GROWTH ANALYSIS

1. *Basic differences from international trade theory.* For regions which are subunits of a national system, external growth factors are of major importance. Although these factors play a role in international trade theory, basic differences between regional analysis and the theory of international trade exist.

On the international level, factors of production are very often assumed to be immobile or to be characterized by a very low degree of international mobility. For regions as subsystems of nations we can expect a higher mobility of factors of production because impediments to factor mobility, such as distance, are less severe on the regional level.

Regions also have a higher intensity of commodity exchange than nations. Let the intensity of interregional interaction be measured by the volume of exports and imports in relation to regional income: $\dfrac{X+M}{2Y}$. Both exports and imports are used in order to avoid the problem that the index is strongly influenced by a trade surplus or a trade deficit. Let the magnitude of the region be expressed by its geographic area or by a mixed index which takes into account both the spatial extension of the area and the volume of its income. Then we can expect the relation between these two variables as indicated in Fig. 4-1.

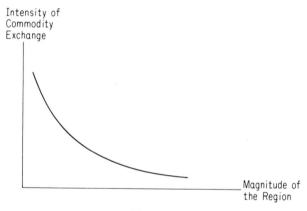

Fig. 4-1

The intensity of commodity interaction between regions decreases with an increase in the magnitude of the area. The larger the region, the lower the intensity of interregional interaction. The smaller the region, the stronger the interaction with other areas and the dependence on the economic processes in other regions.

Boudeville[1] finds that the relation of foreign trade to regional income for the Rhône-Alpes region in France is 68 percent. For a larger system, such as a nation, much lower percentages prevail. But assume that a region as a subsystem of a nation has the same geographic area as a nation. Then the region will be characterized by a higher intensity of interaction because the commodity exchange between nations is subject to political, institutional, social, and historical trade obstacles. Thus Belgium and Holland, with a smaller geographic area than the Rhône-Alpes region, have an intensity of international interaction of 20 and 30 percent.[2] These data indicate that trade barriers such as political and institu-

[1]J. R. Boudeville, "Frontiers and Interrelations of Regional Planning," in E.A.G. Robinson, (ed.), *Problems of Economic Development*, Macmillan, London, 1965, p. 462.
[2]*Ibid.*

tional obstacles are generally not as relevant for a region as for a nation. In the case of a nation the curve in Fig. 4-1 will be shifted downward by the additional trade barriers. We conclude that a region is characterized by a substantially higher degree of openness with respect to commodity exchange.

Finally, regions as subsystems of a nation may force us to rethink international trade theory because they normally belong to a common-currency area. Consequently, all problems of monetary trade theory become irrelevant to regional analysis. Insofar as the monetary theory of international trade is needed for the application of the pure theory of international trade, as in the case of comparative advantage,[3] we have to search for different kinds of explanations.

These considerations, which point out the importance of the external determinants of regional growth, also clearly show that the emphasis of our study has to be shifted. Our analysis of external determinants cannot explain both the expansive and spatial effects as was done in the case of internal growth factors. Therefore the impact of external determinants on the internal spatial structure of the region will be neglected. For purposes of simplification it becomes necessary to assume perfect mobility of factors and commodities within the region. Thus the region melts into a single point for which transport costs and spatial frictions are assumed away. The space dimension, however, is included in our analysis as transportation costs between regions are taken into consideration. The spatial effects of external growth determinants can easily be analyzed by duplicating our procedure in the spatial-impact study of internal factors.

2. *The underlying two-region model.* The external determinants will be analyzed for a two-region model. Two regions, I and II, constitute the national economy. Figure 4-2 illustrates this situation.

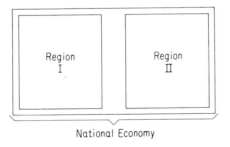

National Economy

Fig. 4-2

Our analysis has to distinguish between regional and interregional products. An interregional product is a commodity which is demanded in both regions (sufficient condition); the product may be produced in one region only. Correspondingly, a regional product is defined as a good which is sold in one region

3Compare Chap. 5, p. 91.

only due to differing regional-demand patterns, high transport costs, or a lack of transport facilities necessary for the product in question.

Whereas in Part I we assumed only one homogeneous aggregate output, we now have to introduce at least one interregional commodity for each region. A single interregional commodity implies conditions which are inconsistent with an interregional approach, either by allowing only one region or by having no interaction.

The assumption of only one interregional commodity for the two-region case implies one of the following. (a) Both regions are completely separated from each other. There is no interaction between the two subunits of the system, e.g., the national economy. In this case we cannot speak of a system of regions because a system requires that its subunits, the regions, interact with each other. (b) The regions are not separated from each other so that interaction is possible and they do not differ in their production conditions. In this case, region I is identical to region II. The subunits melt into one area. If we do not take refuge to additional criteria, such as the social system, there are no specific characteristics for the two subunits. (c) The regions are not separated from each other but differ in their production conditions. The inputs of capital, labor, and technical knowledge, are distributed unevenly among the two regions so that one area has a production advantage for the single interregional commodity. Two cases must be distinguished. (1) If factors of production are completely mobile interregionally (and completely divisible) they will eventually move to the region where the interregional commodity is demanded. As factors move to the place of demand there is no need for an interregional exchange of one interregional commodity. After a series of factor movements the regions will not differ. We have the same result as in (b). (2) If factors of production are completely immobile, it follows logically that one region must have a permanent production advantage. Then interaction cannot take place because the favored region is not interested in trade, and the disfavored region—although interested—cannot offer any commodities in exchange. We reach the same result as in case (a).

From cases (a), (b), and (c) we conclude the following. If two regions are introduced into our analysis, each region must at least produce one commodity which is exchanged interregionally. For a system of three regions we get an analogous solution. The production of only one or only two interregional outputs in a system of three regions does not yield a meaningful result. The minimum requirement in this case is three interregional commodities. Thus we can postulate the following theorem of model construction: The construction of a system of n interconnected regions presupposes a minimum number of n interregional commodities with each region producing at least one interregional good.

From this theorem it follows that our two-region model must contain two interregional commodities. The exchange of these goods represents one form of interregional interaction. The expansion effects of this form of exchange is discussed in Chapter 5. The other form of interregional interaction is the movement of factors of production. Migration of production factors is identical to variations in the availability of inputs and has direct implications for the level of output in different regions due to relation 3-5. Introduction of hypotheses which explain the interregional mobility of factors of production is therefore a first step in extending the growth model to an open region. These hypotheses have to be postulated for the interregional movement of labor and capital, and the transfer of technical knowledge between regions. In order to simplify the analysis, it is assumed throughout Chapter 4 that consumption goods are interregionally immobile and that factor movements represent the only form of interaction between regions. Consumption goods are demanded in the region where they are produced.

B. MOBILITY OF LABOR

Like increases in population, movements of population between regions are not a purely economic but a social phenomenon which cannot be tackled with economic tools alone. Each supplier of labor is integrated into a system of groups by role expectations, their enforcement, and social positions, and these groups are usually concentrated in one geographic area. His behavior, which is determined by the norms of his groups, is characterized by a pattern of perseverance linking the individual to his groups and, via the groups, to a region. Interregional mobility of labor can exist only if processes are started which loosen the ties of the individual with his group.

1. *Aspiration level and reference-group behavior.* The interregional movement of labor can be understood as a social action. Each social action[4] consists of three basic elements—an actor, a situation, and the orientation of the actor to the situation. A social action may be interpreted as a stimulus-response mechanism in which an actor responds to a situation or a change in a situation. The orientation of an actor toward a situation determines his response.

The orientation, in turn, depends on the goals of the individual actor. These goals may not be expressed specifically, but we may assume an "intently rational" man[5] who wants to reach a certain aspiration level. "This subjectively determined threshold is a weighted composite of a set of yardsticks for achievement in the specific realms in which he participates."[6] The achievement level z

---

[4]T. Parsons and E. A. Shils (eds.), *Toward a General Theory of Action*, Harvard U.P. Cambridge, Mass., 1951, p. 53.

[5]H. A. Simon, "A Behavioral Model of Rational Choice," *Quarterly Journal of Economics*, Vol. 69 (1955), p. 114. An excellent discussion of the behavorial aspect of migration is given in J. Wolpert, "Behavorial Aspects of the Decision to Migrate," *Papers and Proceedings of the Regional Science Association*, Vol. 15 (1965), pp. 159–169. On the principle of "bounded rationality," compare H. A. Simon, *Models of Man*, Wiley, New York, 1957, pp. 196–206.

[6]Wolpert, *op. cit.,* p. 162. Compare H. A. Simon, "Theories of Decision-Making in Economics and Behavorial Science," *American Economic Review*, Vol. 49 (1959), p. 263.

thus may be defined as a set of values $z_1, z_2, \ldots, z_n$ which the individual wants to reach.

$$z = \{z_1, z_2, z_3, \ldots, z_n\} \tag{4-1}$$

The achievement level is not fixed at a permanent target level. It depends on the past experience of the individual and on the targets fulfilled by others with whom the actor compares himself. The group which serves as a frame of reference is called the *reference group*.[7] The achievement level of an actor A with respect to any variable z_i (i denoting the elements of Eq. 4-1) depends on the previously realized achievements $^A z_i^{t-1}$, $^A z_i^{t-2}$ and on the achievements of the reference group B, $^B z_i^t$. The performance of the actor in the more recent periods may have greater weights:

$$^A z_i^t = f(^A z_i^{t-1}, ^A z_i^{t-2}, \ldots, ^A z_i^{t-n}, ^B z_i^t) \tag{4-2}$$

If we assume a man with "limited rationality,"[8] he compares his desired achievement level with his actual performance, i.e., his realized achievement level. The realized achievement level indicates the place utility which "refers to the net composite of utilities which are derived from the individual's integration at some position in space."[9] The following cases are conceivable.

(a) The individual may have realized poor targets in the past and, even though his reference group has realized a higher achievement level, he is not dissatisfied with his situation and reduces his aspirations. The social system may provide mechanisms which either (1) enable the individual to reduce his achievement level, or (2) prevent the desired achievement level from becoming too high, or (3) prevent the realization of too high achievement levels and thus induce its reduction.

(b) The individual may be dissatisfied with his performance compared to his reference group in the region. This has two consequences: (1) The individual has a different predisposition for information from other regions. He is open to alternatives, and any signal indicating better opportunities in another area is more likely to be noticed. (2) If dissatisfaction with the given situation is strong enough, the individual starts searching systematically for better opportunities. Information on these opportunities may induce the individual to change his reference group. The worker in region I starts to compare himself with the worker in region II. This is the first step toward becoming a "marginal man"[10] in his old environment. The new reference group reinforces the conflict between the desired and actual achievement level for the individual.

(c) Even if the individual is not originally dissatisfied with his performance compared to his regional reference group, additional information on better eco-

---

[7]R. K. Merton, *Social Theory and Social Structure,* Free Press New York, 1957, p. 225.
[8]H. A. Simon, "A Behavioral Model of Rational Choice," p. 102.
[9]Wolpert, *loc. cit.*
[10]Merton, *op. cit.*, p. 265.

nomic opportunities in another region may induce the choice of a new reference group. This in turn—as in case (b)—may lead to a new desired achievement level. Cases (b) and (c) describe situations which eventually may result in migration.

The willingness of an actor to migrate depends on the reference-group behavior of the individual. The choice of a new reference group which includes persons in a comparable position in another region alienates the actor from his original group and orientates him toward a new group. The more intensive the orientation toward a group outside the region, the greater are the chances for interregional mobility.

2. *Information aspects.* One necessary condition for the orientation toward a group outside the region is the interregional differentiation of those variables which influence the overall attainment level of the individual. This condition, however, is not a sufficient one. The actor needs information on the behavior of the relevant variables in another region. This knowledge is not objectively new in the sense that the society as a whole did not have the knowledge so far, but it represents subjectively new information.[11]

It is tempting to apply the results of mathematical information theory to the information aspect of interregional migration. Mathematical information theory[12] is a formal analysis of information transmission. The information of a signal (or a message) is defined as its ability to reduce the uncertainty of a receiver. A signal with a high probability of occurrence, therefore, conveys little information; whereas a signal with a high statistical rarity or a high surprise value contains more information.[13]

Assume, for instance, that there are eight spatial points (or regions) to which the individual may migrate. The individual is interested to know whether better opportunities exist at these spatial points than at his actual location. In this situation the actor may receive different messages: (1) A higher wage rate is not paid at spatial point 8. (2) A higher wage is not paid at the spatial points 1, 2, 3, and 4. The two statements differ in the reduction of uncertainty and therefore have a different information content. Assume that the actor does not know a priori probabilities for the occurrence of a higher wage rate at the eight

[11]F. Machlup, *The Production and Distribution of Knowledge in the United States.* Princeton U.P., Princeton, N.J., 1962, p. 28.

[12]On information theory: R. L. Meier, *A Communications Theory of Urban Growth,* M.I.T. Press, Cambridge, Mass., 1962, C. Shannon and W. Weaver, *The Mathematical Theory of Communication,* U. of Illinois Press, Urbana, 1949; A. Feinstein, *Foundations of Information Theory,* McGraw-Hill, New York, 1958; F. M. Reza, *An Introduction to Information Theory,* McGraw-Hill, New York, 1961; A. M. McDonough, *Information Economics and Management Systems,* McGraw-Hill, New York, 1963, R. A. Johnson, F. W. Kast, and J. E. Rosenzweig, *The Theory and Management of Systems,* McGraw-Hill, New York, 1963; C. Cherry, *On Human Communication,* M.I.T. Press, Cambridge, Mass. and Wiley, New York, 1957; W. Schramm, "Information Theory and Mass Communication," in B. Berelson and M. Janowitz (eds.), *Reader in Public Opinion and Communication,* Collier, New York, 1966.

[13]Schramm, *op. cit.,* p. 714; Cherry, *op. cit.,* p. 36.

spatial points, so that each point has the same probability of sending a positive signal. Under this assumption statement (1) reduces uncertainty by one eighth; whereas statement (2) reduces uncertainty by one half.

In the latter case, the actor has received one *bit* of information.[14] Thus a bit of information has been transmitted if the number of equally probable signals is reduced by one half. Having defined a basic unit of information we are in a position to apply this concept of mathematical information theory to the migration decision. How many bits of information are necessary to identify the spatial points with a positive signal, i.e., a higher wage. This problem is illustrated in Fig. 4-3 with 0 denoting a *no*-signal and 1 representing a *yes*-signal.

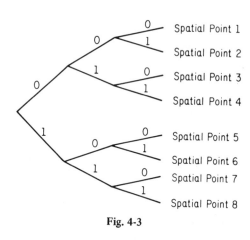

Fig. 4-3

Three *yes-no* answers are sufficient to identify all eight spatial points as a sender of a positive signal. (1) Does the signal come from the first half of the spatial points? (yes or no); (2) From the first fourth part? (yes or no); and (3) From the first half of a fourth part? (yes or no) One bit identifies a (positive) signal from 2 spatial points, 2 bits identify a signal from 2^2 points, 3 bits from 2^3 points, and n bits from 2^n points. It follows that logarithms to the base 2 can be used to measure information in terms of bits, e.g., $\log_2 2^3 = \log_2 8 = 3$.

With probability $p(i) = 1/a$ for an event i, i.e., a higher wage at a spatial point, the necessary information for the identification of event i is $\log_2 a$, with $a = 1/p(i)$. Denoting the information on event i with $h(i)$ we have

$$h(i) = \log_2 a = \log_2 [1/p(i)] = \log_2 1 - \log_2 p(i) = -\log_2 p(i) \quad (4\text{-}3)$$

Equation 4-3 specifies the bits of information that are necessary to identify an event i.[15] Equation 4-3 is the starting point for the derivation of such concepts as average information, relative and absolute entropy, and redundancy.

[14]On the definition of a bit, compare Schramm, *op. cit.*; Cherry, *op. cit.*, p. 170.
[15]Schramm, *op. cit.*, p. 728.

Mathematical information theory is based on a rather specific information concept which is defined in terms of reducing uncertainty. For the explanation of economic behavior, however, the value of a message with respect to the goal system of an actor is of utmost importance. Such a valuation[16] of a message or a signal is not possible by mathematical information theory which, at this stage, is not concerned with the communication of news but with the transmission of signals. In Fig. 4-3, for instance, the 3 bits of information are not too meaningful for an actor since the difference in the wage rate may be negligible. The exact wage rate is not given by binary digits. Admittedly it is possible to inquire the exact level of the wage rate by a series of questions. (Does point 8 pay a higher wage than x dollars, $x + 1, x + 2, x + 3, \ldots$, yes or no?) The bits, however, refer to different economic situations and are not comparable to one another in an economic sense. The bit is merely a unit in counting yes-no signals. Because of these difficulties we here approach the information problem of the migration decision from a sociological point of view.

As any communication system consists of a sender, a receiver, and the communication channels, the communication of the new knowledge depends (a) on the predisposition of the receiver, namely, our actor, (b) on the communication channels, and (c) on the intensity of the information impulse from the sender.

The predisposition of the receiver depends on his degree of satisfaction or dissatisfaction with his actual situation, as has been discussed. He may not notice information flows if he is satisfied with his position, he may be open to incoming information, or he may even actively engage in systematic search for new knowledge on economic opportunities.

The information flows also depend on the structure of the communication system, i.e., the existing information channels. In order to derive conclusions on the distribution of information and its transmission, we would have to develop an interregional communication model which contains the information flows concerning those variables that determine the attainment level of the individual. An important distinction has to be made between formal and informal information flows in such a communication model. Formal information flows are given if organized information channels are used for the transmission of news, such as mass media. Informal information flows arise spontaneously, without any organization; they normally involve a person-to-person relationship, although they may use technical apparatus.[17]

Informal streams of information depend on the frequency of personal contacts, which in turn are a function of social structure, e.g., the membership in

[16]On the evaluation of information: J. Marshak, "Efficient and Viable Organizational Forms," in M. Haire (ed.), *Modern Organization Theory*, Wiley, New York, 1959, p. 319; J. Marshak, "Theory of an Efficient Several-Person Firm," *American Economic Review, Papers and Proceedings*, Vol. 50 (1960), p. 545; J. Marshak, *Economic Theory of Information and Organization* (Mimeographed lecture notes by E. Bössmann, Cowles Foundation, New Haven, Conn.), p. 11.3.

[17]The distinction between formal and informal structures is customary in sociology.

different groups. Normally information channels will correspond to group structures. This means that a large part of information on migration possibilities depends on past migration. Migrants communicate with members of their old group and thus provide important information effects.[18]

Information sent by migrants may, however, be distorted. According to the hypothesis of cognitive dissonance,[19] perceptions and values become consistent with experienced reality. After migration actually takes place, the individual continues to collect information which justifies the decision. This method of information collection implies that some shortcomings of the new situation may be compensated for by the overestimation of favorable information flows. This mechanism also causes distortion of information being sent by the migrants to their original region.[20]

Not only do informal communication flows occur within one group, but information will also flow between different groups. This information is transmitted by persons with multiple-group membership. Informal information flows therefore depend on the following factors:

(1) The social structure: news will normally be transmitted to members of the same group.

(2) The type of information and the value of the new knowledge for the group: information not relevant for a group will not be transmitted. Thus weak elements in an information chain may arise. If, for instance, members of group I who are in a good economic position hear about high wages in another region, this knowledge may not be interesting for this group. The new knowledge may leak away in group I, and group II with potential migrants may never hear about the better opportunities.

(3) The intensity of group membership: the more intense group relations, the more important is the social structure for the derivation of information channels.

Formal information flows make use of an organized communication system; they do not represent person-to-person information. Examples are the recruitment by job offices or the spread of information by mass media. But these formal channels of communication do not ensure a perfect mobility of knowledge about opportunities in other areas.

The distribution of formal information flows depends on the communication space intended by the sender. The area of coverage intended is a function of the type of labor. For top executives, recruiting and consequently information flows are nationwide. The same is not true for other types of labor.[21]

Empirical evidence suggests that mass communication does not influence

[18]P. Nelson, "Migration, Real Income and Information," *Journal of Regional Science,* Vol. 1 (1959), p. 49.

[19]L. Festinger, *Theory of Cognitive Dissonance,* Harper & Row, New York, 1957.

[20]The overestimation of economic opportunities may eventually induce an improvement of these opportunities (self-fulfilling prophecy).

[21]On this point, compare Wolpert, *op. cit.,* p. 164.

individual behavior with the same intensity as informal communication. Person-to-person information flows are necessary to evaluate the news of mass media.[22] Specific migration studies tend to support these findings. Migrants to a war plant in Seattle received 34-53 percent of their information from friends, although there was intensive recruitment by government agencies.[23]

The spatial distribution of informal and formal information flows and the structure of interregional communication systems can be analyzed with simulation models, probability theory, and in terms of network studies and graph theory.[24] If we abstract from those types of labor for which a national labor market exist, we can expect that the intensity of an information impulse decreases with the length of the communication network and is thus a function of distance.

Information on better opportunities in another region depends not only on the predisposition of the receiver and the structure of the communication system but also on the third element of a communication process—the sender. Thus the number of senders and also their distribution over space influences the information flows. Information impulses are also a function of the difference in opportunities. The higher the wage differences, the stronger the information impulse at its origin. If the wage differences do not reach certain thresholds, no information effect may be expected.

3. *Search processes and migration decisions.* In the preceding analysis the actor has been viewed in a passive role as a receiver of information. Reference-group behavior, however, may not only result in a changed predisposition for incoming information but may also lead to a search behavior of the actor. If the actor is characterized by an unlimited rationality his search behavior can be explained in terms of search theory.[25] Search theory has been developed for military and exploratory search problems. Its results are applicable to economic search behavior as well. Search theory assumes that the actor maximizes the probability to find an object with a given search effort. The search problem[26] is described by Eqs. 4-4 through 4-10.

[22]E. Katz and P. F. Lazarsfield, *Personal Influence*; Free Press, New York, 1955.

[23]Nelson, *op. cit.*, p. 63.

[24]D. Cartwright, "The Potential Contribution of Graph Theory to Organization Theory," in M. Haire (ed.), *Modern Organization Theory—A Symposium of the Foundation for the Research of Human Behavior*, Wiley, New York, 1959, pp. 254-271; J. S. de Cani, "On the Construction of Stochastic Models of Population Growth and Migration," *Journal of Regional Science*, Vol. 3 (1961), pp. 1-13.

[25]B. O. Koopman, "The Theory of Search," *Operations Research*, Vol. 4 (1956), pp. 124-346, 503-531; Vol. 5 (1957), pp. 613-626; A. Charnes and W. W. Cooper, "The Theory of Search: Optimum Distribution of Search Effort," *Management Science*, Vol. 5 (1958), pp. 44-50; E. N. Gilbert, "Optimal Search Strategies," *Journal of the Society for Industrial and Applied Mathematics*, Vol. 7 (1959), pp. 413-424; J. C. Griffiths, "Exploration for Natural Resources," *Operations Research*, Vol. 14 (1966), pp. 189-209; J. de Guenin, "Optimum Distribution of Effort: An Extension of the Koopman Basic Theory," *Operations Research*, Vol. 9 (1961), pp. 1-7; G. Stigler, "The Economics of Information," *Journal of Political Economy*, Vol. 69 (1961), pp. 213-225.

[26]On the formal structure of a search problem, compare Koopman, *op. cit.,* Vol. 5 (1957), pp. 614-615; de Guenin, *op. cit.,* pp. 1-4.

An object, i.e., a better opportunity, exists in a space. The location of the object is defined by a random variable X. The probability that the object is located between x and $x + dx$, is given function $g(x)$.

$$Pr = g(x)dx \qquad (x \leqslant X \leqslant x + dx) \tag{4-4}$$

The properties of the function are

$$g(x) \geqslant 0 \tag{4-5}$$

$$\int_{-\infty}^{+\infty} g(x)\, dx = 1 \tag{4-6}$$

Condition 4-6 implies that the object is necessarily located in a given space. It can also be assumed that the actor does not know whether the object is in the space.[27]

The search effort is limited by Φ which is a constant. The properties of the search density $\zeta(x)$ are

$$\zeta(x) \geqslant 0 \tag{4-7}$$

and

$$\int_{-\infty}^{+\infty} \zeta(x)dx = \Phi \tag{4-8}$$

$p[\zeta(x)]$ is the probability to find the object if it is located at x. This function specifies that an actor may glimpse at an object without detecting it. The higher $\zeta(x)$, the greater are the chances of detecting the object. This function introduces the concept of noticeability. This concept, which is taken from military search theory, is also relevant for economic search processes. For instance, one aspect of the noticeability of an economic object is the reaction of the object, i.e., its communication response to search stimuli.

The probability to find an object which is located between x and $x + dx$ is

$$g(x)\, p\, [\zeta(x)]\ dx \tag{4-9}$$

Consequently, the probability of success P is a function of the search effort

$$P = \int_{-\infty}^{+\infty} g(x)\, p\, [\zeta(x)]\ dx = P(\zeta) \tag{4-10}$$

---

[27]de Guenin, op. cit., p. 2. In this case it is assumed that the object has the probability α to be in the space, with $\alpha \leqslant 1$. Equation 4-6 turns into

$$\int_{-\infty}^{+\infty} g(x)\, dx = \alpha$$

$\alpha < 1$ denotes the case in which it is known whether there is an object in the space.

The search problem consists in determining the search density which maximizes the probability of success $P(\zeta)$ subject to the restraints 4-7 and 4-8. The solution of this problem allows the derivation of theorems on the optimal search effort.[28] This approach has, however, certain limitations for our analysis of the migration decision. First, it implies an actor with unlimited rationality whereas we assume an "intently rational" man. Second, an economic theory of search requires the valuation of the search object in terms of the goal system of an actor. Here, however, the problem arises that an object has to be evaluated which is not yet known. Third, search costs may depend on other variables and vary in the process of search.[29] In spite of these difficulties search theory and its combination with information theory represents an interesting approach to mobility analysis. The approach is not restricted to the analysis of the mobility of labor, but may also be applied to the mobility of capital, of commodities, and of firms, i.e., the location decisions of entrepreneurs.

If we give up the stringent assumption of unlimited rationality, only satisfactory alternatives are searched for. The individual is likely to search in a less systematic fashion and to concentrate his search effort on those spatial points which are part of his information horizon. Only when the place utilities of these familiar spatial points do not allow a reduction of the gap between desired and actual attainment levels will new spatial points be added to the search set. Thus the search process with limited rationality is characterized by a process of sequential-information gathering with the set of spatial search points being enlarged after each search failure. If a satisfactory result is found, the actor may end the search process without being certain that better opportunities still exist. On the other hand, easy and quick search results may lead to higher aspiration levels and continued searching.

The hypothesis of a limited search horizon and of sequential-information gathering points out an important obstacle to interregional mobility. The individual concentrates his first search efforts on his old region before orienting his search toward other areas. If he finds a satisfactory place utility in his region, the search process is terminated even if better opportunities in other regions exist. The mechanism of sequential-information gathering forestalls interregional mobility.

A search process cannot be continued indefinitely. Assume the actor has found a problem solution which is satisfactory. Continuing the search involves the risk of losing the satisfactory opportunity (economic variables change, a position is taken).[30] The search process is also limited by search costs. These costs consist in time costs and costs of communication and information gathering. Each additional search effort increases total search costs. Consequently, the

[28] de Guenin, op. cit., p. 6.
[29] J. MacQueen and R. G. Miller, "Optimum Persistence Policies," Operations Research, Vol. 8 (1960), p. 363.
[30] MacQueen and Miller, op. cit., p. 219.

place utility of any new search result must be higher (at least by the additional search costs) than the place utility of an already existing satisfactory alternative. Finally, search costs increase with distance so that the search process is not only limited in time but also in space.

4. *Determinants of labor mobility.* The knowledge of better opportunities is not a sufficient condition for migration to occur. Migration involves transportation costs. These costs must either be earned in a relatively short period[31] or the newly realized attainment level with respect to nonmonetary variables must be valued much higher than the welfare loss from transportation costs. Normally the first condition applies.

Transportation costs vary with distance. We have also seen that the intensity of the information effects depends on distance. Finally, the social system can be assumed to vary with distance, and differences in the social system represent an obstacle to migration. We conclude that the mobility of labor is a function of distance: (a) the greater the distance, the greater the difference in the social systems and the stronger the obstacles to mobility; (b) the greater the distance, the less intense are the formal and informal information effects; (c) the greater the distance, the higher are the search costs; (d) the greater the distance, the higher are the costs of transportation; and (e) the greater the distance, the more intervening opportunities are likely to exist.

The concept of intervening opportunities was developed by Stouffer.[32] "The idea is that the number of people going a given distance s from a point is not a function of distance directly but rather a function of the spatial distribution of opportunities."[33] Stouffer postulates that the number of persons who migrate a distance is directly proportional to the number of opportunities on the periphery and inversely proportional to the number of opportunities in the circle.[34]

Measuring labor mobility as the proportion of migrating workers to total work force, the mobility of labor decreases with distance, as shown in Fig. 4-4.

Substituting for distance with different magnitudes of regions, we can postulate that the mobility of labor declines with an increase in the area under consideration. Regions as subsystems of a nation are characterized by a relatively high intraregional mobility where interregional and international mobility is relatively low. Figure 4-5 illustrates the relationship.

As our analysis is related to interregional problems, a specific range of distance is given. Thus the dependence of mobility on distance is implicitly taken into consideration and need not be introduced explicitly. In a two-region model

[31]G. S. Tolley, "Population Adjustment and Economic Activity: Three Studies," *Papers and Proceedings of the Regional Science Association*, Vol. 11 (1963), p 87.
[32]S. A. Stouffer, "Intervening Opportunities: A Theory Relating Mobility and Distance," *American Sociological Review*, Vol. 5 (1940), pp. 845–867.
[33]S. A. Stouffer, "Intervening Opportunities and Competing Migrants," *Journal of Regional Science*, Vol. 2 (1960), p. 1.
[34]This approach has been developed further in the concept of competing migrants, *ibid.*

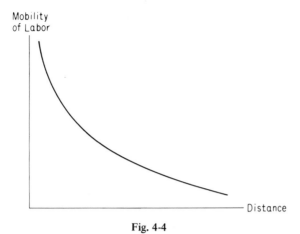

Fig. 4-4

we may also abstract from the problem that the mobility between adjacent regions will be greater than between nonadjacent areas.

Since the dependence on distance is taken into account implicitly, the
interregional mobility of labor may be considered as a function of the distribution of opportunities between regions. The difference in opportunities can be
expressed in terms of variables such as income, rate, and stability of employment,
cost of living, availability of a cultural infrastructure such as educational facilities, social positions, and the amenity factor[35] of a location. For purposes of
simplification we assume that the number of workers migrating to an area depends
on the wage rates in the two regions—the greater the difference in wages, the

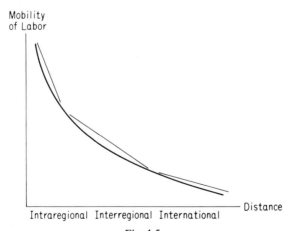

Fig. 4-5

[35] H. S. Perloff *et al.*, *Regions, Resources and Economic Growth*, Johns Hopkins Press,
Baltimore, Md., 1960, p. 72.

stronger is the information effect, the higher (*ceteris paribus*) the possible attainment level at the new location, and the shorter is the period needed to earn the cost of transportation.

The external increase in the labor force of region I, $^{II}dL^I$, is determined by

$$_{t-1}^{II} dL_t^I = f(w_{t-1}^I, w_{t-1}^{II})$$ (4-11)

If $^{II}dL^I$ becomes negative, workers emigrate from I to II. The total increase in the labor supply of region I, dL^I, consists of the internal increase $^IdL^I$ and immigration $^{II}dL^I$,

$$dL^I = {}^IdL^I + {}^{II}dL^I$$ (4-12)

5. Expansion effects. The expansion effects of the interregional movements of workers depends not only on the number of migrants but also on their relative quality with respect to the regional labor supply. Thus the withdrawal effect will be greater if the most capable workers migrate.[36] Normally the age group 20-40 represents the largest part of migrants. It is very likely that this group includes the most efficient workers because younger people will have embodied more technical knowledge. From the point of view of the receiving region, the incoming workers may have reached a higher level of technical knowledge than the one which is available in the region, or they may be characterized by a lower level of skill.

The following analysis ignores these problems and assumes a homogeneous labor force in the system of regions. Under this assumption the expansion effects of migration are determined by relation 3-7. They can be illustrated by an Edgeworth-box diagram.[37] Assume the same capital supply in both regions, but a different labor supply. As seen in Fig. 4-6, we get one Edgeworth box for each region.

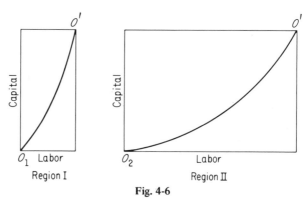

Fig. 4-6

[36] B. Okun and R. W. Richardson, "Regional Income Inequality and Internal Population Migration," *Economic Development and Social Change*, Vol. 9 (1961), reprinted in J. Friedmann and W. Alonso (eds.), *Regional Development and Planning—A Reader*, M.I.T. Press, Cambridge, Mass., 1964, p. 306.

[37] J. Vanek, *International Trade—Theory and Economic Policy*, Irwin, Homewood, Ill., 1962, p. 187.

The lines O_1O' and O_2O' represent the Edgeworth contract curves. They imply production functions which are characterized by decreasing marginal productivities. These contract curves may be used to construct transformation curves.

Let us assume that due to the larger labor supply the wage in region II is lower than in region I and the difference is sufficiently large to induce migration. The reduction in the labor supply of region II is identical to the increase in region I. The contract curve of the region is shifted outward because its production block increases, and the contract curve of region II is shifted inward as its production block is reduced, as shown in Fig. 4-7.

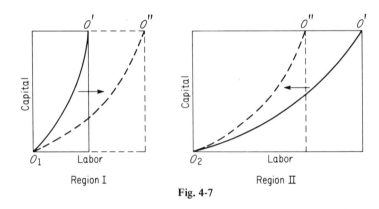

Fig. 4-7

Migration will equalize wages in the two regions, since the marginal productivity of labor in region I decreases and that in region II rises. If labor is completely mobile with zero interregional transportation costs, the final wage difference will be zero. The transformation curve of region I, which represents the production-possibility frontier and the growth potential for a given set of re-

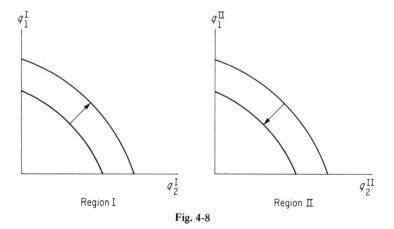

Fig. 4-8

sources, is shifted outward by the immigration of labor. Output increases. The production potential of region II is reduced accordingly (see Fig. 4-8).

The shift of the transformation curve depends on the bias in the production of commodities q_1 and q_2 with respect to labor. Figures 4-6-4-8 demonstrate the effects of migration on the production potential of the two regions.

C. MOBILITY OF CAPITAL

The analysis of the interregional mobility of capital must distinguish three different concepts of capital. First, capital may be defined in terms of the balance of payments. A net capital movement is then the balancing factor between exports and imports.[38] An excess of exports over imports indicates that a region is increasing its claims on the other region and is thus undertaking net foreign investment. Net exports include goods and services, net unilateral transfers, and net income on investment.[39] Second, capital may be defined as a stock of monetary funds. In this case the interregional export of capital is understood as a flow of funds. Third, capital is regarded as an input in the production function.

The three concepts are not identical. For instance, a deficit on current accounts does not mean that a region has imported the input "capital." Assume the trade deficit relates to consumption goods. Then the surplus of imports over exports may be used to set resources free so that they may be allocated to the production of capital units. But this is not necessarily so, since the import surplus may also be used for additional consumption without freeing any resources for capital accumulation. Monetary capital, moreover, is not identical to capital as an input because it includes all assets which are in monetary or in near-money form. As we are interested in regional growth and regard physical capital as the basic determinant of regional output, we will concentrate on the mobility of capital as an input to the production function.

In the case of physical capital goods we need to distinguish between the existing stock of capital and newly produced capital commodities. A large part of the newly produced capital goods is interregionally mobile. This is true for all those investment goods which are to be or can be exported, machinery being the relevant example. Other parts of new capital goods are tied to a specific spatial point in the region where they originate and are therefore no longer mobile (buildings, all infrastructure outlays).

New capital units can be assumed to be more mobile than the existing stock. But once originally mobile capital is connected to land, it becomes functionally immobile. These capital units are integrated into a production process and the costs of taking them out of one technical structure and placing them in a new

[38] J. T. Romans, *Captial Exports and Growth Among U. S. Regions,* Wesleyan U. P., Middletown, Conn., 1965, p. 21.

[39] *Ibid.,* p. 23.

technical environment are normally so high that an economic immobility results. Also, the higher the depreciation of a machine the smaller the chance that it will be moved physically to another area. Thus the existing stock of capital shows some immobility.

Assume the existing physical capital stock is completely immobile and new capital units are mobile. Under this assumption the existing stock may nevertheless be transferred to the other region. Two transfer methods exist: (1) The capital stock of region I is written off and the earned depreciations may be used to buy new machinery which may be sent to region II. The existing capital stock in region I decreases and the stock in region II increases. (2) The second method is to transform the physical capital into monetary units by selling the physical stock to someone who has savings or has accumulated funds in the past. This possibility presupposes, however, that the owner of the existing stock has more information on the higher profit rate in region II than the owner of monetary funds (savings), because otherwise the saver would invest in region II directly. The transformation of physical capital into monetary funds is one way in which an immobile stock of capital may become more mobile.

Capital can move from one region to the other in the following forms: (1) An old or a new machine of region I is exchanged for a commodity of region II. The transfer of a machine reduces the existing stock in region I (old machine) or prevents a potential increase of the capital stock (new machine). If region II offers consumption goods in exchange, the transaction reduces the actual or potential capital stock in region I and increases the capital stock in region II. If region II offers investment goods in return, the capital stocks in the two regions change their composition, but none of the regions loses capital goods. Note that in this case the capital used in a region is also owned by the residents of the area. (2) An old or a new machine may be sent from region I to region II without any commodity flow in return. Region I is still the owner of the machine, and region II has to pay interest charges in each subsequent period. The first case represents an exchange, and the second case is a transfer which is one-sided in the short run.

As soon as money enters the picture the corresponding cases to (1) and (2) are as follows: (3) The monetary counterpart of (1) is that both regions have funds available for the import of commodities from the other region. The physical exchange of commodities is reflected in the exchange of monetary payments between the two regions in one period. (4) Region I has at its disposal monetary capital, namely, funds for investment stemming from saving or earned depreciations. (a) These funds may be lent to region II which buys machines from region I. (b) The monetary capital may be used to free resources in region II from the production of consumption goods. These resources may then be used to build capital in region II.[40] This has the same effect as the transfer of a machine. If the monetary capital represents savings of region I, the potential in-

---

[40]In this case an export surplus is identical to a capital transfer.

crease in the capital stock in region I is not realized. If the monetary capital originates from earned depreciations, the existing stock in region I decreases. Cases (4a) and (4b) are the monetary aspect of case (2); one region gets a higher capital stock at the expense of the other. Although the exchange of commodities [cases (1) and (3)] may influence the capital stock,[41] we concentrate on cases (2) and (4). We now need to explain why capital leaves one region and moves to another.

Capital accumulation in a closed region depends on the demand and supply of investment funds, with savings representing the supply of investment funds and the profit rate determining the demand for investment funds.[42] Capital accumulation in an open region (dK^I) consists of the internal increase $(^IdK^I)$ and the external increase $(^{II}dK^I)$.

$$_{t-1}dK^I_{t+1} = {}_{t-1}^I dK^I_{t+1} + {}_{t-1}^{II} dK^I_{t+1} \qquad (4\text{-}13)$$

The external variation of the capital stock may become negative if capital moves from region I to region II. If the existing stock of capital is immobile, the outflow is limited by the internal increase. Otherwise it may very well surpass the internal increase because the existing capital stock may be reduced by an outflow of old capital units.

The external variation in the capital stock can be regarded as a function of the rates of return in the two regions. If the rate of return is higher in region II than in region I, capital will flow from I to II. If the rate of return is higher in region I, capital will be attracted to this area.

$$^{II}dK^I = f(r^I, r^{II}) \qquad (4\text{-}14)$$

The mobility of capital is restricted by the following factors: (a) The existing stock of capital tends to be largely immobile in a physical interpretation. Increasing its mobility through earned depreciation involves time. (b) A part of the addition to the capital stock is also immobile (e.g., infrastructure capital). (c) As the sources for investment originate mainly within firms, it can be expected that entrepreneurs tend to invest in their own firms and that it requires sizable differences in the rates of return before any entrepreneur will invest his funds in another region. (d) Finally, information obstacles may reduce the mobility of capital as in the case of labor.

The expansion effects of capital transfers can be explained in the same manner as movements of labor. The Edgeworth box of the capital-receiving region is increased and its transformation curve shifts outward. On the other hand, the Edgeworth box of the capital-sending region becomes smaller and its production frontier shifts to the left.

It should be noted that the mobility of capital affects the definition of

---

[41]This problem is analyzed in Sec. D of Chap. 5.
[42]Compare relation (3-8) in Chap. 3.

regional income and consequently our relations 3-26 through 3-29. Regional income is normally defined according to the residents concept. It is the income accruing to the residents of an area. Regional income may be different from regional product which represents the output produced by all factors of production available to an area. As some factors may be owned by residents of another region, income produced is not identical to income received. Also part of the income produced may leave the area in the form of interest payments. On the other hand, the residents of an area may receive interest payments from another region.[43] Because output produced is the decisive variable of supply and income received, the basic determinant of demand, a regional-growth model should include the definitional relationship between output produced (area concept) and income received (residents concept). For purposes of simplicity, however, we ignore these problems.

D. MOBILITY OF TECHNICAL KNOWLEDGE

1. Increases in regional output do not only depend on the internal and external capital and labor supply, but also on the newly realized technical knowledge. Relations 3-22 through 3-25, explaining the technical change of a closed region, therefore have to be changed for an open area. New technical knowledge—information about potential production processes—does not originate in all regions of a national economy at the same time or at the same rate The region which satisfies the following conditions has greater chances to find new technical knowledge. The statements hold only *ceteris paribus*, everything else but the mentioned variables being constant.

The greater the number of problems in the region which are resistant to solutions by traditional means,[44] the greater the dissatisfaction with existing production procedures.

As the existing knowledge is an input for finding new knowledge, the region with the higher level of existing knowledge has greater chances to invent.

Since an invention requires the confrontation of previously unconnected sets of information,[45] the region has greater chances for inventions where different sets of information are more likely to be confronted. Consequently the regional communication system will influence the possibility of inventions.

Inventions may be thought of as the outcome of a systematic search. Therefore a region has greater chances for inventions when it can use more resources for this search effort.

Because large firms tend to use more resources for research than small ones, the region with larger firms has greater chances to make inventions.

[43] A similar problem arises in the case of commuting labor. Our analysis ignores these interregional commuters.
[44] J. Friedmann, "A General Theory of Polarized Development," The Ford Foundation, Urban and Regional Advisory Program in Chile, Santiago, Chile, 1967 (mimeo), p. 11.
[45] *Ibid.*

The search effort is also undertaken in government-supported research institutions. The more of these institutions in an area, the greater the chances for inventions.

From the foregoing *ceteris paribus* statements we can conclude that new technical knowledge is unlikely to originate in all regions at the same rate. Some regions produce more inventions than others, and also produce different types of inventions. New technical knowledge is not ubiquitous at its origin.

2. As the technical horizon changes differently in the regions, the realized increase in technical knowledge depends on the mobility of the new knowledge between regions.[46] If new technical knowledge is completely mobile, the new ideas are available to all regions. The region making fewer inventions experiences an inflow of new ideas in addition to its own inventions during the period. If the new technical knowledge is completely immobile, no inflow of new ideas can occur. Consequently the mobility of new technical knowledge is an important factor for the regional availability of new ideas. The literature often assumes that new and existing technical knowledge is completely mobile.[47] This assumption will be questioned here.

The mobility of new technical knowledge is a communication problem. If new technical ideas are communicated between different regions, the new knowledge is interregionally mobile. With no communication it is immobile. An analysis of the interregional communication flows will therefore allow conclusions on the interregional mobility of technical knowledge. We will distinguish between inventions made by government-supported institutions and by private industry.

Government-supported research organizations which engage in basic research are normally disposed to communicate their research results. The willingness of these institutions to be an active sender is a necessary but not a sufficient condition for the existence of a communication flow. Two other conditions are necessary. First, the communication system must be organized efficiently so that no weak elements exist in a communication chain which can interrupt the information flow. Second, a communication flow presupposes a receiver. The reception of the new ideas requires a certain technical horizon of the receiver which permits understanding of the information; the noticeability of the new technical knowledge also depends on the evaluation of the existing solutions by the receiver. If the receiver is dissatisfied with actual procedures he may be open to new ideas. Thus the predisposition of the receiver influences the effectiveness of communication flows of new technical knowledge even if the senders do not impose any restrictions.

---

[46]For simplifying purposes we assume that the existing stock of knowledge is the same for both regions.

[47]Compare, for instance, "A new manufacturing process or a new machine is, under competition, available to all," G. H. Borts and J. L Stein, *Economic Growth in a Free Market*, Columbia U. P., New York, 1964, p. 81.

Inventions which result from basic research cannot immediately be applied to production procedures. The results of basic research are only the starting point for applied research which is usually undertaken by private firms. Consequently even if a completely equal distribution of "basic" new technical knowledge between regions results, regions may succeed in applying it at different rates. Also the potential receivers are not distributed equally over space. Similarly, as the information impulses originate unequally in space, the number of potential receivers may be larger in one region than in another. Thus the existing spatial structure, i.e., the distribution of industry over space, determines the possible application of the new basic knowledge.

Finally, the distinction between formal and informal communication affects the distribution of new basic technical knowledge. A region may receive more informal information flows than another if it has personal contact with research institutions. This is because the noticeability of a signal may be greater for informal information flows. This type of information flow seems to be important in the regional policy of France where specialization by universities in different scientific fields is a policy variable to attract specific types of industries (atomic science and hydrology in Grenoble, or mechanical engineering in Rouen—the new location of car manufacturers). In these cases the firms near the universities may be better and more quickly informed due to informal communication flows. All these factors lead to some degree of immobility of new technical knowledge.

If the inventions are made by private firms, and if they are the result both of basic and applied research, there is even a stronger tendency for some degree of immobility of new technical knowledge. In addition to the problem of an efficient organization of the communication system and the predisposition of receivers, another factor reduces the mobility of new technical knowledge. We can expect that the inventors are not interested in sending information on their discoveries in order to prevent a worsening of their competitive situation. As the inventors deliberately prevent new knowledge from entering the communication system, one necessary condition for an information flow is not fulfilled—the existence of a sender. The new knowledge is not transmitted and, if we ignore industrial espionage, new applied technical knowledge is likely to be strongly immobile.

One exeption is the deliberate export of new technical knowledge by firms. This case may, however, be more relevant for international trade if firms are not able to establish a branch in a foreign market or to enter the foreign market via exports (political considerations, too low a capacity at home, or risks involved). These enterprises are normally willing to share the new technology with foreign firms thus creating royalty incomes. Such a procedure implies that the home market of the innovating firm is not negatively affected by granting patent licenses to foreign firms. On the interregional level this condition is not so easily fulfilled. Only if the innovating firm produces a purely regional commodity is its market unaffected by letting other firms use the same technical process. We therefore can conclude that this exception to the rule is likely to be unimportant.

Nevertheless, some new ideas may come from other areas. Similarly, as in the case of labor and capital, a distinction has to be made between an internal and an external change of technical knowledge. Let E^I indicate all inventions known in region I, let $^aE^I$ be the autonomous and $^iE^I$ be the induced inventions of region I, and let $^{II}E^I$ define the inventions coming in from region II. Then relation 3-23 becomes

$$E^I = {}^iE^I + {}^aE^I + {}^{II}E^I \qquad (4\text{-}15)$$

3. Not only is technical knowledge as a determinant of regional growth influenced by the mobility of knowledge about inventions but, since technical knowledge consists of inventions and their realization, technical change in a region also depends on the possibilities for making inventions commercially feasible. Even if the regions have the same information on inventions, the potential processes may be realized at different rates in different regions. The successful development of an invention requires certain minimum conditions to be given. If these minimum requirements are equally fulfilled in all regions, no restrictions on the mobility of technical knowledge are imposed. If, however, the requirements are met differently in a set of regions, the mobility of technical knowledge is reduced. The realization of a potential process may be split up into two different elements, the innovation[48] as the first application and the imitation as subsequent realizations of the same process. Innovations are restricted by the following factors.

Existing spatial structure. We may distinguish total and partial innovations. Total innovations change the main production process of an economic organization. Partial innovations influence only a subunit of this production process, leaving the main process basically unaffected. If innovations are partial in the sense that they relate to existing economic structures, the interregional distribution of these structures, e.g., of firms, determines the location of innovations. A partial innovation is not a sufficient reason for changing the location of the existing structure. Thus the existing spatial structure reduces the mobility of partial innovations.

Availability of funds for investment. The availability of funds is an additional restraint on the mobility of technical knowledge. Since these funds come partly from retained earnings, the given spatial structure—the distribution of funds—influences the innovation. The funds also depend on savings and depreciation. Consequently the region with lower savings and lower depreciation will have a smaller chance to innovate. As replacement investment is a function of

---

[48] A different definition is used by R. D. Johnston, "Technical Progress and Innovation," *Oxford Economic Papers*, Vol. 18 (1966), p. 160.

the existing capital stock, a region with a lower capital stock will, *ceteris paribus*, have a lower probability to innovate.

Profit requirements. The innovation will only be undertaken at those locations where certain profit requirements are fulfilled.

Size of firms. If the hypothesis is correct that larger firms are better equipped to innovate because they can compensate the risky innovation in one activity by other activities, the region which has smaller-sized firms has a smaller chance to innovate. If competition between firms can be regarded as a requirement for inventions to be realized, the region with less competition will also innovate less.

Innovative personality. The lack of "innovative personality traits"[49] reduces the chances for an innovation and thus also affects the mobility of technical knowledge.

4. All these factors reduce the mobility of technical knowledge. The other aspect of the realization of new technical knowledge is the imitation of the innovation—the application of new technical knowledge by a second producer. Here the following restrictions on the mobility of technical knowledge arise.

Transmission interval. Competitors of the innovator do not have immediate information on the first realization of the new technical knowledge. A transmission interval[50] exists which indicates the time lapse between the innovating act and the reception of a message of this act by a competitor. The length of the transmission interval depends on the efficiency of the information-gathering agency of the firms and on the competitive structure of industry.[51] The longer the transmission interval, the less mobile is new technical knowledge.

Patent system. Patent regulations may prevent the spread of new technical knowledge. They represent a similar obstacle to the mobility of technical knowledge as information barriers.

Other factors. The availability of funds, profit requirements, and the size of firms are other conditions that influence the imitation of an innovation. They represent similar obstacles as in the case of an innovation. The first three factors also reduce the mobility of new technical knowledge.

Our analysis so far leads to the result that new technical knowledge is only partly mobile in its form as information on new production processes. The realization of new technical knowledge such as innovations and imitations also imposes restrictions on the mobility of new technical knowledge. For purposes of simplicity, relation 3-25 includes only savings and depreciation as possible restrictions of the mobility of technical knowledge. All other factors are neglected.

5. It can be argued that the transfer of machines which embody new

---

[49]Friedmann, *op. cit.*, p. 13.

[50]G. B. Richardson, *Information and Investment: A Study in the Working of the Competitive Economy*, Oxford U. P., Oxford, England, 1960, p. 51.

[51]*Ibid.*, p. 67.

technical knowledge is a substitute for the mobility of technical knowledge. In order to be able to evaluate this position we must introduce certain distinctions.

A firm in region I produces a consumption commodity z and discovers a new process t for the production of this consumption commodity. In this case we can expect that the firm will not pass on its new knowledge but will use it to produce an improved consumption good z'. This new commodity z' is exported to other regions, but the production procedure t is not exported. The new technical knowledge is immobile.

A firm in region I produces an investment good x. The firm introduces a new process t which allows the production of an improved (or new) investment commodity x'. As in the preceding case, the knowledge of the new production process t is not communicated to the other region. Technical knowledge with respect to t is immobile. But x' is a machine embodying technical progress. The innovating firm will try to sell its new product to as many customers as possible. Therefore it will inform the potential users of the new capital good. In contrast to the situation of imitation in which we have a competitive relation between producers, the relation between the producer of the new machine and its users is not competitive. Figure 4-9 illustrates the difference between the two situations.

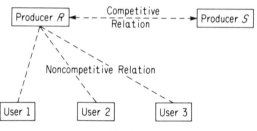

Fig. 4-9

A different adoption of the new machine cannot be due to a lacking willingness of the producer to send information. But the potential users may become aware of the new production possibility in different time periods, depending on their satisfaction with the old processes and their attitude toward change. The information sent by the producer of the new capital good may not be noticed by the potential users because of their specific predisposition. Also, the conditions analyzed for innovations and imitations apply to the problem of adoption. If these conditions differ from region to region, different rates of adoption may be the result. Finally, the rate of adoption depends on the distribution system used by the producer. Selling through subsidiaries or specialized dealers requires a more active participation of the potential users than a salesmen system.[52]

Empirical evidence suggests that the diffusion of a capital good which embodies technical progress goes on with a different intensity over time. Defining an adoption coefficient as the percentage of firms having introduced the new machine, we can expect the behavior of this coefficient for regions I, II, and III to be as indicated in Fig. 4-10.[53]

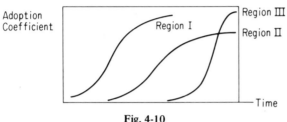

Adoption
Coefficient

Region I

Region III

Region II

Time

Fig. 4-10

Griliches finds such behavior in the case of agricultural adoptions.[54] Similar results are obtained by Mansfield[55] and Rogers.[56] "Measuring from the date of the first successful commercial application, it took 30 years or more for all the major firms to install centralized traffic control, car retarders . . ."[57] Mansfield also found that the number of years which passed before half of the railroad firms had introduced a new process varied from 0.9 to 15 years, the average being 7.8 years.[58]

Thus even if we assume that complete mobility is intended at the production source of the capital commodity, we can expect some degree of immobility. Together with the other arguments presented so far, we come to the conclusion that technical knowledge is immobile to some important degree.

6. For the receiving region the expansion effects of communication of new technical knowledge are similar to an inflow of labor or capital. The information on an invention enables a region to reallocate its resources and to shift its production-possibility curve outward. For the region sending the information the effects are different from an outflow of labor or capital. If a region loses labor or capital to another region its resource base is reduced and output decreases immediately. If a region sends information on its technical knowledge there is no

[53]*Ibid.*, p. 502.
[54]*Ibid.*
[55]E. Mansfield, "The Speed of Response of Firms to New Techniques," *Quarterly Journal of Economics*, Vol. 77 (1963), pp. 290–311; E. Mansfield, "Intrafirm Rates of Diffusion of an Innovation," *Review of Economics and Statistics*, Vol. 45 (1963), pp. 348–359; E. Mansfield, "Technical Change and the Rate of Imitation," *Econometrica*, Vol. 29 (1961), pp. 741–766.
[56]E. M. Rogers, *Diffusion of Innovations*, Free Press, New York, 1962; also compare A. Sutherland, "The Diffusion of an Innovation in Cotton Spinning," *Journal of Industrial Economics*, Vol. 7 (1959), pp. 117–135.
[57]E. Mansfield, "Technical Change and the Rate of Imitation," p. 744.
[58]*Ibid.*

withdrawal effect, as the new knowledge is still available to the sending region unless the area commits itself not to use the technical knowledge. Consequently the production-possibility frontier of the region remains constant. In later periods, secondary effects may occur because the region having received the new technical knowledge becomes more competitive[59] and thus affects the market position of the sender of technical knowledge.

E. MOBILITY OF CONSUMPTION GOODS AS A SUBSTITUTE FOR FACTOR MOBILITY

If factors are completely mobile between regions, no exchange of consumption goods will take place. In this case commodities can be produced at exactly those spatial points where the goods are demanded. Assume that there is an increase in demand for a commodity at a point in space. Assume also that this spatial point originally does not have resources available to satisfy the increased demand. Perfect mobility of factors of production would ensure that these factors would be immediately attracted in the needed quantities by raising the wage or profit rate. Realize, however, that the perfect mobility of factors of production, including technical knowledge, implies the nonexistence of transportation costs and the complete divisibility of resources.

If we reduce the mobility of factors of production, consumption goods will be exchanged between regions. Assume that the interregional mobility of factors of production is zero. If we then have an increase in demand for a commodity, and if the resources needed for the production of this commodity are not available within the region, the increased demand can be satisfied only by an interregional movement of commodities. Therefore we have the following as a theoretical statement: The higher the mobility of factors, the smaller the potential volume left for the movement of consumption commodities, and the lower the mobility of factors, the greater the volume of consumption goods traded between the regions. This alternative relationship between factor mobility and the potential exchange[60] of consumption goods is shown in Fig. 4-11.

A high factor mobility (y_1) will go together with a low volume of exchange (x_1). A low factor mobility (y_2) will lead to a higher volume of trade between regions (x_2).[61]

[59]The expansion effects of a communication of technical knowledge do not expand the Edgeworth box as in the case of capital and labor (Fig. 4-6). In the case of neutral technical change the same production isoquants indicate a higher output level. If technical progress is factor-biased, the shape of the isoquants is changed.

[60]The relation between factor movements and commodity exchange has been analyzed by B. Ohlin, *Interregional and International Trade*, Harvard Economic Studies, Harvard U. P., Cambridge Mass., 1954, p. 167; also compare R. A. Mundell, "International Trade and Factor Mobility," *American Economic Review*, Vol. 67 (1957), p. 320.

[61]Some factors may shift the curve of Fig. 4-11, e.g., technical progress in the transportation sector. Also cumulative relationships between factor movements and commodity exchange exist: Migrated workers may keep up traditional consumption patterns thus increasing import demand. This case is, however, ignored here.

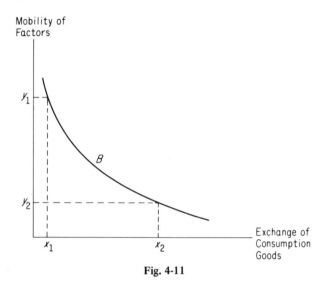

Fig. 4-11

Our analysis of the interregional mobility of factors of production has shown that perfect factor mobility cannot be expected. The following arguments summarize the causes which make for some degree of immobility.

Land is completely immobile. The existence of transportation costs reduces the mobility of the other factors of production. A factor will only move to another region if the interregional difference between factor rewards compensates for transportation costs in a short period.

Factors are not completely divisible. Because of their lumpiness they are not perfectly mobile interregionally.

Each factor is characterized by a pattern of persistence which binds it to its original place. The ratchet effect of retained earnings in the case of capital, the integration of the worker into social groups, the unwillingness of the inventor to communicate are the causes that make for some degree of immobility.

The interregional communication system may include obstacles to information flows of alternative factor uses and spatially differing economic opportunities which cause some factor immobility.

According to the foregoing arguments, factor mobility is reduced to an unspecified point B on the curve in Fig. 4-11. At point B factor movements will be substituted by the interregional movements of commodities.

The analysis of the expansion effects of these two forms of interaction will distinguish the following two cases.

If the increase in demand for a commodity not produced in a region is permanent, factors will move to this point of demand—if they are perfectly mobile. These factor movements happen only once and are not canceled in the next period. The factors stay in the region to which they migrated. Regional output increases in the period when the factors are added to the existing stocks.

Then output remains constant at the new level. If factors are immobile, this type of factor movement is substituted by a permanent movement of commodities.

If demand increases only temporarily for one period, factors will move only for this period and return to their original region at the end of this period. There is an increase in the output of the factor-receiving region in one period, but in the next period the output is reduced to its original level. If factors are immobile, this type of factor movement (with factors only temporarily in the region) is substituted by a movement of consumption goods for one period only. At the end of the period the increased level of exchange of goods is reduced and a contractive effect is the result, just as in the case of remigrating factors.

From the above two cases we see the basic difference between the expansion effects of factor movements and commodity exchange. Whereas a factor movement leads to an increase in output dO as indicated in relation 3-7, only a *change* in the level of commodity movements causes variation of output. Permanent interregional movements of commodities determine the level of output O_t, but they do not affect the increase in output dO. A change in regional output or income can, *ceteris paribus*, only be explained by a variation in the intensity of interregional commodity movements. Consequently it is not necessary for a regional growth model to explain the absolute level of interregional commodity movements. On the contrary, variation in the exchange of commodities is the decisive explanatory variable.

APPENDIX

THE INTERREGIONAL DISTRIBUTION OF NEW TECHNICAL KNOWLEDGE

Set theory may be used to analyze the mobility and spatial distribution[62] of new technical knowledge (compare Section D).

1. *Spatial distribution of information on inventions.* Let us assume an economy A as described in Eq. 2-1. Set A is the possibility set for the occurrence of inventions. In any given period, inventions, however, will only be made at some spatial points, namely, only at those points where the relevant determinants of inventions, e.g., research expenditures, are given. This subset of A may be defined as

$$A_E = \left\{ a/\ a = a_E \right\} \tag{A-1}$$

with a_E denoting a spatial point where an invention takes place.

Set A_E only indicates at which spatial points an invention originates. New technical knowledge will be available at other spatial points of set A if the inventions are communicated to these points. Consequently the communication

[62]Compare H. Siebert, "Zur Interregionalen Verteilung neuen technischen Wissens," *Zeitschrift für die gesamte Staatswissenschaft,* Vol. 123 (1967), pp. 231–263.

of inventions becomes a central problem in the study of the interregional distribution of new technical knowledge.

Formally, the communication process leads to a new set A_{X_E} which includes all those spatial elements a_{X_E} where the information on the new process is available.

$$A_{X_E} = \left\{ a/ \, a = a_{X_E} \right\} \tag{A-2}$$

The communication process will depend on the willingness of the inventor to communicate, on the existing channels of communication, and the predisposition of the receiver. It can be expected that not all spatial points will be informed about the new knowledge. Therefore

$$A \supset A_{X_E} \supset A_E \tag{A-3}$$

The relation between sets A_{X_E} and A_E can be presented by a graph $G_1 = [a_j^i]$. a_i and a_j represent the spatial points. As A_{X_E} and A_E are connected by information flows, j can represent only the spatial points a_E, for only these points can be the origin of an arc. i can represent all spatial points a since in the extreme case the information flows reach all spatial points.

2. *Spatial distribution of innovations.* Let us assume the spatial distribution of all the determinants of an innovation is given by set A_{D_1}, which contains spatial points where the locational requirements for an innovation like capital, transport connections, infrastructure, etc., are met:

$$A_{D_1} = \left\{ a/a = a_{D_1} \right\} \tag{A-4}$$

It can be expected that these minimum requirements for an innovation will not be fulfilled at all spatial points. Consequently

$$A \supset A_{D_1} \tag{A-5}$$

An innovation can only take place at those spatial points which (1) have information on the invention, and (2) meet the minimum requirements for an innovation. Consequently the spatial points where an innovation takes place a_{In}, must be elements of sets A_{X_E} and A_{D_1}. The intersection of these two sets yields set A_{In} which denotes all spatial points with an innovation.

$$A_{In} = A_{X_E} \cap A_{D_1} \tag{A-6}$$

with

$$A_{In} = \left\{ a/a = a_{In} \right\} \tag{A-7}$$

and

$$A_{In} = \left\{ a/a \in A_{X_E} \wedge a \in A_{D_1} \right\} \tag{A-8}$$

From Eqs. A-3 and A-5 follows

$$A_{In} \subset A \tag{A-9}$$

Operations A-1 through A-9 relate to the economy A. If we are interested in the interregional distribution, analogous operations would have to be performed for the two regions I and II.[63]

3. *Spatial aspects of the diffusion of realized new technical knowledge*. The realization of new technical knowledge is not only represented by an innovation but also includes imitation and adoption. The set of spatial points at which an imitation occurs depends on the set A_{D_2}, which includes all those spatial points where the necessary requirements for an imitation, such as capital, the intensity of competition, and other factors, are given:

$$A_{D_2} = \left\{ a/a = a_{D_2} \right\} \tag{A-10}$$

[63] Assume the economy A consists of two regions I and II.
Set A_E consists of two subsets I_E and II_E:

$$A_E = I_E \cup II_E \tag{1}$$

with

$$I_E = \left\{ a/a \in I \wedge a = a_E \right\} \tag{2}$$

and

$$II_E = \left\{ a/a \in II \wedge a = a_E \right\} \tag{3}$$

If the determinants for inventions, like expenditures for research, are distributed differently between the two regions I and II, the number of elements in sets I_E and II_E will not be equal.

$$N_{I_E} \gtrless N_{II_E} \tag{4}$$

Thus (4) indicates an unequal distribution of inventions between the two regions.

The information flows on these inventions can be represented by graphs $G_4 = [a_j^i]$ and $G_5 = [a_j^i]$. In G_4, j can only denote the senders in region I, whereas i in G_2 can stand for all elements in I (intraregional communication) and all elements in II (interregional communication). In G_5, j can only stand for all elements of II_E, whereas i can denote the spatial points of both regions. Defining

$$I_{X_E} = \left\{ a/a \in I \wedge a = a_{X_E} \right\} \tag{5}$$

and correspondingly for II, we have by analogy to Eq. A-3.

$$I_{X_E} \subset I \tag{6}$$

$$II_{X_E} \subset II \tag{7}$$

In both regions, only a subset of all spatial points will have information on the new technical possibilities. If for simplifying purposes we denote I_{X_E} and II_{X_E} as the set of those spatial points which at least have received one information on inventions, then the interregional differentiation in new technical knowledge can be represented by the difference in the number of elements of sets I_{X_E} and II_{X_E}.

Contrary to Eq. A-3, results (6) and (7) can not be expressed by

$$I_E \subset I_{X_E} \tag{8}$$

and correspondingly for II. It is possible in the two-regions case that a spatial point has information on new technical knowledge (a_{X_E}), this information however, may not have come

Assume that the patent system does not impose insurmountable obstacles to imitation, then only those spatial points will imitate which, in addition to the necessary requirements for an imitation, also have information on the innovation. The set of all those spatial points with information on the innovation $a_{X_{In}}$ is defined as

$$A_{X_{In}} = \left\{ a/a = a_{X_{In}} \right\} \tag{A-11}$$

The relation between $A_{X_{In}}$ and A_{In} can be expressed by a graph $G_2 = [a_j^i]$, with j representing all potential senders (all the points where innovation occurred) and i representing all spatial points as possible receivers. It can be assumed that

$$A_{D_2} \subset A \tag{A-12}$$

If there are information obstacles,

$$A_{X_{In}} \subset A \tag{A-13}$$

---

from a sender in I_E but from II_E. Thus it is possible that for point a^1

$$a_{X_E}^1 \in I_E \wedge a^1 \notin I_E \tag{9}$$

Statement (9) is a contradiction to the definition of inclusion, as used in (8). Statement (9) can hold only if the communication obstacles are so strong that no interregional flow of information occurs.

Let I_{D_1} and II_{D_1} indicate the minimum requirements of innovations: Then the set of spatial points where innovations take place is determined by

$$I_{In} = I_{X_E} \cap I_{D_1} \tag{10}$$

$$II_{In} = II_{X_E} \cap II_{D_1} \tag{11}$$

An interregional differentiation in innovations will prevail, if the number of elements in both sets I_{In} and II_{In} is different.

If the number of elements having information on new knowledge and the minimum requirements for innovations are greater in I than in II,

$$N_{I_{X_E}} > N_{II_{X_E}} \tag{12}$$

and

$$N_{I_{D_1}} > N_{II_{D_1}} \tag{13}$$

it does not yet follow that

$$N_{I_{In}} > N_{II_{In}} \tag{14}$$

This is due to the fact that if the corresponding sets with a smaller number of elements are characterized by a greater number of common elements, then the operation of intersection may compensate for the smaller amount of elements. If we assume, however, that the relative distribution of common elements in the corresponding sets (I_{X_E}, I_{D_1}) and (II_{X_E}, II_{D_1}) is the same, it follows from conditions (12) and (13) and operations (10) and (11) that the number of elements in the innovations sets of the two regions must be different.

The intersection of both sets yields a new set which gives all those spatial points where imitation takes place:

$$A_{X_{In}} \cap A_{D_2} = A_{Im} \tag{A-14}$$

From Eqs. A-12, A-13, and A-14, it follows that

$$A_{Im} \subset A \tag{A-15}$$

The set A_A, which denotes all the spatial points where a new product embodying new technical knowledge is adopted by the demand side, is obtained by the intersection of a set with information on the new product A_X with a set indicating minimum adoption requirements A_{D_3}. Set A_X is related to A_{In} and A_{Im} by graph G_3 which represents information flows on the new product.

Regarding A_{In}, A_{Im}, and A_A as the appearance of realized new technical

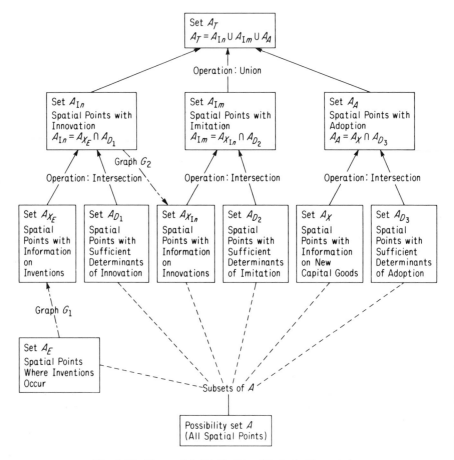

Fig. 4-12. The spatial distribution of technical knowledge.

knowledge, the union of these sets will indicate all the spatial points A_T where technical progress takes place.[64]

$$A_{In} \cup A_{Im} \cup A_A = A_T \qquad (A\text{-}16)$$

with

$$A_T = \left\{ a/a = a_{In} \vee a = a_{Im} \vee a = a_A \right\} \qquad (A\text{-}17)$$

From the above arguments it can be expected that A_T is a subset of A:

$$A_T \subset A \qquad (A\text{-}18)$$

Equation A-18 states that new technical knowledge will not be distributed equally over space.[65] Figure 4-12 represents the process by which A_T is derived.

PROBLEMS

1. If capital and labor are mobile interregionally, regional income is not any longer identical with regional product. Discuss.

2. Evaluate the relevance of communication theory for the interregional movement of labor, capital, and the transfer of technical knowledge.

3. Discuss the relevance of Simon's concept of "limited rationality" for the decision to migrate.

4. Which factors impede the spatial mobility of labor (capital) in a developing nation compared to a developed economy?

5. Read Stigler's article on the "Economics of Information" and apply his ideas to the labor market in a spatial setting.

6. Discuss the basic concepts of mathematical information theory and the theory of search and apply these concepts to the analysis of the interregional mobility of labor (capital).

7. Assume technical knowledge is communicated from region I to region II. Discuss the expansion effects of this transfer in terms of Edgeworth's contract curve and the transformation curve. Does it make any difference whether the technical knowledge is factor-neutral or factor-biased?

8. Factor movements equalize factor prices. Comment.

9. ". . . factor movements act as a substitute for the movements of commodities" (Ohlin).[66] Comment.

---

[64]If we want information on those spatial points where innovations, imitations, and adoptions occur at the same time, the operation of intersection has to be used.

[65]In order to derive results with regard to the distribution of new technical knowledge between regions I and II, a similar procedure as in footnote 53) must be followed for I_{Im}, I_A, II_{Im}, and II_A.

[66]Ohlin, *op. cit.*, p. 169.

chapter 5

Expansion Effects of
Interregional Commodity
Movements

If factors of production are partly immobile, expansion effects will be caused by the alternative form of interregional interaction, namely, the exchange of consumption commodities. The expansion effects of this form of interaction[1] are analyzed in the present chapter. In order to simplify the analysis, we assume throughout Sections A, B, and C that factors of production are completely immobile and that the only form of interregional interaction is the exchange of consumption goods.[2] We therefore reverse our assumption of the previous chapter. In Chapter 4, commodities were assumed to be completely immobile and the mobility of factors was analyzed. Analogously, in the present chapter factors are assumed to be completely immobile and the mobility of commodities is investigated.

Variations in the interregional movements of consumption goods may be attributed to two different phenomena. (1) With a given regional income, a given level of regional demand, and a given production technology, interregional trade barriers are reduced. The result is an intensified interregional exchange. (2) Output, income, and demand of a region may vary as a result of changes in the internal determinants of economic growth. This in turn may precipitate an increase of interregional exchange. In both cases the intensity of interregional exchange varies, but as a consequence of different causes. Whereas in the first case the increase in interregional exchange is the causal factor of a regional expansion, in the second case the causal relationship is reversed. The internal expansion is the agent which then leads to a change in the interregional movement of commodities. Because of the basic differences inherent in both cases, we re-

[1] On the relevance of trade theory for regional analysis: M. L. Greenhut, "Needed—A Return to Classics in Regional Economic Development," *Kyklos,* Vol. 19 (1966), pp. 461–480.

[2] We also assume for Secs. A, B, and C, that investment goods are not exchanged.

quire different hypotheses for the explanation of their expansion effects. We first study the intensified interregional commodity exchange caused by a reduction of interregional trade barriers.

A. ALLOCATION GAINS THROUGH REDUCTIONS OF INTERREGIONAL TRADE BARRIERS

1. For the region—here understood to be a subsystem of a nation—the alternative between a completely closed and a completely open system is not so relevant as in the case of nations. This is attributable to the fact that one important barrier to trade, namely, tariffs, is negligible on the regional level.[3] Nevertheless, some obstacles to interregional trade exist. The transport rates differ for commodities, and interregional transportation costs for some products can be so high—relative to their price—that an area may be treated as a closed region with respect to these commodities. Or the goods of a region may be of such a nature that they require specific transportation facilities which are either not feasible with a given technology or lead to such an increase in the delivered price that the product is not competitive in other regions. Communication obstacles which prevent information flows on export or import markets represent another factor that accounts for the interregional immobility of some commodities. Finally, differences in the social systems of regions can also cause a low level of interregional trade, as such differences may impede the flow of information. Alternatively—and perhaps concurrently—social-system differences may make for such consumption patterns that the products of one region are not demanded in another. Because of all these factors regional production of some commodities takes place behind a bulwark of high transportation costs, transportation facility shortages, insufficient information, and other barriers. If one of these obstacles is reduced, the intensity of interregional exchange increases. We analyze here the effect of a reduction in transportation costs.[4]

2. Assume supply-and-demand conditions in regions I and II are represented by the curves in Fig. 5-1. The horizontal axis denotes the quantities of the commodity in the two areas q^I and q^{II}, and the vertical axis indicates prices. No transportation costs between the two regions exist.

Region I has a production advantage over region II expressed by the supply curve S^I compared to S^{II}. S^I has a lower intercept and/or a lower slope than S^{II}.

---

[3]Historical exceptions are manifold. Compare, for instance, the situation in Germany before the Zollverein in 1833.

[4]On the role of transportation costs in international trade: M. C. Kemp, *The Pure Theory of International Trade*, Prentice-Hall, Englewood Cliffs, N. J., 1964, Chap. 10. The reductions in transportation costs lead to a stronger integration of a national economy. For the solution of this problem, analogies to the theory of customs unions may be established. On historical experience, compare Phyllis M. Deane, *The First Industrial Revolution*, Cambridge U. P., Cambridge, England, 1967, Chap. 5; On economic integration: B. Balassa, *The Theory of Economic Integration*, Irwin, Homewood, Ill., 1961; P. Streeten, *Economic Integration*, A. W. Sythoff, Leiden, Netherlands, 1964.

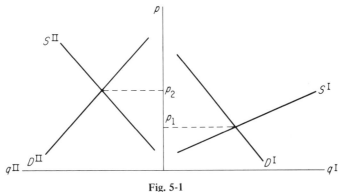

Fig. 5-1

Note that in the second quadrant the supplied quantities q^{II} also increase with a rising price. With demand conditions D^I and D^{II}, p_1 and p_2 indicate the regional prices if no exchange takes place. If exchange is introduced and if transportation costs are ignored, region II will import from region I. In order to determine the quantity imported, we construct the excess-demand curve of the two regions. Line E^I in Fig. 5-2 indicates the excess demand of region I in the first quadrant with $D^I > S^I$ and the excess supply of region I in the second quadrant with $D^I < S^I$. The excess-demand function of region I intersects the price axis at p_1.

We also construct the excess-demand curve E^{II} of region II which intersects the p-axis at p_2. Curve E^{II} shows the excess supply of region II in the first quadrant ($D^{II} < S^{II}$) and excess demand in the second quadrant ($D^{II} > S^{II}$). The intersection of the two curves yields the equilibrium price and the equilibrium quantity of interregional exchange. These variables are determined where the excess supply of region I equals the excess demand of region II. The price p_0 lies between the two original prices; $p_1 < p_0 < p_2$. Quantity q_0 in the second quad-

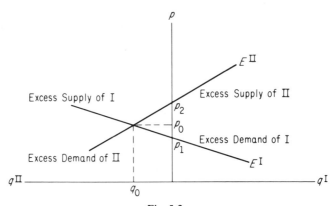

Fig. 5-2

rant represents imports to region II (exports from I). Producers in region II have to accept a lower price and must reduce their quantity, as part of the demand of region II is now satisfied by region I.

The existence of interregional transportation costs affects the excess-supply curves of both regions by shifting them upward. The delivered price for the excess supply of regions I and II is higher by the amount of the transportation costs (see Fig. 5-3).

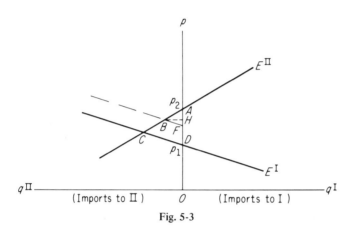

Fig. 5-3

The upward shift in the delivered price of region I affects the equilibrium solution. If the transportation costs per unit are equal to DA, the delivered price of excess supply of region I is equal to OA. At this price region II can supply the total quantity demanded in the area. No trade takes place. Transportation costs close region II with respect to the imports of the specific commodity.

Transportation costs of DF lead to a new equilibrium at B. Compared to point C, price increases and the volume of imports to region II are reduced. Define the difference between the original equilibrium prices $p_2 - p_1$ as the competitive range—namely, that price range in which producers in regions I and II compete. The scope of this competitive range depends on the slope of the excess-demand curves and on the magnitude of transportation costs per unit. If transportation costs are equal to DA, the competitive range shrinks to zero. If transportation costs are DF, the competitive range is equal to FA. Thus the existence of interregional transportation costs provides protection against competition.

Our analysis started from a world of no spatial frictions between regions and showed the effects of introducing transportation costs. The competitive range becomes smaller and the volume of commodity movements is reduced. For regional growth theory we follow opposite reasoning. We begin with a situation of high transportation costs such as those depicted by DA in Fig. 5-3. No exchange takes place in this situation. Technical change in the transport sector which results in lower transport rates or improved transport facilities widens the competitive range and opens the region for specific products. As transportation costs are reduced, the shift in the excess-supply curve of region I becomes smaller, resulting in more commodities being sold to the other region. Products which had been purely regional goods at one point in time now become interregional commodities through a reduction in transportation costs.

3. Let a column vector represent all commodities produced in region I. Order these products according to their interregional price differences so that the commodity with the highest positive difference heads the list. Define the price difference as the mill price in region I (p^I), plus the transportation costs to region II ($^I t^{II}$), minus the mill price charged by firms in region II (p^{II}):

$$\Delta p = p^I + {}^I t^{II} - p^{II} \qquad (5\text{-}1)$$

Figure 5-4 shows the column vector of all n commodities produced in region I.

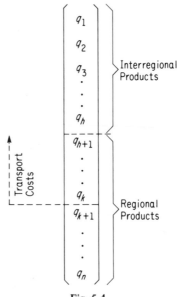

Fig. 5-4

All those commodities which satisfy the condition

$$p^I + {}^I t^{II} < p^{II} \qquad (5\text{-}2)$$

for at least some quantities, are interregional commodities. They are represented in Fig. 5-4 by products $q_1, \ldots, q_h$. All products of region I for which

$$p^I + {}^I t^{II} > p^{II} \qquad (5\text{-}3)$$

cannot be exported and are therefore regional commodities. They are represented by products $q_{h+1}, \ldots, q_n$. Regional products can be broken up into two groups. Products $q_{h+1}, \ldots, q_k$ are limited to the region because of transportation costs. For these products the mill price charged by firms in region I is lower than the mill price of firms in II, $p^I < p^{II}$; but the existence of transportation costs prevents the export of these commodities. If transportation costs decline, this group of regional goods may become interregional commodities.

The other group of regional products $q_{k+1}, \ldots, q_n$ is characterized by the condition that their mill price p^I is higher than mill price p^{II}; $p^I > p^{II}$. In the extreme case the commodity is not demanded in region II. Then p^{II} is zero. This group of commodities is not affected by a reduction in the transportation costs. An increase in the exchange of these commodities could result only if the demand conditions in region II or the production conditions in region I would change. This group of products is not, however, relevant to our analysis. We also construct a vector of region II commodities, with products being ordered in the opposite way. The vectors of the two regions are shown in Fig. 5-5.

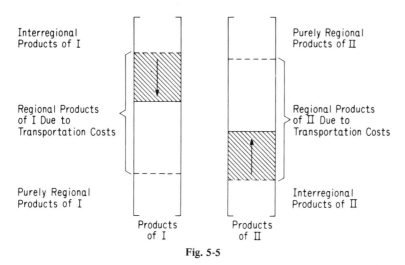

Fig. 5-5

Both vectors include commodities whose regional character is the result of high transportation costs. A reduction in transportation costs will therefore reduce the number of regional commodities and enlarge the set of interregional products. The cross-hatched areas in both vectors indicate the increase in the set of commodities which are newly introduced to interregional trade. The increase in trade depends on the initial level of transportation costs, their reduction, and on the difference between the mill price of the product in the two regions.

4. The increase in interregional interaction leads to an interregional specialization of production which results in a more efficient use of factors of production in the two-region system. Let us assume for simplicity that in the original situation the interregional transportation costs are so high that no trade takes place. Also assume first-degree homogeneous production functions, with de-

clining productivities to both factors. Each region produces commodities q_1 and q_2. The production-possibility curves for regions I and II are drawn in Fig. 5-6. Points P_1 and P_2 represent the production and consumption points of the two regions before interregional exchange takes place. At these points the transformation curves are tangent to the regional indifference curves. They represent the relative price lines or the terms of trade before trade.

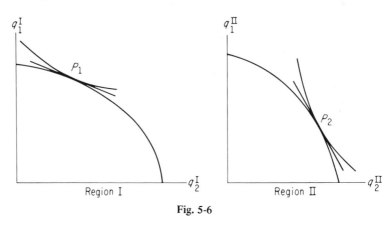

Fig. 5-6

     Allocation gains from trade due to a reduction of trade barriers are shown in Fig. 5-7. To derive Fig. 5-7, rotate the production block of region II 180 degrees and move the production block of region II so that the equilibrium points P_1 and P_2 of Fig. 5-6 overlap.

     After trade, both regions reach a consumption point on a higher indifference curve. This is made possible by (1) a reallocation of resources in both regions, and (2) an increased exchange of commodities. The new optimal-production situation for both regions is represented by point E. At E the production blocks of the two regions are tangent to each other and the rates of transformation of the two commodities are equal. The production block of region II, though unchanged in its shape, has been shifted outward. Region I reallocates its resources by moving from P_1 to E, thus producing more of commodity q_2 and less of q_1. Region II specializes in the production of q_1 and reduces its output of q_2. Region II moves along its production frontier until it reaches point E.

     For the new production equilibrium at point E, new interregional terms of trade are established. With these terms of trade region I realizes point C as its new consumption point. Region I exports commodity q_2, namely, that good in whose production it has a relative advantage. Section CD represents exports of region I. Region I imports commodity q_1. ED indicates the imports of region I. The exchange of commodities enables region I to reach a higher indifference curve after trade. Since the exports of region I are identical to the imports of region II, and since the imports of I are the exports of II, region II reaches the same consumption point C. This point will also be situated on a higher indiffer-

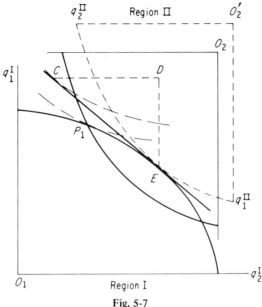

Fig. 5-7

ence curve for region II. Note that the consumption points of both regions lie outside their production frontiers and that this is made possible by trade.

The movement from P_1 to E can be explained by the principle of comparative advantage. This hypothesis postulates that a region specializes in the production of that commodity for which it has a comparative production advantage. The relative advantage is the result of different factor endowments among regions. A region will export those commodities which can be produced with the relatively abundant factor of production, and it will import those commodities which are produced by a relatively scarce factor. The existence of a comparative advantage is, however, not a sufficient condition for interregional specialization, as exports and imports depend not on relative advantages but on absolute price differences. Consequently the comparative-advantage hypothesis holds only if comparative advantages are translated into absolute price differences.

In international trade theory the link between these variables is the demand for foreign currency. Assume country I has an absolute price disadvantage in both commodities but it has a comparative advantage in one commodity. At the start the cheaper products of country II will be demanded. This leads to an increased demand for foreign currency. The foreign currency becomes more expensive as the exchange rate (currency II/currency I) goes up. The original absolute price disadvantage of country I will eventually be changed, since its products become less expensive for country II. At the same time the absolute price advantages of country II will be reduced and each country ends up with an absolute price advantage for that product for which it had a comparative advantage at the start.

This mechanism of transforming a comparative advantage into an absolute price difference does not work on the regional level because exchange rates do not exist. The following process may lead to the same result: If region II has an absolute price advantage in both commodities, region I first demands commodities produced in region II, which therefore must produce larger quantities of both commodities. By assumption, its production activities are subject to declining marginal productivities. With an increase in production, the prices of the two commodities must rise. This increase may be so substantial that region I becomes competitive in that commodity for which it has a comparative advantage. Also, as entrepreneurs can be expected to increase the output of the sector with the highest productivity first (comparative advantage of region II), they have to withdraw resources from the other sector by bidding up their prices. This also makes for an eventual translation of comparative advantage into absolute price differences.

5. As Haberler[5] has shown, a reallocation of resources is not a necessary condition for gains from trade. If a reallocation of resources is not possible because of intersectorial immobility of factors, or nonflexible factor prices, gains may still arise, but on a smaller scale. Figure 5-8 describes the allocation gains. If a reallocation of resources between two activities q_1 and q_2 is not possible, the original production points of both regions go unchanged. Unlike Fig. 5-7, the production block of region II is not shifted to the right.

Curve AB is the production-possibility curve of region I. ST is the corresponding curve for region II. Insofar as a reallocation of resources is excluded, a movement along the curves is not possible. Both regions produce at the same point on their production-possibility curves as before trade (point E). Nevertheless both regions can benefit from trade. After the reduction of trade barriers, new terms of trade emerge which are defined for constant-production quantities q_1 and q_2 in the two regions. With the new terms of trade represented by PP', ED denotes imports of I (= exports of II), and CD indicates exports from I (= imports of II). Introduce indifference curves I$'$ for region I and II$'$ for region II. After trade, region I is at point C on the higher indifference curve II$'$. Region II also realizes a higher indifference curve.

6. As a result, we postulate the hypothesis that a reduction of trade barriers results in a more efficient allocation of resources. Letting $d^A O$ represent allocation gains and γ indicate variations in trade obstacles (such as changes in the transportation costs or variations in the information system), we have the functional relationship

$$d^A O = f(\gamma) \tag{5-4}$$

[5]G. von Haberler, "Some Problems in the Pure Theory of International Trade," *Economic Journal,* Vol. 60 (1950), p. 233; S. B. Linder, *An Essay on Trade and Transformation,* Wiley, New York, 1961, p. 24.

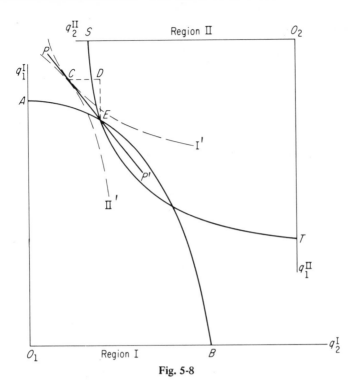

Fig. 5-8

A reduction in trade obstacles leads to higher allocation gains. The variable γ depends primarily on technical progress in the transportation sector. The allocation gains of the total system are partitioned between the two regions depending on the change in the terms of trade. The gains are greater for region I than for region II if the terms of trade[6] are relatively more favorable to region I. Relation 5-4 therefore has to be rewritten

$$d^A O = f(\gamma, dP) \qquad (5\text{-}5)$$

Finally, we assume that the allocation gains depend on the level of regional income.[7] The higher the income of a region, the greater the allocation gains. Compare a region with a low income Y_0 with another region having a high income Y_1. The Y_0-area is likely to have fewer resources with a smaller amount of resources having to be reallocated. On the other hand, the Y_1-region has more resources, and the reallocation of more resources may result in higher allocation gains. Consequently

$$d^A O = f(\gamma, dP, O) \qquad (5\text{-}6)$$

---

[6] For the determination of the terms of trade, compare Sec. C of this chapter.
[7] Linder, *op. cit.*, p. 62.

In order to incorporate the allocation gains into our model, we go back to Eq. 3-29, which states that the increase in real regional income is the minimum of either the increase in potential output or the increase in demand in real terms:

$$dY^a = \min (dO, dD) \tag{5-7}$$

This equation was developed for a closed region and must now be reinterpreted. For an open region, the change in the supply side is equal to the variation in potential output and the commodities imported, dO and dM. The change in demand is equal to the variation in internal demand dD^i, plus export demand dX. The increase in actual real income dY^a is restricted by the change in the supply side or by the change in the demand side. Consequently, for an open region, Eq. 5-7 becomes

$$dY^a = \min \left\{ (dO + dM), (dD^i + dX) \right\} \tag{5-8}$$

If supply is the limiting factor, the allocations gains are indicated by the increase in imports. The changes in exports and imports are functions of the variations in trade obstacles.

$$dX = f(\gamma) \tag{5-9}$$

$$dM = f(\gamma) \tag{5-10}$$

If γ equals zero, no increases in exports and imports can be expected (*ceteris paribus*) and no allocation gains exist.

B. EXPANSION EFFECTS OF INCREASES IN INTERREGIONAL DEMAND

1. Increases in interregional commodity movements are not only the result of reductions in trade barriers but may also be attributed to purely intraregional changes of certain variables. The preference pattern of a region may change over time, or regional income may rise due to internal determinants of economic growth. Both cases lead to an increase in demand for the products of the other region. Growth occurring in region I transmits impulses to region II and thus induces development there.

The dependence of the expansion of an area on export demand is the basic theme of the export-base theory.[8] The export base is defined as the set of all

[8] D. C. North, "Location and Regional Economic Growth," *Journal of Political Economy*, Vol. 63 (1955), pp. 243–258; C. M. Tiebout, "Exports and Regional Economic Growth," *Journal of Political Economy*, Vol. 64 (1956), pp. 160–164; Greenhut, *op. cit.;* H. S. Perloff, E. S. Dunn, E. F. Lampard, and R. F. Muth, *Regions, Resources and Economic Growth*, Johns Hopkins Press, Baltimore, Md., 1960, p. 55; W. Hochwald, "Dependence of Local Economies upon Foreign Trade: A Local Impact Study," *Papers and Proceedings of the Regional Science Association*, Vol. 4 (1958), pp. 259–271; L. Fouraker, "A Note on Regional Multipliers," *Papers and Proceedings of the Regional Science Association*, Vol. 1 (1955), pp. 1–8; G. M. Meier, "Economic Development and the Transfer Mechanism," *Canadian Journal of Economics and Political Science*, Vol. 19 (1953), pp. 1–19. The theory of the export base can be traced back to W. Sombart, "Der Begriff der Stadt und das Wesen der Städtebildung," *Archiv für Sozialwissenschaft und Sozialpolitik*, Vol. 25 (1907), p. 1.

those production activities which are undertaken to satisfy interregional demand. These are the interregional or basic commodities produced by a region. The secondary or nonbasic activities produce for regional demand. The theory postulates that the growth of a region depends on the performance of the export sector—"it is the ability to develop an export base which determines regional economic growth."[9] The increase in demand for the interregional production activities of a region stimulates production in the export sector, which in turn has feedbacks on purely regional activities.

This approach, which has been formulated by North,[10] Tiebout,[11] and Andrews,[12] stresses the demand side as an important factor of economic development. The theory may therefore be expressed in an analogous form to the international multiplier. The reader is referred to the standard texts on this subject, both in the theory of international trade and regional economics.[13]

Our formal model can incorporate the theory of the export base by introducing an additional determinant for the change in exports and imports. The change in exports of region I depends on the variation of income in region II. Imports of region I are a function of income in I. Equations 5-9 and 5-10 then become

$$dX^I = f(\gamma, dY^{II}) \qquad (5\text{-}11)$$

and

$$dM^I = f(\gamma, dY^I) \qquad (5\text{-}12)$$

The increase in exports (and imports) influences the basic equation of our model, relation 5-8. The change in export demand makes for a greater increase in demand, and the rise in imports represents an increase in supply. The theory of the export base concentrates on the rise in export demand. Thus it appears as one special case of our general model, being included in dX of Eq. 5-8. As the export-base theory relates changes in exports directly to the rise of income in other regions, it implicitly assumes a constant level of trade barriers so that γ becomes zero. Then Eqs. 5-11 and 5-12 represent the starting equations for the derivation of the multiplier.[14]

2. The theory of the export base has received the greatest attention of all

[9]Tiebout, *op. cit.*, p. 164.

[10]North, *op. cit.*

[11]Tiebout, *op. cit.*

[12]R. B. Andrews, "Mechanics of the Urban Economic Base," *Land Economics,* Vol. 29 (1953), pp. 161-167, 263-268, 343-350; Vol. 30 (1954), pp. 52-60, 164-172, 260-269, 309-319; Vol. 31 (1955), pp. 47-53, 144-155, 245-256, 361-371; Vol. 32 (1956), pp. 69-84.

[13]J. Vanek, *International Trade: Theory and Economic Policy*, Irwin, Homewood, Ill., 1962, p. 101; J. Vanek, "The Foreign-Trade Multiplier (Appendix E)," in C. P. Kindleberger, *International Economics*, Irwin, Homewood, Ill., 1963, p. 659; H. O. Nourse, *Regional Economics*, McGraw-Hill, New York, 1968, Chap. 7.

[14]On the derivation of the multiplier, compare Appendix B of Chap. 7.

efforts to explain regional growth. The following limitations of the approach should be noted.

According to the theory of the export base, the decisive explanatory variable for an increase of regional output is a rise in interregional demand. This implies that productive capacity is sufficiently large to satisfy the increased demand. Thus the theory of the export base must assume that at the beginning of the growth·process (1) potential resources are not fully utilized, or (2) resources are attracted from other regions. The second case is explicitly allowed only for the later stages of regional development.[15] For this case to occur in earlier stages of development would require an explanation of why resources are not attracted to those regions where interregional demand actually increases. Since this case can be ruled out, the assumed high production elasticity of the region with respect to increases in interregional demand implies that resources are sufficiently available in the region. At the original stage of development the production potential is not fully utilized. Only under this assumption does the basic hypothesis of the export-base theory hold. And only in this case can the process be approximately handled with the aid of an interregional multiplier. If factors of production are not sufficiently available, the increase in demand results in higher prices, and, as a corollary, a monetary rather than a real multiplier is the outcome. Our model takes these limitations into consideration in that the increase in demand is only one factor for the development of actual income. If the increase in demand surpasses the increase in supply, it does not contribute to actual real income.

Regional development is not only a function of interregional demand, but may also depend on regional demand and its composition. This conclusion can be reached from the availability hypothesis formulated by Kravis[16] for international trade. Similarly, as regions demand only those commodities which they either do not produce at all or do not produce in sufficiently large quantities, they also supply those goods which they produce for their intraregional demand.[17] Establishing an export base requires production and selling experience which a region gains in the regional markets. Thus the set of regional products determines in large measure the potential set of exportables.[18]

Whereas the theory of the export base postulates that the export base determines the production of regional commodities (relation 1), the opposite relation may be relevant too, at least for long-run analysis. The set of regional products presents the possibility set for exports in the future (relation 2). This second relationship has been neglected by the theory of the export base. (See Fig. 5-9.)

[15] Tiebout, *op. cit.,* p. 166.

[16] I. Kravis, "Availability and Other Influences on the Commodity Composition of Trade," *Journal of Political Economy,* Vol. 64 (1956), p. 143.

[17] This point illustrates a so far totally neglected problem, namely the integration of regional growth theory and the theory of the growth of the firm.

[18] Linder, *op. cit.,* p. 87.

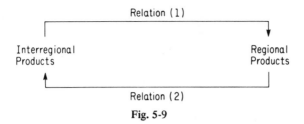

Fig. 5-9

The theory of the export base does not specify whether the additional inter-regional demand also includes investment goods. A purely demand-oriented multiplier along Keynesian lines treats investment commodities in the same fashion as consumption goods. But this procedure reveals an important disadvantage of the export-base approach. Capacity effects which are highly important for growth are completely neglected. The export of investment goods represents a stimulus to economic growth as demand increases, but at the same time it is a withdrawal of potential additional capital from the region. Conceivably the regions may import other capital goods in exchange for the export of machines, but alternatively the area may import consumption goods. The import of consumption goods will usually not[19] increase production capacity. Different results in terms of economic growth may be obtained, depending on whether or not exports and imports include investment goods. All these problems connected with the capacity effect of exports and imports are neglected by the export-base theory.

The theory of the export base has not yet completely resolved the problem of the carryover.[20] As a result of an increase in demand for interregional products, the demand for regional products rises. An aggregative analysis can indeed work with a basis multiplier.[21] But a more detailed study implies sectorial disaggregation requiring appeal to input-output models or to semi-input-output frameworks[22] for the explanation of the carryover. Alternatively, a disaggregated multiplier may also provide more detailed information.[23]

The above approach cannot explain the increase in its central variable—that it, the rise in external demand. The increase in interregional demand is introduced exogenously into the model, somewhat like a *deus ex machina*, starting the whole growth process. The theory of the export base can explain growth only for a single region; it is unable to describe the growth process for a system

---

[19]Only if the imported consumption goods are used to set resources free for the production of capital goods, an expansion effect is experienced.

[20]G. M. Meier, *Leading Issues in Development Economics,* Oxford U. P., New York, 1964, p. 371.

[21]Tiebout, *op. cit.,* p. 160.

[22]J. Tinbergen, "Projections of Economic Data in Development Planning," *Planning for Economic Development in the Caribbean,* Caribbean Organisation Hato Rey, Puerto Rico, 1963.

[23]J. Airov, "Fiscal-Policy Theory in an Interregional Economy: General Interregional Multipliers and Their Application," *Papers and Proceedings of the Regional Science Association,* Vol. 19 (1967), pp. 83–108.

of regions, as the internal determinants of growth are not taken into consideration. For smaller regions such as urban areas it may be permissible to regard growth as a function of interregional demand. The larger the region, however, the more important become the other factors of economic development.

The theory of the export base does not include demand shifts between regions. Such interregional shifts[24] in demand are caused by changes in preference patterns and in the conditions of production in the various regions. Abrupt changes in the consumption behavior of a multiregion system may thus favor the commodities of region I and disfavor the products of region II. Also, increases in factor prices or a worsening of the production conditions in region I (such as a lower quality of inputs or a decline in the entrepreneurial performance), may make region II more competitive. Finally, the production conditions in region I may improve. All these processes are not taken into account.

The export-base theory neglects changes in the terms of trade. This procedure is due to the assumption of a high production elasticity with respect to an increase of demand. Changes in absolute prices are neglected and consequently the terms of trade remain constant. The following analysis of the factors influencing interregional trade sets out clearly this simplifying assumption of the export-base theory.

C. EXPANSION EFFECTS THROUGH VARIATIONS IN THE INTERREGIONAL TERMS OF TRADE

If internal determinants of growth occur within a region, the model we have constructed so far predicts an increase of regional income. The present section shows that this result may not be reached if variations in the terms of trade are taken into consideration.[25] The following differences between this and previous sections should be noted.

As in the treatment of the problem of the previous section, we seek an answer to the question of how regional impulses of expansion are transmitted to other areas by means of interregional interaction. But whereas the previous section stresses the demand side and concentrates on the exporting region, we now introduce supply conditions and also the effects on the importing area.

The analysis also differs from the previously discussed problem of allocation gains caused by way of a reduction of interregional trade barriers. In both cases the terms of trade change. But whereas the first problem relates to gains from the reallocation of resources (due to a reduction of interregional trade barriers),

---

[24] Perloff et al., op. cit., p. 70.

[25] The relevance of variations in the terms of trade for regional analysis has been pointed out by Pfister and Streeten: R. L. Pfister, "The Terms of Trade as a Tool of Regional Analysis," Journal of Regional Science, Vol. 3 (1961), pp. 57–64; P. Streeten, "Reply to Professor Davin's Introductory Report," Théorie et Politique de l'Expansion Régionale, Actes du Colloque International de l'Institut de Science Economique de l'Université de Liège, Brussels, Belgium, 1961.

we analyze a different problem in this section: How do additional internal growth determinants affect the expansion of open regions?

We do not here compare a situation without (or with a low) level of exchange with a situation having (more intensive) trade. Rather we compare two situations where the second is characterized by a larger availability of internal growth factors. The difference between the two problems is pointed out in the adjoining table.

Situation I	Situation II	Result
No (low level of) interregional exchange	(Higher level of) interregional exchange due to reductions in interregional trade barriers	Allocation gains from increased trade
No (low) internal growth	Increased internal growth	Welfare effects from variations in the terms of trade

In both cases the intensity of interregional exchange and the terms of trade are likely to change. These variations are, however, due to different causes. In the case of allocation gains, trade barriers are reduced, exchange increases, and—as a result—the terms of trade change. The causal factor is a reduction of trade obstacles. The process is not influenced by internal growth factors. In the second case, trade barriers are not reduced but at least one of the areas experiences internal development. This affects the level of interregional exchange and may lead to a change in the terms of trade.

In order to determine the effects of internal growth determinants on regional welfare (measured by the availability of commodities in a region), we assume two originally stagnant areas. Factors of production are immobile. The trade balance has neither deficit nor surplus. Now internal growth factors appear in region I. They can influence interregional exchange in such a way that the quantities of exports and imports change differently for constant terms of trade. The expansion in region I, which results in an increase in income, may lead to a rise in imports. Exports, on the other hand, are likely to stay constant because income in region II does not change. Thus internal growth determinants may lead to a disequilibrium in the trade balance of the two regions. For the disequilibrium to disappear, the interregional terms of trade must change.[26]

[26] H. G. Johnson, *International Trade and Economic Growth*, Harvard U. P., Cambridge, Mass., 1967, p. 67. The discussion has been initiated by J. R. Hicks, "An Inaugural Lecture," *Oxford Economic Papers*, Vol. 8 (1956), pp. 223-228. Also compare A. Asimakopulos, "A Note on the Productivity Changes and the Terms of Trade," *Oxford Economic Papers*, Vol. 9 (1967), pp. 225-228; Kemp, *op. cit.*, p. 81.

I. Variations in the Terms of Trade as a Necessary Consequence of Internal Expansion

The terms of trade are defined as the relative price of the export and import commodities. They are also referred to as the *barter terms of trade*. Let P_X indicate the price of the export commodity (or the price index of all export goods) and let P_M stand for the price of the imported good (or the price index of all imported products). Then the terms of trade are defined as

$$P = \frac{P_X}{P_M} \tag{5-13}$$

1. The fact that internal determinants of growth may lead to a change in the interregional terms of trade can be shown diagrammatically with the help of a transformation curve. As shown in Fig. 5-10, an increase in one factor, e. g.,

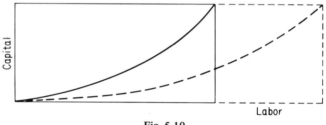

Fig. 5-10

labor, enlarges one side of the Edgeworth box. This leads to a new contract curve whose points are characterized by new factor-price relations. The resources will be reallocated according to the new factor prices.

The new contract curve results in a new production-possibility frontier. The shift in the production-possibility curve depends in part on the factor intensity of the two commodities with respect to the increasing factor. If the production of commodity q_1 is labor-intensive and if that of q_2 is capital-intensive, an increase of labor shifts the point of maximum production of q_1 farther away from the origin than q_2. The maximum point of production is defined as that production situation in which all resources are used for the production of one commodity only. If on the other hand the production of q_2 is labor-intensive, the maximum output of q_2 will be shifted farther away from the origin than that of q_1. (See Fig. 5-11.)

As interregional exchange takes place before the shift of the transformation curve, it can be assumed that an optimal allocation is originally given which corresponds to the original terms of trade P_1. These terms of trade are determined by a common tangent to the production blocks of both regions (E_1). A shift of the production-possibility curve of region I may lead to a change in the interregional terms of trade as shown in Fig. 5-12. It is assumed that the production block of region II does not change.

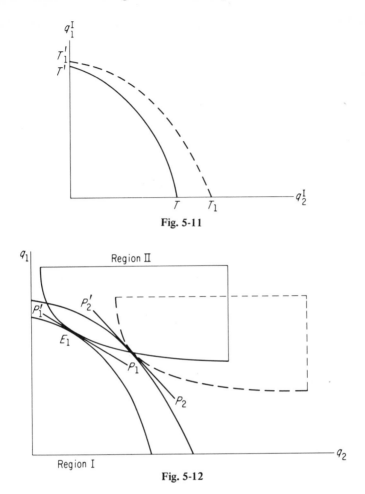

Fig. 5-11

Fig. 5-12

Technical progress also results in a change of the transformation curve. The variation of the transformation curve depends on the factor intensity in the production of the two commodities q_1 and q_2 and on the factor neutrality or factor bias of technical knowledge. Let q_2 represent the export commodity and q_1 the import substitute—or, in short, the import commodity. Then the shift of the production-possibility curve depends on the bias of technical progress with respect to the export and import goods.

Technical progress is export-biased if the use of all resources shifts the maximum-production point of the export commodity q_2 farther from the origin than the maximum-production point q_1 of the import substitute. The transformation curve becomes steeper. Technical progress is import-biased (import substituting) if the maximum-production point for the import substitute q_1 is shifted farther out than q_2. Technical progress is neutral with respect to export and import activities if both points of maximum production are affected in the same way.[27]

These considerations point out the nature of the problem of allocation gains due to increased intensity of interregional interaction. In the previous case allocation gains arose from the determination of an optimum of two production blocks. The transformation curves were given and did not change, as shown in Fig. 5-7. On the other hand, the study of the effect of internal growth factors on the terms of trade assumes an interregional optimum of specialization and the enlargement of at least one production block (Fig. 5-12). The terms of trade change in both cases—but they change as a result of quite different catalysts.

2. The preceding analysis demonstrates that internal determinants of growth result in variations of the interregional terms of trade. These variations influence the level of regional income if we define regional income as the set of commodities available to a region. If the terms of trade deteriorate for a region, more commodities have to be exported to allow the same level of imports. An improvement in the terms of trade, on the other hand, results in an increase in available commodities. The welfare losses Ω may be approximately measured by the increase in the costs (in terms of additional imports) of the original level of imports. The gains in welfare can be expressed by the decrease in costs of the original level of imports.[28]

$$\Omega = M\frac{\dot{P}}{P} \qquad (5\text{-}14)$$

where $\dot{P}$ indicates the derivative of the terms of trade with respect to time.

Condition 5-14 can be derived in the following way. In any period, equality of exports and imports is established by the terms of trade. If X and M denote quantities, then

$$XP_X = MP_M \qquad (5\text{-}15)$$

Using Eq. 5-13, Eq. 5-15 becomes

$$X = \frac{M}{P} \qquad (5\text{-}16)$$

where P indicates the terms of trade. Differentiating X with respect to time and letting dotted variables indicate time derivatives, we have[29]

$$\dot{M} - \dot{X}P = M\frac{\dot{P}}{P} \qquad (5\text{-}17)$$

---

[27] It is assumed that technical progress in the transportation activities between regions does not affect the production possibility curves of the regions.

[28] Johnson, *op. cit.*, p. 69; B. Södersten, *A Study of Economic Growth and International Trade*, Almquist-Wiksell, Stockholm, Sweden, 1964, p. 47.

[29] The differentiation yields

$$\dot{X} = \frac{P\dot{M} - M\dot{P}}{P^2}$$

Rearranging, we get Eq. 5-17.

If $\dot{M} > \dot{X}P$, the region can import more than it has to export at constant terms of trade. The right-hand side of Eq. 5-17 measures the additional imports made possible. If $\dot{M} < \dot{X}P$, the area has to export more than it can import. The right-hand side becomes negative and the area experiences a welfare loss. Thus $M\dfrac{\dot{P}}{P}$ measures the welfare effects of changes in the terms of trade.

The welfare effect measured by Eq. 5-14 depends on the change in the terms of trade. The change in the terms of trade is defined as

$$\dot{P} = \frac{d\left(\dfrac{P_X}{P_M}\right)}{dt} \tag{5-18}$$

Differentiating Eq. 5-18, we have

$$\dot{P} = \frac{P_M\dot{P}_X - P_X\dot{P}_M}{P_M^2} \tag{5-19}$$

Assuming identical export and import prices originally, the terms of trade change according to

$$\dot{P} \gtreqless 0 : \dot{P}_X \gtreqless \dot{P}_M \tag{5-20}$$

The terms of trade improve if the export price increases more than the import price. In this case $\dot{P}$ is positive and the welfare effect must also be positive. Ω then indicates the quantity by which exports can decrease without reducing the original level of imports. If the change in the terms of trade is negative, the import price rises more than the export price. The welfare effect is therefore negative. Ω then specifies the increase in exports necessary if the region is to maintain imports at the same level.

The existence of the welfare effect necessitates a revision of our basic equation 5-8. In this relation the minimum value of the increase in supply or demand determines the increase in real income. The increase in exports is treated as a rise in demand and the increase in imports as a rise in supply. Relation 5-8, however, does not consider changes in the terms of trade. If the terms of trade vary, the absolute level of imports becomes important insofar as a deterioration in the terms of trade associates a lower level of imports with a given amount of exports. On the other hand, an improvement in the terms of trade allows more imports with a given level of exports. In order to include these welfare effects of changes in the terms of trade, relation 5-8 becomes

$$dY^a = \min\left\{ (dO + dM), (dD^i + dX) \right\} + \Omega \tag{5-21}$$

If the region has a zero import level, changes in the terms of trade do not lead to any welfare losses because no additional commodities have to be exported in order to maintain the zero level of imports. This is also true if the terms of trade do not change.

For simplicity, let us assume that the increase in supply is the relevant restraint to the increase in real income. Then two effects on regional income can be distinguished. Effect I determines the potential increase in supply caused by an internal increase in the factors of production. Effect II indicates the change in the availability of commodities caused by a change in the terms of trade. Let dY^P indicate the change in income for a constant terms of trade. Then the overall change in actual real income is given by

$$dY^a = dY^P + \Omega \qquad (5\text{-}22)$$

If Ω is positive for the expanding region, the increase in real income—stemming from the increase in internal determinants of growth (and defined for constant terms of trade)—is reinforced. The internally stagnant region II ($dY^P = 0$) experiences a worsening of its terms of trade and a decrease in its real income.

If Ω is negative for the expanding region, the increase in income ascribable to internal expansion is reduced. For the internally stagnating region II, Ω is positive and real income there rises. Region II thus receives a growth stimulus from region I.

The extreme case may arise in which for the expanding region we have

$$\vdash \Omega \vert > \vert dY^P \vert \qquad (5\text{-}23)$$

Although internal determinants of growth are available, the reduction in real income due to the deterioration of the terms of trade is so strong that the net effect is a decrease in real income in the originally expanding area. This case is referred to in the literature as *immiserizing growth*.[30]

II. Analysis of the Conditions for a Variation in the Terms of Trade

1. In order to analyze the possible effects of an additional regional growth determinant on the interregional terms of trade (and thus on regional expansion), we assume a two-region model with the following characteristics. Region I produces two commodities $^{I}q_1^{I}$ and $^{I}q_2^{I}$. The first superscript indicates the region where the commodity is produced, the second where it is demanded. $^{I}q_1^{I}$ is the import substitute, $^{I}q_2^{II}$ the export commodity. Region II produces the two goods $^{II}q_1^{I}$ and $^{II}q_2^{II}$. $^{II}q_1^{I}$ is the export commodity, $^{II}q_2^{II}$ is the import substitute. These definitions and the interrelations between the two regions are delineated in Fig. 5-13.

2. Assume that originally an equilibrium situation exists in the balance of payments. Also assume that the economic expansion only influences commodity q_1. There is no change in the supply or demand of commodity q_2. Then the terms of trade remain constant if the condition

$$\begin{array}{ccc} \text{Total supply of} & = & \text{total demand for} \\ \text{commodity } q_1 & & \text{commodity } q_1 \end{array} \qquad (5\text{-}24)$$

is fulfilled.

[30] J. Bhagwati, "Immiserizing Growth—A Geometrical Note," *Review of Economic Studies*, Vol. 25 (1958), pp. 201–205.

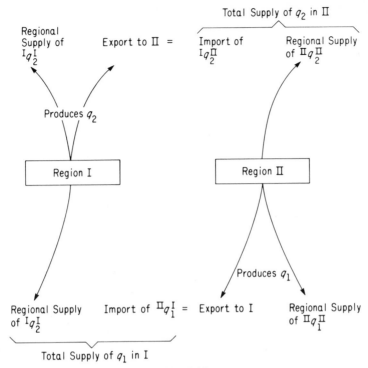

Fig. 5-13

For simplicity let us assume that q_1 which is imported by region I is not demanded in region II at all. Total demand for q_1 is then identical to the demand of region I. Total supply of commodity q_1 consists of quantities produced at home and of imports.

At any moment of time, the terms of trade bring the supply and demand of commodity q_1 into equilibrium. Starting from such an equilibrium situation, the terms of trade will not change, if

$$\frac{\text{Increase in supply}}{\text{of } q_1 \text{ by I}} + \frac{\text{increase in supply}}{\text{of } q_1 \text{ by II}} = \frac{\text{increase in demand}}{\text{for } q_1 \text{ by I}} \quad (5\text{-}25)$$

The variables of this condition can be determined algebraically[31] and with the help of Fig. 5-14.[32]

The quantity M of the import substitute supplied by region I is a function

[31] Compare J. Bhagwati, "International Trade and Economic Expansion," *American Economic Review*, Vol. 48 (1958), pp. 941–953; B. Södersten, "Foreign Trade and Economic Growth: The Marginal Aspect," *International Economic Papers*, No. 11 (1962), pp. 184–195.

[32] J. Bhagwati, "Immiserizing Growth—A Geometrical Note," p. 201; J. Black and P. Streeten, "The Balance and the Terms of Trade and Economic Growth," Appendix I in P. Streeten, *Economic Integration*, A. W. Sythoff, Leiden, Netherlands, 1964.

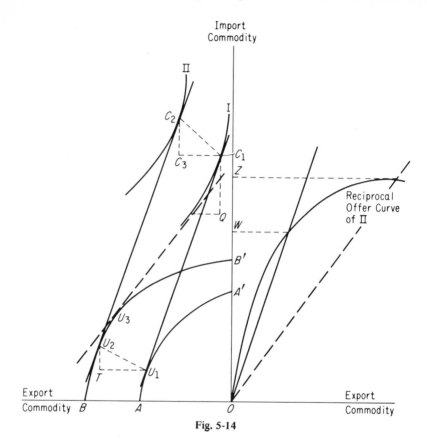

Fig. 5-14

of time and of the terms of trade, which, in turn, also change with time:

$$M = f[t, P(t)] \qquad (5\text{-}26)$$

The change in supply of the import substitute in region I is given by

$$\frac{dM}{dt} = \frac{\partial M}{\partial P} + \frac{\partial M}{\partial P} \cdot \frac{dP}{dt} \qquad (5\text{-}27)$$

The first term of Eq. 5-27 indicates the increase in the production of the import substitute due to economic expansion (expansion effect). An increase in resources or in technical knowledge enables the region to produce more of commodity q_1. Diagrammatically, internal determinants of growth shift the production block of region I (AA') to the left (BB'). Section TU_2 indicates the increase in production of the import substitute in region I.

The second term of Eq. 5-27 measures the change in supply of commodity q_1 due to a change in the terms of trade. A variation of the terms of trade leads to a reallocation of resources represented by a movement along the transformation curve $(U_2 U_3)$. The reallocation of resources results in a variation of supply (allocation effect).[33]

Supply can also be increased if a change in the terms of trade results in greater exports by region II. Assuming that

$$X = f[P(t)] \qquad (5\text{-}28)$$

we have

$$\frac{dX}{dt} = \frac{\partial X}{\partial P} \cdot \frac{dP}{dt} \qquad (5\text{-}29)$$

The increase in supply is determined by the offer curve of region II. Section WZ indicates the variation in the supply of X.

The demand for commodity q_1 is a function of income and the terms of trade:

$$C = f[Y(t), P(t)] \qquad (5\text{-}30)$$

The change in demand over time is given by

$$\frac{dC}{dt} = \frac{\partial C}{\partial Y} \cdot \frac{dY}{dt} + \frac{\partial C}{\partial P} \cdot \frac{dP}{dt} \qquad (5\text{-}31)$$

The first term indicates the change in demand due to a change in income (income effect). The terms of trade are assumed to be constant. Diagrammatically, the terms of trade line may be interpreted as a budget constraint limiting the consumption of the region. An increase in income shifts the budget line outward. For constant interregional terms of trade the change in demand is given by section $C_2 C_3$ in Fig. 5-14.

The second term indicates the change in demand due to a change in price (price effect). It is represented by a movement along the indifference curve $C_1 Q$.

Collecting the variations of demand, Eq. 5-31, and supply, Eqs. 5-27 and 5-29, we have the condition for an equilibrium in the balance of trade:

$$\overbrace{\frac{\partial C}{\partial Y} \cdot \frac{dY}{dt} + \frac{\partial C}{\partial P} \cdot \frac{dP}{dt}}^{\substack{\text{Variations} \\ \text{in demand}}} = \overbrace{\frac{\partial M}{\partial t} + \frac{\partial M}{\partial P} \cdot \frac{dP}{dt} + \frac{\partial X}{\partial P} \cdot \frac{dP}{dt}}^{\substack{\text{Variations} \\ \text{in supply}}} \qquad (5\text{-}32)$$

Solving for dP/dt, we get an expression for the variation in the terms of trade:

$$\frac{dP}{dt} = \frac{\dfrac{\partial C}{\partial Y} \cdot \dfrac{dY}{dt} - \dfrac{\partial M}{\partial t}}{\dfrac{\partial M}{\partial P} + \dfrac{\partial X}{\partial P} - \dfrac{\partial C}{\partial P}} \qquad (5\text{-}33)$$

[33]This effect overlaps with the allocation gains which are due to a reduction of interregional trade barriers (Sec. A).

Rearranging terms, we have

$$\frac{dP}{dt} = \frac{\dfrac{1}{Y} \cdot \dfrac{dY}{dt} \cdot \dfrac{Y}{C} \cdot \dfrac{\partial C}{\partial Y} \cdot C - \dfrac{1}{M} \cdot \dfrac{\partial M}{\partial t} \cdot M}{-\dfrac{C}{P} \cdot \dfrac{P}{C} \cdot \dfrac{\partial C}{\partial P} + \dfrac{M}{P} \cdot \dfrac{P}{M} \cdot \dfrac{\partial M}{\partial P} + \dfrac{X}{P} \cdot \dfrac{P}{X} \cdot \dfrac{\partial X}{\partial P}} \tag{5-34}$$

Define the following growth rates and elasticities:

$$r_Y = \frac{1}{Y} \cdot \frac{dY}{dt} = \text{relative growth of income in region I}$$

$$r_M = \frac{1}{M} \cdot \frac{\partial M}{\partial t} = \text{relative growth of home production of the import commodity}$$

$$\sigma = \frac{Y}{C} \cdot \frac{\partial C}{\partial Y} = \text{income elasticity of demand with respect to imports}$$

$$\zeta = \frac{P}{M} \cdot \frac{\partial C}{\partial P} = \text{demand elasticity of region I with respect to the terms of trade}$$

$$\eta_I = \frac{P}{M} \cdot \frac{\partial M}{\partial P} = \text{supply elasticity of region I with respect to the terms of trade}$$

$$\eta_{II} = \frac{P}{X} \cdot \frac{\partial X}{\partial P} = \text{supply elasticity of region II with respect to the terms of trade}$$

Substituting these definitions into Eq. 5-34 and writing dP/dt as $\dot{P}$ we have

$$\dot{P} = \frac{r_y \cdot \sigma \cdot C - r_M \cdot M}{-\dfrac{C}{P} \cdot \zeta + \dfrac{M}{P} \cdot \eta_I + \dfrac{X}{P} \cdot \eta_{II}} \tag{5-35}$$

Equation 5-35 specifies the conditions for a change in the terms of trade. In order to determine the direction of the change in the terms of trade, we first discuss whether the denominator is positive or negative. The supply elasticity of region I has been defined as the relation of the relative change in the quantity supplied to the relative change in the terms of trade. Let us assume a positive change in the terms of trade. We then have to specify whether the production of the import substitute increases or decreases. From relation 5-20 we know that

$$\dot{P} > 0 \quad : \quad \dot{P}_X > \dot{P}_M \tag{5-36}$$

One of our simplifying assumptions was that the supply and demand of commodity q_2, the export good of region I, does not change. Consequently, the price of the export commodity of region I is constant; $\dot{P}_X = 0$. From condition 5-36 it follows that $\dot{P}_M < 0$. Since the improving terms of trade ($\dot{P} > 0$) imply a fall in the price of the import substitute, the quantity of import substitutes supplied will decrease. The denominator of the elasticity coefficient η_I is positive, the numerator is negative. The elasticity coefficient is negative. The same is true for the supply elasticity of region II.

The price elasticity of demand is positive; a fall of the price of the import substitute leads to an increase in demand. As a fall in the import price implies a positive change in the terms of trade, the denominator of the coefficient ζ is positive, the numerator is also positive. The coefficient is positive, but due to the negative sign in front of the first term of the denominator of Eq. 5-35, the first term is negative. Because of the negative supply elasticities, all terms of the denominator are negative. The condition for a change in the terms of trade is

$$\dot{P} \gtreqless 0 : r_M M \gtreqless r_Y \cdot \sigma \cdot C \qquad (5\text{-}37)$$

The first term indicates the increase of regional supply of the import substitute, the second term denotes the increase in demand for the commodity. *Ceteris paribus*, the terms of trade vary according to the supply surplus or supply deficit of the region. If the increase in demand for the imported commodity is stronger than the increase in domestic supply, $\dot{P} < 0$, and the terms of trade deteriorate. If the increase in domestic supply is larger than the rise in demand, $\dot{P} > 0$, and the terms of trade improve.

The variation in the terms of trade also depends on the demand-and-supply elasticities of the regional system. The larger the denominator—the elasticity factor—the smaller the necessity for a variation of the relative prices.[34] The result can be easily explained: high demand-and-supply elasticities indicate that the economy can react very quickly to price changes. Quantity changes are possible immediately and the necessity of price changes is reduced.

3. Relation 5-14 may be rewritten in a more general form as

$$\Omega = f(dP) \qquad (5\text{-}38)$$

Welfare gains and losses are here a function of the variation of the terms of trade. Changes in the terms of trade also occur in the case of allocation gains. As the same variable affects similar growth influences in our model, an empirical application of the model encounters the difficulty of isolating unambiguous effects of the same variable on different phenomena. It is not a sufficient criterion for the isolation of allocation gains that they are precipitated by increased intensity of interregional interaction, because the intensity of trade also varies in the case of internal growth determinants and their welfare effects. One possible approach to a clear delineation of these two effects may be to determine the causes of changes in the intensity of interregional exchange. If the additional interregional trade is due to the reduction of trade barriers, allocation gains clearly obtain (relation 5-6). If it is attributable to internal expansion, we have welfare effects according to relation 5-14. Our abstract possibility analysis uses both relations.[35]

---

[34] B. Södersten, "Foreign Trade and Economic Growth: The Marginal Aspect," p. 189.

[35] At this point we have to mention another case of our model in which one determinant enters into two equations and in which the question of identification may be raised. Relation (5-8) contains the increase in interregional demand as a determinant of regional income. The same variable also influences the variation of the terms of trade and the welfare effects. As our possibility analysis attempts to include all (also alternative) growth determinants, the model includes all these relations.

4. Relation 5-35 specifies only the conditions for the change in the terms of trade. It does not explain how specific variables influence the terms of trade. Technical progress may, for example, have different effects on the terms of trade. If technical progress occurs in that industry of region 1 which produces an import substitute, domestic supply increases and demand for imports is reduced. The relative price of region II's exports must therefore fall, causing the terms of trade to improve in favor of region I. If technical progress is realized in the export industry of region I, output increases and the price of exports is likely to fall. The terms of trade therefore worsen for region I. Other effects of economic expansion, such as the effects of increases in demand, must also be considered. The solution of this problem requires not only specification of the conditions for the variations in the terms of trade, but also hypotheses relating the terms of trade to other variables such as technical progress. This problem has not yet been solved and remains one of the many open questions of our subject.[36]

D. REVIEW OF INTERREGIONAL INTERACTIONS AND THEIR EXPANSION EFFECTS

1. In Part II we analyzed the interregional migration of factors of production and the movement of commodities in a *ceteris paribus* world. In Chapter 4 the interregional mobility of factors and their expansion effects were considered under the simplifying assumption that no commodity exchange takes place. In Chapter 5 the interregional exchange of commodities was analyzed under the assumption that factors of production are interregionally immobile. As illustrated in Fig. 5-15, we have concerned ourselves with two extreme cases characterized by sections I and II of curve AA'.

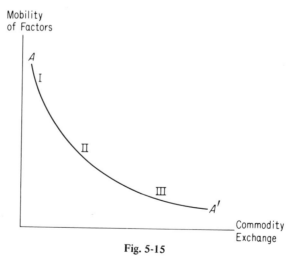

Fig. 5-15

[36] Compare the nomenclature of Johnson, *op. cit.*, p. 82.

A more realistic analysis presumably must allow for both forms of inter-action at the same time and thus relates to section II of curve AA'. This follows from the fact that both forms of interaction exist in the real world. It also de-rives from our theoretical analysis—our considerations of Chapter 4 point to imperfect factor mobility. If only partial mobility of factors obtains, there is room for the alternative form of interaction, the movement of consumption goods.

It seems plausible that the hypotheses we have postulated for the mobility of factors with no commodity exchange also hold if consumption goods are exchanged. We can also expect that the relations determining the expansion effects of commodity movements hold if factors are only partially mobile. Commodity movements and their expansion effects would be excluded only if perfect factor mobility existed. This condition, however, is not fulfilled. Similarly, perfect mobility of consumption goods can be thought of as exclud-ing factor movements, but this case also does not arise. Consequently the estab-lished system of relation does not have to be changed if both forms of inter-action exist.

Figure 5-16 summarizes our discussion of the interregional forms of inter-action. In the case of factors of production we distinguish the migration of workers, the transfer of capital goods, and the communication of technical knowledge. The mobility of labor and capital is connected with a direct with-drawal effect for the region giving up these factors. The communication of technical knowledge will have an indirect effect in changing the competitive situation of the sending region.

As factors are not completely mobile, commodity movements exist. These commodity movements may also have expansion effects. An increase in inter-regional demand generates an increase in regional income if the production system of the region is highly elastic with respect to increases in demand. Our model takes export demand into consideration only insofar as demand must be sufficient to utilize the production potential. In contrast to the purely demand-oriented expansion effects of the export-base theory, the analysis of variations in the terms of trade takes the supply side explicitly into account. These varia-tions may represent welfare gains or losses for the regions engaging in trade. Finally, with factors being only partially mobile, a reduction in interregional trade barriers leads to allocation gains from trade.

2. Our analysis has heretofore ignored some problems relevant to the study of interregional interaction which are far from solution.

Factor movements influence the interregional exchange of commodities in a very general form by reducing the intensity of exchange for all commodities. But they may also have specific effects on import demand and on the supply of export commodities, in turn influencing the commodity terms of trade. Thus the immigration of labor may lead to an increase in import demand if the immigrating workers continue to demand the products of their original region due to constant-consumption patterns. This may lead to a deterioration in the

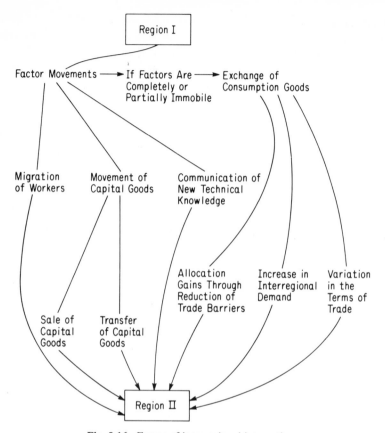

Fig. 5-16. Forms of interregional interaction.

terms of trade.   Or immigration may primarily affect the labor supply in the export- or import-substitute sector, thereby changing the terms of trade. Or the communication of new technical knowledge may benefit the import-substitute sector.   In this case the region will become less dependent on trade.   Similarly, incoming capital may favor the export sector, or the sector producing import substitutes.   In all cases, factor movements have analogous effects on the relative exchange position of the factor-receiving region as an internal increase of a growth determinant.   In addition, the relative exchange position of the factor-losing region is also affected.   If technical knowledge is communicated to the import-substitute sector of region II, the export sector of region I will be negatively affected.

In order to ascertain the variation of the interregional terms of trade as a result of factor movements, the conditions for changes in the terms of trade must be applied to a regional system with mobile factors. Hypotheses would have to be postulated which specify the relation between factor movements and the terms of trade. Such hypotheses presuppose information on the interdependence between internal factor increases and the terms of trade. This knowledge is, however, not yet available. We therefore leave this problem unsolved.

3. Another question yet to be solved is the expansion effect of the interregional exchange of investment goods. On the one hand, investment goods may be treated in the same way as capital movements. On the other, the exchange of investment goods resembles the exchange of consumption commodities. The question arises whether relations which explain the trade of consumption commodities may also be used for analyzing the exchange of investment goods.

(a) The similarity of the movement of investment goods to a capital transfer becomes apparent in a disaggregated analysis. Assume the new capital good is not used for the replacement of depreciated machines. Then the export of an investment commodity from region I to region II increases the capital stock in region II. It has therefore the same expansion effect for the receiving region as a capital transfer. For the region giving up the investment good, the export represents a loss of a capital unit. If the region would not have exported the investment good, it would have had a larger capital stock, enabling it to produce a higher output. We conclude that if we analyze only one side of the exchange of investment goods the same effects exist as in the case of a capital transfer—withdrawal of a capital good in one region, inflow of the capital good in the other area; reduction of potential output in one area, expansion effect on potential output in the other region. So far the analogy to the capital transfer is reasonable.

But an exchange of commodities is not a one-sided phenomenon. The region importing the capital good must offer goods in return. These may be investment or consumption goods. Assume region II offers investment goods in exchange. In this case we have the same effect as above, but with signs reversed. The export of the investment goods leads to lower growth in region II and to higher growth in region I. Consequently, if we split the exchange of investment goods into two components of one-sided transfers, these components may be treated in the same way as a capital transfer. The overall effect of trade in investment goods is, however, indeterminate because the loss of an investment good by one region may be matched by the import of another investment commodity.

One possible approach to a solution of this problem would be to determine the net export of investment commodities. This trade surplus of investment goods has the same effect as a transfer of a capital unit. Regions which import more investment goods than they export increase their capital stock and realize higher output levels in the future. This approach would require the discovery of relations which explain the net exports of investment goods.

(b) Another way to introduce the exchange of investment goods into our model is to treat the transfer not as a net transfer of capital but as a specific type of commodity movement and to apply similar relations to those derived for the exchange of consumption goods. We then have to analyze the analogous use of the relations postulated for allocation gains, the interregional multiplier, and welfare effects.

The application of the multiplier to the exchange of investment goods is not too promising. The multiplier relation analyzes only the demand side, whereas exports and imports of investment goods represent variables which affect long-run production capacity.

Another approach to specify the allocation gains of the movement of invest-ment goods is to determine allocation gains by analogy to relation 5-6. Whereas the exchange of consumption goods leaves the production blocks unaffected— while shifting a constant block so that an optimum can be reached (Fig. 5-7)— the exchange of investment goods has a different effect. An inflow of invest-ment goods shifts the transformation curve to the right because more resources become available. Such an outward shift of the production-possibility curve, however, would also have resulted had no investment goods been exported. Nevertheless we can expect the production-possibility curve to be affected by the exchange of investment goods. There is a net expansion effect from the trade of investment goods, which is explained by the fact that the region can produce the imported investment goods only at a relative disadvantage. No hypotheses specifying the net change of the production block from the trade of investment commodities are available.

Finally, the transmission of growth impulses via changes in the interregional terms of trade may also be applied to the exchange of investment goods. This is so because the relative prices of these commodities can both improve and deteriorate. If a region realizes technical progress by importing investment goods, it becomes less dependent on imports of consumption and—possibly— investment goods. The terms of trade may therefore change. In this case the welfare effects cannot be measured by appealing only to additional exports or imports, for additional exports and imports of investment goods must be weighted in terms of their expansion or contraction effects. We would be im-pelled to measure the additional output arising from any capacity effect that a larger importation of investment goods might imply.

Our analysis should also include the case of investment goods being traded against consumption goods. In this case, allocation gains through the reduction of trade barriers and welfare effects from variations in the terms of trade may also result.

In Section D we have pointed out some of the unsolved problems of inter-regional growth determinants. Only the most decisive factors are included in our model. For simplicity we assume that the interregional exchange of investment goods has expansion effects similar to those precipitated by the exchange of consumption goods.

PROBLEMS

1. Discuss the historical relevance of reductions in transportation costs for the integration of national markets.

2. Show in a diagram the gains from trade (a) with reallocation of resources, (b) without reallocation of resources. Compare the two cases.

3. Demonstrate the difference between allocation gains (reduction in transportation costs) and welfare gains (internal expansion) in a diagram.

4. Formulate the interregional multiplier. (Compare Appendix B of Chapter 7.)

5. "It is the ability to develop an export base which determines regional economic growth" (Tiebout).[37] Comment.

6. Discuss the interrelations of the theory of the growth of the firm and of regional growth theory.

7. How does technical change in region I affect the interregional terms of trade?

8. Interregional factor movements influence the interregional commodity terms of trade. Explain.

9. Interregional commodity movements tend to equalize factor rewards. Explain.

10. Assume regions I and II both produce commodities q_1, and $q_2 \cdot q_1$ is exported by region I. q_2 is exported by region II. Assume region I experiences economic growth. Neither demand for nor supply of q_2 changes. Only q_1 is affected by the expansion in region I. Assume:

(a) The quantity of commodity q_1 produced by region I, $^{S}q_1^{I}$, is a function of time and the terms of trade,

$$^{S}q_1^{I} = f[t, P(t)]$$

(b) The quantity of commodity q_1 produced by region II, $^{S}q_1^{II}$, depends on the terms of trade:

$$^{S}q_1^{II} = f[P(t)]$$

(c) The quantity of q_1 demanded by region I, $^{D}q_1^{I}$, is given by

$$^{D}q_1^{I} = f[Y(t), P(t)]$$

(d) The quantity of q_1 demanded by region II, $^{D}q_1^{II}$, is a function of

$$^{D}q_1^{II} = f[P(t)]$$

Follow a similar procedure as in Eqs. 5-25 through 5-37 and derive a condition for the improvement or deterioration of the terms of trade. Express this condition in terms of elasticities and rates of change. Take into account the value of the elasticities ($\gtrless 0$) and discuss under what condition $dP/dt \gtrless 0$.

[37] Tiebout, *op. cit.*, p. 164.

part **III**

THE COMBINATION OF INTERNAL AND EXTERNAL GROWTH DETERMINANTS

chapter **6**

Formal Structure of the Model

In the previous two parts we have analyzed the internal and external determinants of growth. Our basic theme was to study the influence of each growth factor on regional income and to explain the behavior of the growth factors in terms of other variables. By studying the different growth determinants we have split up the problem of regional growth into its basic components. The following two chapters integrate these basic elements of regional expansion into a consistent model and indicate the use of the model for an explanation of empirical problems. The hypothetic-deductive system, which we formulate both in a general way and in specified equations, must be able to explain the observable phenomena and processes of reality and to predict[1] the events of the future. The empirical problem to which our theoretical system will be applied is the analysis of interregional growth differentials. Before the implications of the model on growth differences can be derived, the equations of the model have to be presented.

A. A GENERAL SYSTEM OF EQUATIONS

In order to construct a general model we collect the relevant hypotheses from parts I and II. Although the model includes quite a number of variables, we can consider only the most simple functional relationships from the previous chapters.

The central relation of the model determines the actual increase in real income as the minimum increase of supply or demand. Implicity, an equilibrium between supply and demand is assumed to prevail originally. All variables relate to region I unless otherwise stated.

$$_{t-1}dY^a_{t+1} = \min\left\{ (_{t-1}dO_{t+1} + {}_{t-1}dM_{t+1}), (_{t-1}dD^i_{t+1} \right.$$
$$\left. + {}_{t-1}dX_{t+1}) \right\} + {}_{t-1}\Omega_{t+1} \qquad (6\text{-}1)$$

The increase in potential output depends on the increase of factors of production in the region

[1] An explanation may be defined as a forecast for the past.

$$_{t-1}dO_{t+1} = f(_{t-1}dK^I_{t+1},\,_{t-1}dL^I_{t+1},\,_{t-1}dT^I_{t+1}) \qquad (6\text{-}2)$$

The increase in the capital stock of region I is the sum of the internal increase and the external increase flowing to region I. The first superscript indicates the origin of a variable; the second denotes the destination. Thus $^{II}dK^I$ characterizes the movement of capital from region II to I; $^IdK^I$ is the internal increase of capital:

$$_{t-1}dK^I_t = _{t-1}^I dK^I_t + _{t-1}^{II} dK^I_t \qquad (6\text{-}3)$$

The internal increase in capital depends on the demand for investment funds (J) and savings (S). The demand for investment funds is a function of the rate of return:

$$_{t-1}^I dK^I_t = f(_{t-1}J^I_t,\,_{t-1}S^I_t) \qquad (6\text{-}4)$$

$$_{t-1}J^I_t = f(r^I_{t-1}) \qquad (6\text{-}5)$$

The external increase of the capital stock flowing to region I (which may be positive or negative) is determined by the rates of return in the two regions:

$$_{t-1}^{II} dK^I_t = f(r^I_{t-1},\,r^{II}_{t-1}) \qquad (6\text{-}6)$$

Let arrows ($\rightarrow$) indicate functional relationships and braces ($\frown$) denote identities. Then Fig. 6-1 illustrates relations 6-3 through 6-6.

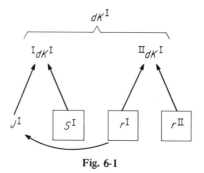

Fig. 6-1

The increase in the labor supply also consists of an internal and an external variation:

$$_{t-1}dL^I_t = _{t-1}^I dL^I_t + _{t-1}^{II} dL^I_t \qquad (6\text{-}7)$$

The internal increase in the work force is a function of the change in population and the wage rate in the region. The inflow of labor depends on the wage rates in the two regions.

$$_{t-1}^I dL^I_t = f(dB,\,w^I_{t-1}) \qquad (6\text{-}8)$$

$$_{t-1}^{II}dL_t^I = f(w_{t-1}^I, w_{t-1}^{II})$$ (6-9)

The change in the labor supply is shown in Fig. 6-2.

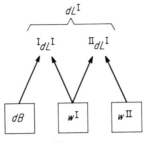

Fig. 6-2

The change in technical knowledge is also explained by a set of equations, although the variables involved are nonoperational. The variation in realized technical knowledge is a function of inventions E, the change in the capital stock and depreciation (θ):

$$_{t-1}dT_t^I = f(E_{t-1}, {}_{t-1}dK_t^I, {}_{t-1}\theta_t)$$ (6-10)

Inventions are split up into an inflow of information on new technical possibilities from the other region $^{II}E^I$ and internal inventions $^I E^I$. Internal inventions are a function of research expenditures (R):

$$E_{t-1} = {}^I E_{t-1}^I + {}^{II} E_{t-1}^I$$ (6-11)

$$^I E_{t-1}^I = f(_{t-2}R_{t-1})$$ (6-12)

Figure 6-3 demonstrates the relationship.

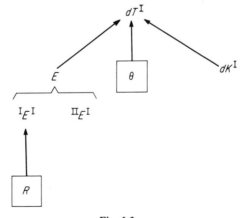

Fig. 6-3

The increase in internal demand is defined as

$$_{t-1}dD^i_{t+1} = {}_{t-1}dC_{t+1} + {}_{t-1}dJ^I_{t+1} \tag{6-13}$$

with

$$_{t-1}dC_{t+1} = f(_{t-1}dY^a_{t+1}) \tag{6 14}$$

The change in investment demand is defined as the difference between two flows:

$$_{t-1}dJ^I_{t+1} = {}_tJ^I_{t+1} - {}_{t-1}J^I_t \tag{6-15}$$

Investment demand $_{t-1}J_t$ is determined by Eq. 6-5. A similar relation gives

$$_tJ^I_{t+1} = f(r^I_t) \tag{6-16}$$

Figure 6-4 depicts the change in internal demand.

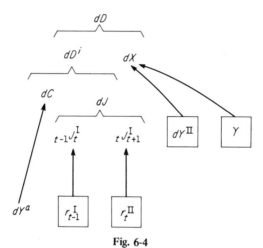

Fig. 6-4

The change in imports depends on reductions of interregional trade barriers and on the change in income of region I:

$$_{t-1}dM_{t+1} = f(_{t-1}dY^a_{t+1}, {}_{t-1}\gamma_{t+1}) \tag{6-17}$$

A similar function holds for exports, the only difference being that the change in exports of region I is a function of the increase of income in region II:

$$_{t-1}dX_{t+1} = f(_{t-1}dY^{II}_{t+1}, {}_{t-1}\gamma_{t+1}) \tag{6-18}$$

Finally the welfare effect Ω is a function of changes in the terms of trade:

$$_{t-1}\Omega_{t+1} = f(_{t-1}dP_{t+1}) \tag{6-19}$$

The model contains 19 equations and 32 variables. It can be closed by assuming that the following variables are given.

The factor rewards are determined exogenously:

$$r^{I}_{t-1} = \overline{r^{I}_{t-1}} \tag{6-20}$$

$$r^{II}_{t-1} = \overline{r^{II}_{t-1}} \tag{6-21}$$

$$r^{I}_{t} = \overline{r^{I}_{t}} \tag{6-22}$$

$$w^{I}_{t-1} = \overline{w^{I}_{t-1}} \tag{6-23}$$

$$w^{II}_{t-1} = \overline{w^{II}_{t-1}} \tag{6-24}$$

The following variables are also assumed to be given:

$$dB = \overline{dB} \tag{6-25}$$

$$_{t-1}S^{I}_{t} = \overline{_{t-1}S^{I}_{t}} \tag{6-26}$$

$$_{t-1}\theta_{t} = \overline{_{t-1}\theta_{t}} \tag{6-27}$$

$$^{II}E^{I}_{t-1} = \overline{^{II}E^{I}_{t-1}} \tag{6-28}$$

$$_{t-2}R_{t-1} = \overline{_{t-2}R_{t-1}} \tag{6-29}$$

$$_{t-1}\gamma_{t+1} = \overline{_{t-1}\gamma_{t+1}} \tag{6-30}$$

$$_{t-1}dP_{t+1} = \overline{_{t-1}dP_{t+1}} \tag{6-31}$$

$$_{t-1}dY^{II}_{t+1} = \overline{_{t-1}dY^{II}_{t+1}} \tag{6-32}$$

Assumptions 6-20 through 6-32 close the model and make it formally consistent.[2] They point out that a large part of variables are not explained within the model. The explanation of these variables within the model would require additional relationships and would make the structure of the model much too complex for our purposes.

The structure of the model is represented in Fig. 6-5. The model contains three different types of variables. (1) The exogenous variables—those that are not explained within the model but are indicated by a square. (2) The central variable—that variable which the model tries to explain: the increase in actual real income. (3) Explaining variables—the variables that influence the central variable and which are determined within the model.

[2]This statement presupposes that the functional relationships of the model are independent of each other (no contradictions, no double determination). On the problem of consistency, compare R. K. Popper, *The Logic of Scientific Discovery*, Basic Books, New York, 1959, pp. 71–72, 91–92.

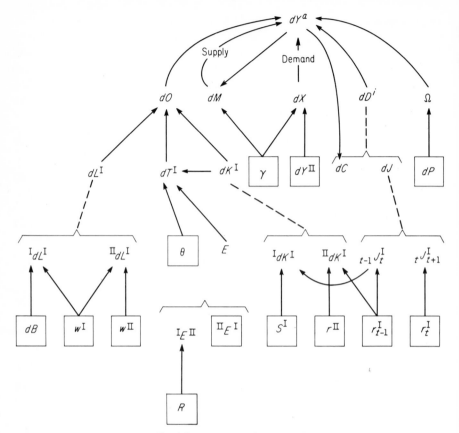

Fig. 6-5. Structure of the model.

B. THE TREATMENT OF EXTERNAL ECONOMIES

Equations 6-1 through 6-32 represent an aggregated model and do not take into account external economies. These are defined as *interdependencies* among different activities. These interdependencies may exist between consumption activities, between production activities, and between a consumption activity and a production activity. We here concentrate on interdependencies within the production sector.

According to Scitovsky,[3] we may distinguish technological and pecuniary

---

[3]T. Scitovsky, "Two Concepts of External Economies," *Journal of Political Economy*, Vol. 62 (1954), pp. 143-151; on external economies compare also P. Bohm, *External Economies in Production*, Stockholm Economic Studies Pamphlet Series, Uppsala, Sweden, 1964; H. B. Chenery, "The Interdependence of Investment Decisions," in M. Abramovitz (ed.), *The Allocation of Economic Resources, Essays in Honor of B. F. Haley*, Stanford U. P., Stanford, Calif. 1959, pp. 82-120. Compare also the distinction between localization and urbanization economies, W. Isard, *Location and Space Economy*, M.I.T. Press, Cambridge, Mass., p. 172.

external economies or diseconomies. Technological externalities represent inter-dependencies in the *volume structure* of production functions, i.e., interdependencies between physically measured inputs and outputs. Let $q_1, q_2, \ldots, q_n$ denote outputs and let $v_1, v_2, \ldots, v_n$ indicate inputs used in the different n activities. Then technological external economies exist if output q_1 is not only a function of the input v_1, but also of the output level of other activities and the inputs in other processes:

$$q_1 = f(v_1; q_2, \ldots, q_n, v_2, \ldots, v_n) \qquad (6\text{-}33)$$

Technological external economies are interdependencies outside the market. They play a role in static-equilibrium theory and in the discussion of the pareto optimum.[4] The relevance of these effects for economic development is questionable. Thus Scitovsky says "The examples of external economies given by Meade are somewhat bucolic in nature, having to do with bees, orchards, and woods. This, however, is no accident: it is not easy to find examples from industry."[5] One example from industry is the improvement of the labor force in an area by the firm which undertakes a training program. Or mining activities may lower the water table and thus reduce productivity in agriculture.

Pecuniary external effects are interdependencies among different production activities via the market mechanism. They relate to the *price structure* of production functions and represent relations between the price variations of inputs and other outputs and their effects on the level of production.[6] Let p_{q_1} and p_{q_2} indicate the output prices, and let p_{v_1} and p_{v_2} denote the input prices. If pecuniary external economies exist, the output of a firm not only is dependent on its output and input prices, but also is a function of the output and input prices of other activities:

$$q_1 = f(p_{q_1}, p_{v_1}; p_{q_2}, p_{v_2}) \qquad (6\text{-}34)$$

As price changes represent a phenomenon of a dynamic economy, pecuniary external economies will be revealed only in a process of development.[7] If resources are allocated by the market mechanism, the external economies of future periods cannot be anticipated and are thus not taken into consideration for the allocation of resources. As the process of development reveals these externalities, reallocative adjustments become necessary. These, however, may not be easily possible if the existing structures are lumpy and if they are characterized by long life. Consequently the market mechanism may lead to a nonoptional allocation of resources if the allocation problem is defined for a dynamic world. Examples of this type of externalities are numerous. Technical change in activ-

---

[4] J. F. Henderson and R. E. Quandt, *Microeconomic Theory—A Mathematical Approach*, McGraw-Hill, New York, 1958, p. 212.

[5] Scitovsky, *op. cit.*, p. 145.

[6] A slightly different definition is used by Scitovsky.

[7] P. H. Cootner, "Social Overhead Capital and Economic Growth," in W. W. Rostow (ed.), *The Economics of Take-off into Self-Sustained Growth*, St. Martin's, New York, 1963, pp. 261–284.

ity 1 may lead to lower output prices. If the output of activity 1 is an input for activity 2, and if the output price of activity 2 is reduced, the output level of activity 2 will be affected. A similar outcome can be expected if activity 1 is characterized by internal economies. Reductions in the transport rates and improvements in the technical infrastructure are other important examples for pecuniary external economies.

Economists so far have not succeeded in measuring external economies. One method to quantify at least part of these effects is the industrial-complex analysis.[8] Another possible approach would be to use an input-output model and follow the backward and forward linkages[9] as guide lines for possible pecuniary interdependencies. Once a price variation occurs, these linkages are used to calculate the effect of the price change on the level of different activities. A round-by-round calculation would have to be made for any change in one of the different activities.

The difficulty in estimating pecuniary external economies stems from the fact that the concept is so broadly defined that some of our determinants, like changes in technology, are included in this concept. Their estimation—similarly as in the case of technological externalities—requires a *ceteris paribus* world where everything which can possibly influence q_1 is constant—except our factor called "external economies."

From the definition of external effects as interrelations among different activities follows that they cannot be explicitly incorporated into an aggregate model since an aggregate framework contains only one activity by definition. Therefore no effort will be made to express external effects formally. They will, however, be taken into consideration in our verbal argumentation.

C. A SPECIFIC TWO-REGION MODEL

The model represented in Eqs. 6-1 through 6-32 is a system of general relationships. It has the advantage to include a great number of variables, but it has the disadvantage that its relations are not specified. As it is difficult to derive the implications of a model if its equations are unspecified, we have to specify at least the most important relations of our model. For purposes of simplicity we assume that the supply side is the limiting factor and that the demand side can be neglected. We also concentrate on the interregional movement of factors of production and ignore the interregional exchange of commodities. Although the model is a reduced form of our more general framework, it will be formulated for the two-region case, whereas our general framework is only related to one open region.

[8] W. Isard, *Methods of Regional Analysis; an Introduction to Regional Science*, M.I.T. Press, Cambridge, Mass., 1960, Chap. 9.

[9] This procedure is proposed by A. O. Hirschman, *The Strategy of Economic Development*, Yale U. P., New Haven, Conn., 1965, pp. 104–105.

Let the production function of region I be given by a Cobb-Douglas function,[10] with α_I indicating the level of technical knowledge and a_I and $(1 - a_I)$ the production elasticities of capital and labor.

$$O_I = \alpha_I \cdot K_I^{a_I} \cdot L_I^{(1 - a_I)} \qquad (6\text{-}35)$$

The change in output of region I can be calculated by differentiating output in Eq. 6-35 with respect to time. For simplicity, let the time derivative of a variable be indicated by a dot, so that $dO/dt = \dot{O}$ or $dK/dt = \dot{K}$.[11] Defining the total differential, using Eq. 6-35 and rearranging terms, we get[12]

$$\frac{\dot{O}_I}{O_{II}} = \frac{\dot{\alpha}_I}{\alpha_I} + a_I \frac{\dot{K}_I}{K_I} + (1 - a_I) \frac{\dot{L}_I}{L_I} \qquad (6\text{-}36)$$

Assuming a similar production function in region II, we have as the growth rate for region II

$$\frac{\dot{O}_{II}}{O_{II}} = \frac{\dot{\alpha}_{II}}{\alpha_{II}} + a_{II} \frac{\dot{K}_{II}}{K_{II}} + (1 - a_{II}) \frac{\dot{L}_{II}}{L_{II}} \qquad (6\text{-}37)$$

Let us assume all variables except the change in capital and labor are given. These two factors of production can change internally and through interaction with the other region. We first analyze changes in the capital stock. Define $_{II}\dot{K}_I$ as the quantity of capital moved from region II to region I. The dot indicates that $_{II}\dot{K}_I$ is not a stock variable but a flow variable. The movement of capital from region II to region I depends on the difference in the rates of return in the two regions. The larger the difference, the more of the existing stock in region II is likely to move. $_{II}\dot{K}_I$ is also a function of the capital stock in region II as this variable limits the possible outflow of capital. If K_{II} indicates the capital stock of region II at the beginning of a period, and if we neglect additional capital units in region II for a moment, we have

[10] The reader not familiar with the properties of the Cobb-Douglas-Function is referred to G. C. Archibald and R. G. Lipsey, *An Introduction to a Mathematical Treatment of Economics*, Weidenfeld and Nicolson, London, 1967, pp. 215–229.

[11] As time subscripts are not needed for the following analysis, we let subscripts indicate the regions.

[12] Regarding O, α, K and L as function of time and remembering that

$$\frac{d(u \cdot v \cdot w)}{dx} = \frac{du}{dx} \cdot v \cdot w + \frac{dv}{dx} \cdot u \cdot w + \frac{dw}{dx} \cdot u \cdot v \qquad (1)$$

and that for $O = f[K(t)]$

$$\frac{dO}{dt} = \frac{\partial O}{\partial K} \cdot \frac{dK}{dt} \qquad (2)$$

the total differential of O with respect to time is given by

$$\dot{O}_I = \alpha_I \cdot K_I^{a_I} \cdot L_I^{1-a_I} + a_I \alpha_I \cdot K_I^{a_I-1} \cdot L_I^{1-a_I} \cdot \dot{K}_I + (1 - a_I) \alpha_I \cdot K_I^{a_I} \cdot L_I^{-a_I} \cdot \dot{L}_I \qquad (3)$$

Introducing O_I as defined in Eq. 6-35 into each term of the right-hand side and dividing both sides by O_I, we have 6-36.

$$_{\mathrm{II}}\dot{K}_{\mathrm{I}} = f(r_{\mathrm{I}}, r_{\mathrm{II}}, K_{\mathrm{II}}) \tag{6-38}$$

Equation 6-38 can be specified in the following way:

$$_{\mathrm{II}}\dot{K}_{\mathrm{I}} = {}_{\mathrm{II}}j_{\mathrm{I}}\left(\frac{r_{\mathrm{I}} - r_{\mathrm{II}}}{r_{\mathrm{I}}}\right)K_{\mathrm{II}} \tag{6-39}$$

The term $\left(\dfrac{r_{\mathrm{I}} - r_{\mathrm{II}}}{r_{\mathrm{I}}}\right)$ indicates the relative difference in the rates of return. $_{\mathrm{II}}j_{\mathrm{I}}$ is a mobility coefficient. It can be interpreted as the elasticity of the capital stock in region II with respect to differences in the rates of return. It is defined as the relation between the relative quantity of capital moved and the relative difference in the rate of return:

$$_{\mathrm{II}}j_{\mathrm{I}} = \frac{\dfrac{_{\mathrm{II}}\dot{K}_{\mathrm{I}}}{K_{\mathrm{II}}}}{\dfrac{r_{\mathrm{I}} - r_{\mathrm{II}}}{r_{\mathrm{I}}}} \tag{6-40}$$

The mobility coefficient $_{\mathrm{II}}j_{\mathrm{I}}$ reflects the obstacles to the movement of capital. It is positive only for the case that the rate of return in region I is higher than in region II. The coefficient is zero for $r_{\mathrm{II}} > r_{\mathrm{I}}$. Thus

$$r_{\mathrm{I}} > r_{\mathrm{II}} \to {}_{\mathrm{II}}j_{\mathrm{I}} \geqslant 0 \tag{6-41}$$

$$r_{\mathrm{II}} > r_{\mathrm{I}} \to {}_{\mathrm{II}}j_{\mathrm{I}} = 0 \tag{6-42}$$

$_{\mathrm{II}}j_{\mathrm{I}}$ may take any value from zero to infinity, whereas both the relative change in capital (numerator of 6-40) and the relative difference in the rates of return (denominator of 6-40) cannot exceed unity.

The product of the mobility coefficient with the relative difference in the rates of return cannot exceed unity, as this would mean that more capital would be moved than is actually available. This condition can be expected to be fulfilled in reality.[13]

[13] As $_{\mathrm{II}}\dot{K}_{\mathrm{I}}$ cannot surpass the existing capital stock in II, we have

$$_{\mathrm{II}}\dot{K}_{\mathrm{I}} \leqslant K_{\mathrm{II}} \tag{1}$$

For (1) to hold, the product of the mobility coefficient with the relative difference in the rates of return is limited by unity:

$$_{\mathrm{II}}j_{\mathrm{I}}\left(\frac{r_{\mathrm{II}} - r_{\mathrm{I}}}{r_{\mathrm{II}}}\right) \leqslant 1 \tag{2}$$

or

$$_{\mathrm{II}}j_{\mathrm{I}} \leqslant \frac{r_{\mathrm{II}}}{r_{\mathrm{II}} - r_{\mathrm{I}}} \tag{3}$$

For $r_{\mathrm{I}} > r_{\mathrm{II}}$, the mobility coefficient becomes zero. For $r_{\mathrm{II}} > r_{\mathrm{I}}$, the lowest limit for $_{\mathrm{II}}j_{\mathrm{I}}$ is 1, if r_{I} is zero. If r_{I} approaches r_{II}, the limit of $_{\mathrm{II}}j_{\mathrm{I}}$ is infinity. This problem of having a restraint for the mobility coefficient can be avoided if the movement of capital is not made a function of the existing stock in the other region.

The increase in capital in region I may also be due to an inflow of capital which has been newly created in the same period in region II. Let us denote the internal increase in capital in region II as $\dot{K}_{II}^i$. Defining the mobility coefficient of additional capital as $_{II}j_I'$ the inflow of capital from this source is given by

$$_{II}\dot{K}_I' = {_{II}j_I'}\left(\frac{r_I - r_{II}}{r_I}\right)\dot{K}_{II}^i \tag{6-43}$$

The same restrictions apply to this mobility coefficient:

$$r_{II} > r_I \rightarrow {_{II}j_I'} = 0 \tag{6-44}$$

Relations 6-39 and 6-43 specify the total amount of capital coming from region II. An outflow of capital from I to II will occur if the rate of return is higher in region II than in region I:

$$_I\dot{K}_{II} = {_Ij_{II}}\left(\frac{r_{II} - r_I}{r_{II}}\right)K_I \tag{6-45}$$

$$_I\dot{K}_{II}' = {_Ij_{II}'}\left(\frac{r_{II} - r_I}{r_{II}}\right)\dot{K}_I^i \tag{6-46}$$

$_Ij_{II}$ denotes the mobility of the existing capital stock in region I, $_Ij_{II}'$ indicates the mobility of the additional capital stock in I. The following restrictions apply:

$$r_I > r_{II} \rightarrow \begin{cases} _Ij_{II} = 0 \\ _Ij_{II}' = 0 \end{cases} \tag{6-47}$$

The total change in the capital supply of region I, $\dot{K}_I$, is identical to the inflow from region II, plus the internal increase of capital in region I, minus the outflow of capital from the region. The inflowing capital may be attracted from the existing capital stock in region II or the additional capital in II. The outflow from region I may reduce the additional capital in I or the existing capital stock in I.

$$\dot{K}_I = {_{II}j_I}\left(\frac{r_I - r_{II}}{r_I}\right)K_{II} + {_{II}j_I'}\left(\frac{r_I - r_{II}}{r_I}\right)\dot{K}_{II}^i + \dot{K}_I^i$$
$$- {_Ij_{II}}\left(\frac{r_{II} - r_I}{r_{II}}\right)K_I - {_Ij_{II}'}\left(\frac{r_{II} - r_I}{r_{II}}\right) \cdot \dot{K}_I^i \tag{6-48}$$

The increase in the capital stock of region II is given by

$$\dot{K}_{II} = {_Ij_{II}}\left(\frac{r_{II} - r_I}{r_{II}}\right)K_I + {_Ij_{II}'}\left(\frac{r_{II} - r_I}{r_{II}}\right)\dot{K}_I^i + \dot{K}_{II}^i$$
$$- {_{II}j_I}\left(\frac{r_I - r_{II}}{r_I}\right)K_{II} - {_{II}j_I'}\left(\frac{r_I - r_{II}}{r_I}\right)\dot{K}_{II}^i \tag{6-49}$$

By the same procedure we can postulate hypotheses for the interregional mobility of labor. Let $_{II}\dot{L}_I$ indicate the interregional migration of workers from II to I. $_{II}\dot{L}_I$ is determined by a mobility coefficient $_{II}\epsilon_I$, the relative wage difference, and the existing labor supply in region II:

$$_{II}\dot{L}_I = {}_{II}\epsilon_I \left(\frac{w_I - w_{II}}{w_I} \right) L_{II}$$

(6-50)

A similar relation is obtained for the mobility of the additional labor force in II:

$$_{II}\dot{L}'_I = {}_{II}\epsilon'_I \left(\frac{w_I - w_{II}}{w_I} \right) \dot{L}^i_{II}$$

(6-51)

Postulating similar functions for the inflow of labor to region II, we have for the increase in labor in the two regions:

$$\dot{L}_I = {}_{II}\epsilon_I \left(\frac{w_I - w_{II}}{w_I} \right) L_{II} + {}_{II}\epsilon'_I \left(\frac{w_I - w_{II}}{w_I} \right) \dot{L}^i_{II} + \dot{L}^i_I$$
$$- {}_{I}\epsilon_{II} \left(\frac{w_{II} - w_I}{w_I} \right) L_I - {}_{I}\epsilon'_{II} \left(\frac{w_{II} - w_I}{w_{II}} \right) \dot{L}^i_I$$

(6-52)

and

$$\dot{L}_{II} = {}_{I}\epsilon_{II} \left(\frac{w_{II} - w_I}{w_{II}} \right) L_I + {}_{I}\epsilon'_{II} \left(\frac{w_{II} - w_I}{w_I} \right) \dot{L}^i_I + \dot{L}^i_{II}$$
$$- {}_{II}\epsilon_I \left(\frac{w_I - w_{II}}{w_I} \right) L_{II} - {}_{II}\epsilon'_I \left(\frac{w_I - w_{II}}{w_I} \right) \dot{L}^i_{II}$$

(6-53)

For the mobility coefficients, the following restrictions hold:

$$w_I > w_{II} \rightarrow \begin{cases} {}_I\epsilon_{II} = 0 \\ {}_I\epsilon'_{II} = 0 \end{cases}$$

(6-54)

$$w_{II} > w_I \rightarrow \begin{cases} {}_{II}\epsilon_I = 0 \\ {}_{II}\epsilon'_I = 0 \end{cases}$$

(6-55)

The increase in the capital stock and the labor supply in the two regions can be substituted into Eqs. 6-36 and 6-37. Equations 6-36, 6-37, 6-48, 6-49, 6-52, and 6-53 represent a two-region model, excluding the demand side and the interregional exchange of commodities and concentrating on the increase in productive capacity and on the interregional movement of factors of production. This model will be used in the following analysis, although reference will also be made to our more general framework.

PROBLEMS

1. Define technological, pecuniary (negative and positive) external effects, social costs, social benefits, and agglomeration economies. How are these terms interrelated?

2. Discuss the methods which have been used to estimate external economies.

3. Rewrite model 6-35 through 6-55 in a simpler fashion by assuming that the quantity of a factor moved only depends on differences in the factors rewards. Interpret the mobility coefficients for this case. Derive an expression for growth differentials and discuss it in a *ceteris paribus* analysis.

4. Discuss which difficulties arise if model 6-35 through 6-55 is to be disaggregated. Try to formulate a regional growth model with an input-output framework. Which problems do emerge? (References on input-output analysis are found in the preceding Chapter 9.)

chapter 7

Implications of the Model: Theorems on Regional Growth Differentials

The model constructed in Eqs. 6-1 through 6-32 represents a *possibility analysis* of regional economic growth discussing the conceivable determinants of an increase of regional income in a world where no government exists. This general framework may be used as the starting point for the analysis of five different problems.

First, the model can explain the actual growth of a single region by analyzing the internal and external determinants of economic growth and their effects on the increase of regional income. This is basically the question we have discussed so far. Second, the model represents a general framework for the historical study of the development of regions. In this case we would analyze how a region has grown over time, which of the possible growth determinants were at work, and their specific role in the regional development process. Possibly the model could contribute to the improvement of existing stage "theories" of regional development.[1] Third, the model can be used to determine the development potential of a region by indicating the potential increase of regional income over a period of time. Such a forecast can be made if the production function can be successfully specified and if projections for the different growth determinants are made. Fourth, questions concerning the relation of regional and national economic growth may be studied. Can national development be explained as the outcome of expansion processes in different regions? How does national growth affect the economic activities in the spatial subsystems of a national economy? Can a concept of leading regions be meaningfully defined—by

---

[1] H. S. Perloff *et al., Regions, Resources and Economic Growth*, Johns Hopkins Press, Baltimore, Md., 1960, p. 59; D. C. North, "Location Theory and Regional Economic Growth," *Journal of Political Economy*, Vol. 63 (1955), pp. 243–258.

analogy—with the concept of leading sectors?[2] Will the expansion of an economy be likely to be regionally balanced or unbalanced?[3] Finally, the model may be used for the explanation of growth differences between regions. It is this last question that will interest us in this chapter.

A. THE RELATION BETWEEN INTERREGIONAL INCOME DIFFERENCES AND GROWTH DIFFERENTIALS

The existence of differences in regional incomes is well established in the literature of regional science. Hanna[4] has ranked the states of the United States according to their per capita income. In 1953 Delaware headed the list with $2,448 and Mississippi closed it with $878, with an average per capita income for the country of $1,788. The studies of Borts[5] and others[6] agree with these results. A similar trend is found in European countries.[7]

Differences in regional-income per capita may reflect to some extent differences in the ownership of capital by different regions. If region I owns capital being used in region II, its income, according to the residents concept, is higher than its regional output, measured according to the area concept. It is safe to assume that only a small part of interregional income differences is attributable to this factor, and it can be expected that regional products show similar differences as regional incomes.

Differences in regional products can be represented by a concentration curve with the y-ordinate indicating regional output as a proportion of national output and the x-axis measuring the area of the regions as a percentage of the total area of the nation. Assume we have only regions I and II with both regions having the same area. Then Fig. 7-1 illustrates a situation in which region I produces more than three-quarters of a total national output.

Different levels of regional output at any moment of time may be interpreted as a static phenomenon and may be explained with static theory, or they may be thought of as the outcome of a dynamic process and may therefore be explained by a dynamic approach. Consequently one way to explain interre-

---

[2] W. W. Rostow, "Leading Sectors in the Take-Off," in W. W. Rostow (ed.), *The Economics of Take-Off into Self-Sustained Growth*, St. Martin's, New York, 1963, pp. 1–21.

[3] N. Hansen, "Unbalanced Growth and Regional Development," *Western Economic Journal*, Vol. 4 (1965), pp. 3–14.

[4] F. A. Hanna, *State Income Differentials, 1919-1954*, Duke U. P., Durham, N. C., 1959, p. 30; F. A. Hanna, "Analysis of Interstate Income Differentials—Theory and Practice," *Regional Income, Studies in Income and Wealth, National Bureau of Economic Research*, Vol. 21, Princeton U. P., Princeton, N. J., 1957, pp. 113–185.

[5] G. H. Borts, "An Approach to Measuring Regional Growth Differentials," *Papers and Proceedings of the Regional Science Association*, Vol. 4 (1958), pp. 207–220.

[6] Perloff *et al.*, *op. cit.*, p. 24; W. R. Thompson, *A Preface to Urban Economics*, Johns Hopkins Press, Baltimore, Md., 1967, Chap. 3.

[7] H. Giersch, "Probleme der regionalen Einkommensverteilung," in W. G. Hoffmann (ed.), *Probleme des räumlichen Gleichgewichts in der Wirtschafts-Wissenschaft, Schriften des Vereins für Sozialpolitik*, Vol. 14, Duncker & Humblot, Berlin, Germany, 1959.

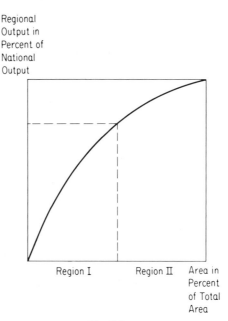

Fig. 7-1

gional income differences is to study the location advantage[8] of regions and to determine the industrial composition that is likely to result from these advantages. The industrial structure of the region permits conclusions on the differences of regional product. In contrast to this approach, which basically uses a static-location theory, we can interpret interregional income differences as the result of dynamic processes of economic growth. Then differences in the level of regional output at a point of time are the outcome of different rates of growth of output over a series of time periods. It is this dynamic approach to the problem of interregional income differences that is used here. Therefore the main objective in the following analysis will be to specify the conditions under which differences in the growth rates of two regions will occur.

B. IMPLICATIONS ON GROWTH DIFFERENTIALS: THE SPECIFIC MODEL[9]

Initially, to specify the conditions for the existence of growth differentials, the simplified two-region model of Eq. 6-36, 6-37, 6-48, 6-49, 6-52, and 6-53 is used. The model neglects the demand side and the movement of commodities

[8] On location advantage, compare W. Isard, *Location and Space Economy*, M. I. T. Press, Cambridge, Mass., 1956; M. L. Greenhut, *Plant Location in Theory and Practise*, U. of North Carolina Press, Chapel Hill, 1956.

[9] The reader is urged to go through Appendix A in order to understand the implications of the model and the following discussion.

between regions. As a direct implication of the model, a condition for the existence of growth differences between regions I and II is

$$\frac{\dot{O}_I}{O_I} > \frac{\dot{O}_{II}}{O_{II}} : \frac{\dot{\alpha}_I}{\alpha_I} + (r_I - r_{II})\left(\frac{U}{r_I} + \frac{V}{r_{II}}\right) G + a_I k_I + (1 - a_I) l_I >$$

$$\frac{\dot{\alpha}_{II}}{\alpha_{II}} + (w_{II} - w_I)\left(\frac{T}{w_I} + \frac{Z}{w_{II}}\right) E + a_{II} k_{II} + (1 - a_{II}) l_{II} \tag{7-1}$$

The derivation of this formula is given in Appendix A.[9] The terms $\dfrac{\dot{O}_I}{O_I}$ and $\dfrac{\dot{O}_{II}}{O_{II}}$ indicate the growth rates of output. k_I and k_{II} are the rates of internal growth of the capital stock; l_I and l_{II} are the corresponding rates for labor. G, E, U, V, T, Z are simplifying terms as defined in the appendix. The discussion of condition 7-1 becomes easier if it is analyzed in a *ceteris paribus* fashion. For convenience it is assumed that both regions start from the same output level. Then the following implications of the model can be derived.

1. The growth rate of region I will be higher than that of region II if it realizes a higher rate of technical change. If all other variables in the two regions are identical, condition 7-1 becomes

$$\frac{\dot{O}_I}{O_I} > \frac{\dot{O}_{II}}{O_{II}} : \frac{\dot{\alpha}_I}{\alpha_I} > \frac{\dot{\alpha}_{II}}{\alpha_{II}} \tag{7-2}$$

This condition implies that region I makes more technical discoveries and can realize them at a higher rate. New technical knowledge must be partly immobile for this condition to be fulfilled. Condition 7-2 could also imply that both regions have the same rate of discovery (or region II may have a higher one), but region I has better possibilities to realize the new technical knowledge. This case, however, may be regarded as unlikely.

In the long run, the export of capital goods embodying the new technical knowledge and information flows on the new production processes will reduce the differences in the rates of realized technical knowledge, but at the same time, new differences may arise.

THEOREM 1. Growth differences between regions will be higher, the stronger the differences in the rate of inventions and the lower the mobility of technical knowledge.[10]

2. Growth differences also depend on the rates of internal growth of capital and labor. Assume the differences in factor rewards are zero and the production elasticities of capital and labor are identical for the two regions. Then condition 7-1 becomes

[10]This statement does not include technical change in interregional transportation systems.

$$\frac{\dot{O}_I}{O_I} > \frac{\dot{O}_{II}}{O_{II}} : k_I + l_I > k_{II} + l_{II} \tag{7-3}$$

This condition reflects the relevance of internal factors of economic development.

THEOREM 2.   The greater the accumulation of capital and the higher the increase of the labor supply of region I compared to region II, the greater its rate of growth.

3. The growth rates of the two regions are a function of the production elasticities of the different factors. Assume the mobility of factors between regions is zero and let the increase in capital be the same in both regions so that $k_I = k_{II} = k$. Similarly for labor, $l_I = l_{II} = l$. Let b denote the production elasticity of labor. Instead of condition 7-1, we have

$$\frac{\dot{O}_I}{O_I} > \frac{\dot{O}_{II}}{O_{II}} : \frac{(a_1 - a_{II})k}{(b_{II} - b_1)l} > 1, \text{ for } b_{II} > b_I \tag{7-4}$$

Region I will grow at a higher rate if its production advantage in capital (expressed as the difference between the production elasticities of this factor) is greater than the production advantage of region II with respect to labor.

THEOREM 3.   The greater the weight of a factor in the production function, the higher the growth rate of the region with an increase in that specific factor.

4. The difference in regional growth rates depends on the interregional mobility of factors of production. Assume region I creates capital through savings. In a *ceteris paribus* world, with given constant technical knowledge, the rate of return of capital will fall in region I. Define r as the real rate of return, r^M as the monetary rate of return, and p as the price of output. As a region produces only one output by assumption, p also indicates the price level. Assuming a perfectly competitive regional market for each region,

$$r = \frac{r^M}{P} = \frac{\partial O}{\partial K} \tag{7-5}$$

The real rate of return r is determined by the marginal productivity of capital.[11] A lower rate of return in region I compared to region II therefore implies a lower marginal productivity.

[11] In perfect competition the monetary price of a factor of production is given by its marginal value product:

$$r^M = p \frac{\partial O}{\partial K}$$

Rearranging, we get Eq. (7-5).

$$r_I < r_{II} = \frac{\partial O_I}{\partial K_I} < \frac{\partial O_{II}}{\partial K_{II}} \qquad (7\text{-}6)$$

If capital is mobile, it will leave region I and flow to region II. A growth differential is prevented through the mobility of capital. If region I experiences an increase in its labor supply, a similar result holds. The wage rate will fall and labor will move to region II.

THEOREM 4. The more immobile an internal growth determinant, the greater the growth differential. The greater the interregional mobility of an internal growth factor, the lower the growth differential. This statement also applies to technical knowledge (compare Theorem 1).

5. Assume, contrary to case 4, that region I has both a higher profit rate and a higher wage rate. These higher factor rewards reflect higher marginal productivities of both factors. Under these assumptions region I will attract both factors of production and thus increase its growth rate—if factors are mobile.[12] But what will happen if one region has a higher profit rate and the other region pays a higher wage? Suppose that region I has a higher profit rate and region II has a higher wage:

$$r_I > r_{II}, \; w_{II} > w_I \qquad (7\text{-}7)$$

From Eq. 6-47, the mobility coefficients of capital $_Ij_{II}$ and $_Ij'_{II}$ are zero in this case. Also, from Eq. 6-55, $_{II}\epsilon_I$ and $_{II}\epsilon'_I$ are zero. Neglecting the weights G and E, and ignoring any effects on the growth differences from k_I, k_{II}, l_I and l_{II}, Eq. 7-1 reduces[13] to:

$$\frac{\dot{O}_I}{O_I} > \frac{\dot{O}_{II}}{O_{II}} : \frac{(r_I - r_{II})}{r_I} (_{II}j_I K_{II} + {}_{II}j'_I \dot{K}^i_{II}) > \frac{(w_{II} - w_I)}{w_{II}} (_I\epsilon_{II}L_I + {}_I\epsilon'_{II}\dot{L}^i_I) \qquad (7\text{-}8)$$

Assume the difference in the factor rewards is the same for both regions so that

---

[12] This statement does not contradict Theorem 4. Different marginal productivities imply the interregional immobility of at least one other factor: they may reflect (1) different technologies, (2) different organizational levels, or (3) different internal changes of factors of production.

[13] This procedure implies as necessary conditions:

$$G = E \qquad (1)$$

namely,

$$\frac{a_I}{K_I} + \frac{a_{II}}{K_{II}} = \frac{(1 - a_I)}{L_I} + \frac{(1 - a_{II})}{L_{II}} \qquad (2)$$

and

$$a_I k_I + (1 - a_I) l_I = a_{II} k_{II} + (1 - a_{II}) l_{II} \qquad (3)$$

Assumptions (2) and (3) do not contradict each other.

$$\frac{r_I - r_{II}}{r_I} = \frac{w_{II} - w_I}{w_{II}} = \lambda \qquad (7\text{-}9)$$

Also assume no increase in the capital stock and the labor supply. Then the condition for a higher growth rate of region I is

$$\frac{\dot{O}_I}{O_I} > \frac{\dot{O}_{II}}{O_{II}} : {}_{II}j_I K_{II} > {}_I \epsilon_{II} L_I \qquad (7\text{-}10)$$

Neglecting the existing stocks of capital and labor, region I will grow at a higher rate if the mobility of capital is greater than the mobility of labor. This is due to the fact that region I can attract more resources (capital) than it has to give up (labor):

$$\frac{\dot{O}_I}{O_I} > \frac{\dot{O}_{II}}{O_{II}} : \frac{{}_{II}j_I}{{}_I \epsilon_{II}} > 1 \qquad (7\text{-}11)$$

For the same degree of capital and labor mobility, it follows from condition 7-8 that region I will grow at a higher rate if it has a smaller labor stock than the capital stock of region II. This implies that it has to give up less resources than it can attract. For the same degree of factor mobility for both capital and labor condition 7-10 becomes

$$\frac{\dot{O}_I}{O_I} > \frac{\dot{O}_{II}}{O_{II}} : \frac{K_{II}}{L_I} > 1 \qquad (7\text{-}12)$$

Assume that the existing stock of capital and labor are completely immobile, but allow mobility for additional capital and additional labor. Then condition 7-8 becomes

$$\frac{\dot{O}_I}{O_I} > \frac{\dot{O}_{II}}{O_{II}} : {}_{II}j_I^i \dot{K}_{II}^i > {}_I \epsilon_{II}' \dot{L}_I^i \qquad (7\text{-}13)$$

For the same increase in capital and labor, region I will grow at a higher rate than region II if additional capital is more mobile than additional labor. For the same degree of mobility, region I will grow at a higher rate if the increase in labor of region II is greater than the increase in capital in region I. This implies that region I can attract more factors than it has to give up.

If we allow for the mobility of the existing stocks and the variations of both factors, the growth rate of region I will *ceteris paribus* be higher than that of region II if the mobility of the existing and the additional capital stock are higher than the mobility of the existing and additional supply of labor.

$$\frac{\dot{O}_I}{O_I} > \frac{\dot{O}_{II}}{O_{II}} : {}_{II}j_I K_{II} + {}_{II}j_I' \dot{K}_{II}^i > {}_I \epsilon_{II} L_I + {}_I \epsilon_{II}' \dot{L}_I^i \qquad (7\text{-}14)$$

Assume region II has an advantage in that labor coming from the existing stock in region I is more mobile than the existing stock of capital in II. Then output in region I will grow faster than that in region II only if the mobility of the additional capital in region II is larger than the mobility of the additional labor supply in region I.

6. The difference in factor prices reflects the relative scarcity or abundance of a factor in a region. High factor prices indicate a relatively strong scarcity and low prices a relative abundance.

THEOREM 5. The more mobile the scarce factor of a region (for which it pays the higher reward) and the less mobile the abundant factor (for which it pays the lower reward), the greater the inter-regional growth difference.

Assume capital increases in region I and labor increases in region II, then, *ceteris paribus,* the profit rate will fall in region I, and the wage rate will decrease in II. Capital moves from I to II and labor in the opposite direction. If in this case capital is more mobile than labor, region II will have a higher growth rate. If labor is more mobile than capital, region I will grow quicker.[14]

These considerations can also be applied to other growth determinants. Assume region I realizes capital-using technical change and region II accumulates capital. If technical knowledge is relatively immobile and capital is relatively mobile, region I will withdraw capital from II. Or if the increase in capital in II is immobile and the increase in technical knowledge in region I is mobile, then region II will attract technical knowledge from region I. The accompanying table gives some examples.

Region I	Region II
$\dot{K}$ (immobile)	$\dot{L}$ (mobile)
$\dot{K}$ (mobile)	$\dot{L}$ (immobile)
dT (immobile)	$\dot{K}$ (mobile)
dT (immobile)	$\dot{K}$ (mobile) / $\dot{L}$ (mobile)
dT (mobile)	$\dot{K}$ (immobile)

If both factors are equally mobile and if the differences in rewards are similar, no growth differences will arise. If both factors are immobile, a growth difference can exist only if a region is more successful than its competitors in stimulating the internal development of growth factors.

[14]G. H. Borts and J. L. Stein, *Economic Growth in a Free Market*, Columbia U. P., New York, 1964, pp. 12, 50; G. H. Borts and J. L. Stein, "Growth and Maturity in the United States—A Study of Regional Structural Change," *Schweizerische Zeitschrift für Volkswirtschaft und Statistik*, Vol. 98 (1962), p. 298.

THEOREM 6. A growth differential can exist only if differing factor mobilities prevail. A permanent growth differential presupposes some immobility of at least one factor. Historically, natural resources can be regarded as this factor.[15]

7. Another condition for the existence of a growth differential can be derived from condition 7-8 assuming identical mobilities for capital and labor. Then

$$\frac{\dot{O}_I}{O_I} > \frac{\dot{O}_{II}}{O_{II}} : \frac{r_I - r_{II}}{r_I} > \frac{w_{II} - w_I}{w_{II}} \tag{7-15}$$

THEOREM 7. For a given degree of factor mobility, the higher the relative difference in the profit rates in favor of region I and the lower the relative difference in the wages in favor of region II, the greater the growth differential.

8. Once a factor movement has occurred, the incentives for further factor movements are reduced. Suppose that capital has been attracted to region I by a higher rate of return. Due to the assumption of declining marginal productivities, the rate of return in region I will fall. At the same time, the rate of return in region II will rise because the capital stock has decreased and because a lower capital stock has, *ceteris paribus,* a higher rate of return. Consequently the mobility of factors will tend to equalize[16] the factor rewards in the two regions. Thus the inducements for further migration are reduced.

C. IMPLICATIONS ON GROWTH DIFFERENTIALS: THE GENERAL FRAMEWORK

The discussion of the existence of interregional growth differentials so far relates to a specific but rather simplified model. This model explicitly ignores some factors of economic development which are, however, included in the more general framework of equations 6-1 through 6-32 or in the verbal analysis. For instance, the specific model does not include external economies and the interregional exchange of commodities. In this section theorems are derived relating to these factors.

1. The difference in the growth rate of regions depends on the mobility of external economies. The mobility of external economies is not defined as the physical movement of a variable, as in the case of labor or capital, but as the spatial extent of the interdependence between activities. External economies are

---

[15] Compare the concept of industrial poles in the writings of A. Predöhl, e.g., *Das Ende der Weltwirtschaftskrise—Eine Einführung in die Probleme der Weltwirtschaft*, Rowohlt, Hamburg, Germany, 1962, p. 79.

[16] Compare G. H. Borts, "The Equalization of Returns and Regional Economic Growth," *American Economic Review*, Vol. 50 (1960), pp. 319–349.

interregionally mobile if they are not limited to activities of a region. They are interregionally immobile if they exist only between the activities of a region.[17] Agglomeration economies[18] are immobile external economies.

THEOREM 8. The more immobile external economies are interregionally, the greater the growth differential. The more mobile external economies, the smaller the growth differential.

Technological external economies tend to decrease with distance, therefore they are likely to be immobile interregionally. Pecuniary external economies are basically mobile as these interdependencies follow market linkages between firms. A detailed mobility analysis of pecuniary external economies is rather difficult, since the concept is vaguely defined. Pecuniary external economies can be expected to be more important intraregionally than interregionally. A region is defined as the set of spatial points for which the intensity of interaction is stronger than with other spatial points. The stronger the interaction, the greater is the number of backward and forward linkages between different activities. As pecuniary external economies follow these linkages they are likely to occur more often within the region than between regions.

The growth differential will be reduced if external economies become more mobile.[19] As externalities depend on the intensity of interregional interaction, an increase in interregional trade will, *ceteris paribus,* reduce the immobility of external economies and consequently reduce the growth differentials.

2. As growth differentials depend on the mobility of factors, it follows that all processes that increase the mobility of factors reduce the difference between regional growth rates. Two important processes that affect the interregional factor mobility are the equilization of regional social structures and technical progress in the interregional transportation systems.

THEOREM 9. The stronger the tendencies to equalize regional social characteristics, such as social structures, attitudes, behavior, and institutions, the greater the mobility of factors and the smaller the growth differences between regions.

This theorem mainly relates to labor, but it may also be applied to other factors. The smaller the difference between social systems, the less severe is the

---

[17] The concept of mobile and immobile external economies has been introduced by E. A. G. Robinson, *The Structure of Competitive Industry*, Harcourt, New York, 1932, pp. 140–142.

[18] On agglomeration economies, see Isard, *op. cit.*, Chap. 8; A. Weber, *Theory of the Location of Industry*, U. of Chicago Press, Chicago, 1929.

[19] This statement holds only *ceteris paribus*. An increase in the mobility of external economies increases the mobility of commodities. This implies more trade, and more trade may bring relatively more gains for one region than for the other. This in turn affects the growth differential.

stress for immigrating workers to adjust to the new social environment and the greater, *ceteris paribus,* the inducement to migrate. The development of a greater homogeneity of society and the reduction of differences in the social systems of different geographic areas normally goes hand in hand with an improvement of nationwide news media. Establishing mass-communication systems for a set of regions will tend to create a better information system, thus increasing the number of information signals on economic variables in other regions. This knowledge relates not only to labor mobility but also to the transfer of capital and of technical knowledge. A similar effect is caused by changes in the transportation system.

THEOREM 10. The stronger technical change in the interregional transportation systems, the greater the mobility of factors and the smaller the growth differential.

3. So far we have neglected the analysis of possible reinforcements of the original growth differential. Such reinforcing effects[20] are not included in the specific model but are part of the general framework. Assume capital, labor, or technical knowledge increases in region I. Let the factor in question be interregionally immobile. Only under this assumption will a growth differential arise. And only if a growth differential exists, is the analysis of a reinforcing effect relevant.

The reinforcement effect may consist in the inducement of an internal or an external determinant of economic growth. A higher output allows increased savings and an internal capital accumulation, and makes possible more research expenditures which eventually may lead to an increased technical knowledge. The rise in output also results in higher internal demand, which may improve the profit situation of the entrepreneurs and may induce additional production. These reinforcement effects on internal variables arise because these internal variables are a function of the level of output which is originally increased.

Whereas the reinforcing effects on internal growth determinants are similar, the effects with respect to external variables differ, depending on the variable which originally causes the growth differential.

Let region I experience an increase in technical knowledge which is not communicated to region II. Assume that this technical change is factor neutral. Then according to Hicks[21] the ratio of the marginal productivities of capital to labor will remain constant for a given capital-labor intensity. The marginal productivities of capital and labor rise. This implies a higher rate of return and a

---

[20] The reinforcing effects are identical to Hirschman's polarization effects. A. O. Hirschman, *The Strategy of Economic Development*, Yale U. P., New Haven, Conn., 1965, p. 187; also compare the backwash effect described by G. Myrdal, *Rich Lands and Poor*, Harper & Row, New York, 1957, p. 27.

[21] Compare F. H. Hahn and R. C. O. Matthews, "The Theory of Economic Growth: A Survey," *Surveys of Economic Theory*, Vol. 2, Macmillan, London, 1965, pp. 47–48.

higher wage rate. The higher factor rewards will attract capital and labor to the region if these factors are mobile. Thus immobile technical knowledge induces the inflow of another growth factor into region I and reinforces the original growth difference. Contrary to the reinforcement with respect to internal variables, the induced movement of capital and labor has a dual effect. It represents a contraction of output in region II and an expansion of output in region I. Due to the withdrawal effect, the inducement of an external variable has a stronger influence on the growth differential than the inducement of an internal variable.

Assume the increase in technical knowledge of region I is capital using (labor saving). Then the ratio of the marginal productivity of capital to labor rises for a given capital intensity.[22] This implies that before any reallocation of capital and labor can occur, the ratio of the rate of return to the wage rate rises. This may come about in five different cases: (1) Both the rate of return and the wage rate rise, but the rate of return increases more than the wage rate. (2) The rate of return rises and the wage rate remains constant. (3) The rate of return rises and the wage rate falls. (4) The rate of return remains constant and the wage rate falls. (5) Both the rate of return and the wage rate fall, but the wage rate decreases more than the rate of return. The last two cases can be ruled out, since technical progress must increase the marginal productivity of at least one factor. Capital-using technical knowledge increases the rate of return.

Case (1) has a similar reinforcing effect as neutral technical knowledge, the only difference being that region I will attract relatively more capital than labor. In case (2) no labor is çoming into region I, since the wage rate remains constant. Ceteris paribus we can, however, expect a stronger inflow of capital. In case (3) region I may lose labor due to the falling wage rate. But this contraction effect is likely to be more than compensated for by the inflow of capital. Thus in the case of factor-biased technical change a reinforcing effect also results.

If region I experiences an increase in capital or labor and if these factors are immobile, no reinforcement effect with respect to external variables may arise. Assume capital increases in region I. Then the rate of return will fall. Since capital is immobile it does not leave the region. If the production system of the region is flexible, the factors of production will be reallocated and the region increases its capital-labor ratio. With a flexible production system, the wage rate is unlikely to rise and no labor will be withdrawn from the other region. If, however, the production system is characterized by fixed production coefficients, the increase in capital can be utilized only if the labor supply can be increased. In this case the wage rate must rise and labor may be attracted to the region. An internal increase in capital only leads to the inducement of an external variable in two cases. (1) The fall in the rate of return brings about an increase in the wage rate. Then labor will be attracted to the region. (2) Region II realizes new technical knowledge but does not have the funds available to

[22] Ibid.

realize it. Because of the immobility of capital, the new ideas will be attracted to region I where investment funds are available. The analysis of an increase of labor will lead to a similar result.

If capital, labor, or technical knowledge increases, the reinforcing effect on internal variables is similar. The reinforcing effects of these three factors differ, however, with respect to external variables.

THEOREM 11. Original growth differentials being caused by internal changes in growth determinants tend to be reinforced through the mechanisms of the model. The reinforcing effect will not arise if factors are completely mobile as the immobility of factors is a precondition for the original growth differential.

Theorem 11 may be restated with respect to external growth determinants if we distinguish between autonomous and induced growth determinants. Assume an increase in technical knowledge is the autonomous factor. If this growth determinant is interregionally immobile it can induce other determinants—e.g., it may attract additional capital.

THEOREM 12. If an autonomous growth factor is interregionally immobile, the growth differential will be greater the higher the mobility of the induced variable. Immobile technical change has the strongest reinforcement effect of all growth determinants.[23]

One aspect of technical change is resource innovations. We have already mentioned that historically it was the immobility of this growth determinant which caused interregional differences in economic activities.[24] An increase in the mobility of factors does not always lead to a weakening of the growth differential. On the contrary, the growth difference may become greater if the induced resource is more mobile. From Theorem 12 an important policy implication follows. If regional economic policy attempts to reduce growth differentials, it must increase the mobility of all factors. If an important growth determinant remains immobile, the increased mobility of other growth factors reinforces growth differentials and thus moves the economy further away from the desired situation.[25] If one condition of the first-best solution (i.e., perfect mobility of *all* factors) cannot be established, the first-best solution has to be substituted by a

---

[23] Note the resemblance to the impact analysis of technical change on the intraregional structure in Chap. 3.

[24] The reinforcing effect of an immobile growth determinant may become even more apparent if we engage in a disaggregated analysis. Only a disaggregated study can point out the linkages relevant for a growth pole. Compare F. Perroux, "La Firme Motrice dans la Région et la Région Motrice," *Théorie et Politique de l'Expansion Régionale*, Actes du Colloque International de l'Institut de Science Economique de l'Université de Liége, Brussels, Belgium, 1961, pp. 257–305; Hirschman, *op. cit.,* Chap. 6.

[25] On the theory of second best, compare R. G. Lipsey and K. Lancaster, "The General Theory of Second Best," *Review of Economic Studies*, Vol. 24 (1956–57), pp. 11–31; C. C.

second-best solution. This second-best solution of a policy attempting to reduce interregional growth differences does not permit to increase the mobility of induced factors. On the contrary, it can only be reached by establishing mobility restraints for the induced growth determinants.

4. We have established that the immobility of an internal increase of factors of production accounts for growth differentials. We also have established that factor immobility is substituted by commodity exchange. Consequently the question must be asked whether commodity movements will cancel the growth differential caused by factor immobility. Let region I experience an increase in capital and let this increase in capital be immobile. Then, according to our theorems so far, region I will have a higher growth rate. But how is this growth differential affected by the change in the commodity movement? If we use the theory of the export base, an additional resource allows higher exports which increase regional income. But the theory of the export base does not give the total picture. Assume region I is originally characterized by a comparative advantage in the production of the capital-intensive commodity. Then an increase in capital will increase this comparative advantage. A greater quantity of exportables can be produced. With a constant production situation and given demand patterns of region II, the price of the exportable has to fall. The terms of trade deteriorate for region I. In this case, region II would benefit from the immobile increase in capital of region I through a more favorable exchange rate for the traded commodities. The original growth differential will be weakened through the change in the terms of trade.

Suppose, however, that region I has a comparative advantage in the production of the labor-intensive commodity and that it imports the capital-intensive commodity. An internal increase in capital, which is immobile, will affect the allocation of resources and will lead to an increased production of the import substitute. Region I becomes less dependent on imports. In this case the terms of trade may improve. The growth differential will be reinforced.

A similar outcome can be expected if both regions increase one of their resources and if these resources are immobile. Assume capital increases in I and labor is augmented in II. Then both regions will reallocate their resources according to the new factor endowment. The terms of trade may improve or deteriorate for a specific region. Thus a growth differential—if it arises in this case[26] — may be reinforced or weakened by the exchange of commodities.

Morrison, "The Nature of Second Best," *Southern Economic Journal*, Vol. 32 (1965–66), pp. 49–52.

A converse theorem to 12 cannot be formulated. It cannot be stated: if the original determinant is mobile, the growth differential will be smaller the greater the mobility of the induced factor. This statement does not have any meaning, as the mobility of the autonomous determinant will prevent any growth differential to arise. Consequently the interregional mobility of the induced variable is completely irrelevant.

[26] Whether a growth differential results, depends on the conditions specified in theorems (2) and (3).

THEOREM 13.   A growth differential caused by the immobility of factors may be reinforced or weakened by the movement of commodities. The reinforcing effect is a function of changes in the terms of trade.[27]

Theorem 13 does not exclude one of the two outcomes. Both cases, a reinforcement and a weakening of the original growth differential, are possible. This also relates to the case of allocation gains which result from reductions of trade barriers. Allocation gains mean only that both regions gain from trade, but they do not imply that both regions' gains are of the same magnitude. The partitioning of the allocation gains among regions is a function of the change in the terms of trade.

A relationship cannot be established between the mobility of commodities and growth differentials via the effects of trade on the regional growth rates. However, there may be a link between growth differentials and the mobility of commodities via other variables. Some arguments suggest that an increase in the mobility of commodities reduces growth differentials. Pecuniary external economies are more mobile as commodities are more mobile. Also, new technical knowledge may be transferred to another region via the movement of commodities embodying technical progress. The higher the interregional exchange of commodities the greater are the chances for an interregional transfer of technical knowledge. These arguments are, however, not sufficient to allow the conclusion that a perfect mobility of commodities prevents or even weakens growth differences between regions. On the contrary, a high mobility of commodities allows wide markets, larger plant sizes, and economies of scale—all factors which possibly could lead to a growth difference between regions. No conclusive result on the relevance of the mobility of commodities for interregional growth differentials can be derived.

D. FURTHER IMPLICATIONS ON GROWTH DIFFERENTIALS: LEVELING EFFECTS

In the previous two sections the conditions for the existence of regional growth differentials have been analyzed. Let us assume that some of the factors operate which make for a higher growth rate in favor of region I. The question then arises as to whether any processes will be started which will reduce this growth differential. Autonomous changes both in region II and in region I may of course bring about an equalization of growth rates. Region II may, for instance, increase its internal labor supply, or the entrepreneurial quality of region I may deteriorate. Except for these autonomous changes, growth in region II may also be induced by the increase in output of region I. We call this induced

---

[27]Commodity movements lead to an equalization of factor rewards. But this does not imply an equalization of growth rates.

expansion a *leveling effect*.[28]   In what follows, three different ways are discussed   .·
in which leveling effects may operate.

1. Whereas external economies have to be immobile in order to lead to a
growth differential (Theorem 8), we get the following for the negative pecuniary
external effects.

THEOREM 14.   The more immobile the negative pecuniary external effects,[29]
the stronger the leveling effect.

If pecuniary diseconomies are limited to a region, they slow down the expansion of that area without affecting other regions adversely. If they are mobile interregionally, they impair other areas negatively. A leveling effect exists
only if the immobile external effects occur in the region with the growth advantage. If they prevail in the slowly growing region, the growth differential will
be increased.

An important case of pecuniary external diseconomies is the increase in input prices. If we can show that in the process of economic development input
prices rise, then negative pecuniary external economies exist. If the price increases for an interregionally mobile input, the price rise will not be limited to
the expanding region only. Then all regions are affected in a similar way and a
leveling effect cannot be expected. Assume the wage increases in a strongly expanding region due to an increase in demand. If workers can be attracted from
other regions, these regions also experience a wage rise as their labor supply is
reduced by emigration. Thus the mobility of labor protects the expanding region against a very large wage increase and forces a higher wage upon the slowly
expanding area. Both tendencies prevent a leveling effect. If labor is immobile,
the wage rise will only be felt in the expanding region.

In order to find possible leveling effects we have to search for price increases
of immobile factors. Land is the most important example. In the process of regional economic growth, the demand for land will increase. First, an increase in
production requires a spatial expansion of firms. Second, demand for residential
land rises with an increase in the number of workers (population) and with
changes in consumption patterns. Third, additional social overhead capital has
to be created in the process of growth, which also increases the demand for land.

Increased demand due to these factors is confronted with an unaugmentable
supply. Higher prices for land are the immediate result. The originally expanding region I experiences higher costs of production. Price rises of the input land

---

[28]This effect is identical to Hirschman's trickling down and Myrdal's spread effect,
Hirschman, *op. cit.,* p. 187; Myrdal, *op. cit.,* p. 31.

[29]Technological diseconomies are neglected. A similar result holds as in the case of
pecuniary external diseconomies: The more immobile the negative technological external
effects, the greater the leveling effect. We can expect that technological interdependencies
are limited to the region and therefore tend to be interregionally immobile. With increasing distance the probability of technological interdependence between production activities
decreases.

cannot be transferred directly to other regions, as land is immobile. Eventually the competitive situation of the region with respect to some products is negatively affected due to the price rise of the immobile factor. Thus the case may arise that firms in region I can no longer export their commodities since production in region II is competitive.

In this case the leveling effect does not only consist of a weakening of the expansion in region I, but also of induced growth in region II by making this area more competitive.

THEOREM 15.   Price increases of immobile factors in an expanding region lead to an interregional leveling effect. The strongest leveling effects can be expected from price variations of land.

With a price increase of the immobile factor of production, mobile factors may be used as substitutes. Thus an increase in the price of land may result in substitution of capital. Then the regional price of capital will go up, and if capital is mobile it will be attracted to the area increasing the rate of return in the other regions.

THEOREM 16.   The easier it is to substitute an immobile factor by a mobile factor, the less immobile are the pecuniary external economies and the smaller is the leveling effect.

If we want to draw a conclusion for regional policy which tries to reduce regional growth differentials, we reach—it seems—a contradictory result. On the one hand, regional policy has to support the leveling effects and to prevent the interregional spillover of price rises. This can be done if the immobility of factors is kept up or even increased. On the other hand, the policy with the same goal of reducing interregional income differences has to increase the mobility of factors in order to weaken the growth differential.

This contradiction can easily be resolved. Leveling effects can, by definition, occur only if a growth differential exists originally. Regional growth policy, therefore, has to weaken the growth differential in the sense of a causal therapy. A stimulation of the leveling effect represents a neutralization policy which cures the symptoms but does not change the cause. This neutralization policy is superfluous if the causal therapy succeeds in reducing the growth differential.

2. The leveling effect may also be explained with the help of the interregional multiplier. An increase in the income of region I leads normally to an increased import of commodities from other regions. As the propensity to import is relatively high for spatial subsystems of a nation, the increased export demand represents a strong stimulus for the slowly (or not) growing region.

We now ask whether or not the leveling effect could be so strong that region II will finally have a higher induced expansion than region I where the growth originally occurred. If the induced income does not lead to a rise in import demand so that there is no feedback on region I, we have the following set of relationships. The original increase in income in region I is given by

$$\dot{Y}_{\mathrm{I}} = \overline{\dot{Y}}_{\mathrm{I}} \tag{7-16}$$

The change in imports $\dot{M}_{\mathrm{I}}$ is a function of the change in income in region I. m_{I} denotes the marginal propensity to import,

$$\dot{M}_{\mathrm{I}} = m_{\mathrm{I}} \cdot \dot{Y}_{\mathrm{I}} \tag{7-17}$$

By definition,

$$\dot{M}_{\mathrm{I}} = \dot{X}_{\mathrm{II}} \tag{7-18}$$

The induced increase in income in region II is

$$\dot{Y}_{\mathrm{II}} = \frac{1}{s_{\mathrm{II}}} \cdot \dot{X}_{\mathrm{II}} \tag{7-19}$$

if region II does not import any commodities. Substituting Eq. 7-17 into Eq. 7-19, we have

$$\dot{Y}_{\mathrm{II}} = \frac{1}{s_{\mathrm{II}}} \cdot m_{\mathrm{I}} \dot{Y}_{\mathrm{I}} \tag{7-20}$$

Consequently

$$\dot{Y}_{\mathrm{II}} > \dot{Y}_{\mathrm{I}} : m_{\mathrm{I}} > s_{\mathrm{II}} \tag{7-21}$$

For region II to expand stronger than region I, the propensity to import of region I must be larger than the savings propensity of region II.

If a feedback effect from the growth of region II is allowed, an additional leakage for region II and a new inducement for the growth of region I is introduced. As can be seen from Appendix B, the change in the regional incomes with respect to an autonomous change in investment demand A is

$$\frac{dY_{\mathrm{II}}}{dA} > \frac{dY_{\mathrm{I}}}{dA} : m_{\mathrm{I}} > s_{\mathrm{II}} + m_{\mathrm{II}} \tag{7-22}$$

The increase in income of region II will be higher than that of region I if the propensity to import of I is greater than the propensity to import of II plus the savings propensity of II. This result can be expected only for a backward area with a low marginal propensity to save (no capital formation) and a low level of imports from the other region. The result is therefore rather unlikely for most cases. It also cannot be expected in the real world of more than a two-region system. Then the import propensity of region I with respect to region II is reduced, since the total import propensity of region I must be split up between different regions. Condition 7-21 is then less likely to be fulfilled. Also, with economic expansion in region I, the import propensity of region I may decline with an increase in regional size.[30] Finally, it should be realized that the multi-

[30] W. R. Thompson, *A Preface to Urban Economics,* Johns Hopkins Press, Baltimore Md., 1967, p. 164.

plier represents only a demand-oriented analysis. Under these restrictions we have the following.

THEOREM 17. The interregional multiplier has leveling effects. A complete compensation of the growth differential is unlikely.

3. Leveling effects can also be explained by a deterioration of the terms of trade for the expanding region (an improvement in the terms of trade for the nongrowing region). Two tendencies point out that a deterioration of the terms of trade may occur in the process of economic development. First, prices of factor inputs may rise due to the increased demand in the expanding area. Second, export demand of the expanding region may decrease. Higher factor prices reduce the competitiveness of a region and make for a reduction of exports and an increase of imports. Imports also rise as a consequence of higher regional income. Lower exports and higher imports must alter the interregional terms of trade. Thus the deterioration in the terms of trade incorporates both leveling effects already discussed in Theorems 15 and 17. Both theorems could also be expressed as follows.

THEOREM 18. The increase in import demand and the price rise of immobile factor inputs leads to a deterioration of the interregional terms of trade for the expanding region and will thus cause leveling effects.[31]

Figure 7-2 summarizes the leveling effects.

Leveling effects presuppose a high degree of commodity mobility, as the mechanisms of Fig. 7-2 will operate only if the level of commodity exchange be-

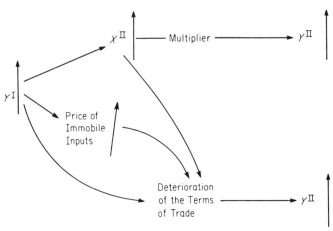

Fig. 7-2

---

[31]The deterioration of the terms of trade may be reinforced or weakened by non-induced changes in those variables that influence the terms of trade.

tween regions is high. At this point our mobility discussion is logically closed. Leveling effects occur only if a growth differential exists. The existence of a growth differential presupposes factor immobility. Factor immobility is substituted by the mobility of consumption commodities. Consequently leveling effects will go together with a high mobility of commodities.

4. The discussion of growth differentials has centered on the following effects. First, there is an original growth difference caused by a change in a growth determinant in one of the regions. Assume that these growth factors appear only in region I. Second, the occurrence of these growth determinants may induce further growth factors in region I. This is a *reinforcing effect*. Third, one aspect of the induced growth of region I is the attraction of resources from region II. We call this the *withdrawal effect*. The withdrawal effect represents only part of the reinforced differentiation, as growth in a region may also induce factors internally. Fourth, the originally nongrowing region II may receive growth stimuli from region I. We call this the *leveling effect*. Assuming that region II experiences only induced development, the described effect results in the following types of regions.

(a) *Regions with autonomous growth.* For region I it is likely that the original growth effect plus the induced growth effect, which possibly includes the attraction of resources from region II, is greater than the brake mechanism represented by the leveling effect:

$$\frac{\text{Original}}{\text{growth effect}} + \frac{\text{induced}}{\text{effect}} > \frac{\text{leveling}}{\text{effect}}$$

From the discussion of the leveling effect it is unlikely that it can compensate for the original growth effect by which it was induced. Price rises of immobile factors of production can be expected only if a strong expansion of output has already occurred. These price rises cannot compensate an existing growth differential completely. The disappearance of a growth differential via the interregional multiplier implies a rather unrealistic situation. An induced variation in the terms of trade is also unlikely to be so strong as to totally compensate the growth advantage of a region. Also, it should be noted that region II may experience a withdrawal effect of resources. Region I can be expected to have a stronger expansion than region II. This type of region corresponds to Perroux's growth pole[32] and to Friedmann's[33] core region.

(b) *Regions with induced growth.* Region II may expand if the induced growth is stronger than the withdrawal of resources,

$$\text{Leveling effect} > \text{withdrawal effect}$$

[32] F. Perroux, "Note sur la notion de pôle de croissance," *Economie Appliquée,* Paris, Vol. 8 (1959), pp. 307-320.

[33] J. Friedmann, *Regional Development Policy–A Case Study of Venezuela,* M. I. T. Press, Cambridge, Mass., 1966, Chap. 2; compare also J. Friedmann, "A General Theory of Polarized Development." The Ford Foundation, Urban and Regional Advisory Program in Chile, Santiago, Chile, 1967 (mimeo), p. 22.

It can be expected that this type of region will expand at a much lower rate than type (a). This case may be circumscribed as an *induced growth pole.*

(c) *Stagnating regions.* Region II stagnates if the induced growth from region I is identical to the withdrawal effect:

Leveling effect = withdrawal effect

(d) *Contracting region.* Finally, the pull of the originally growing region I on the resources of region II may be so strong that the leveling effect is weaker as compared to the loss of resources. In this case region II contracts,

Leveling effect < withdrawal effect

Regions of the type (b), (c), and (d) represent three different cases of the periphery.[34] This classification of regions represents a starting point for regional growth policy.

E. OPEN QUESTIONS

In Chapters 2-7 we constructed a general framework of regional economic growth which should be interpreted as a possibility analysis. The following problems are still unsolved.

First, the model has not yet been empirically estimated. Some of the variables have not been put into an operational form and some relationships have not been specified, even on a theoretical level. Thus the interregional exchange of commodities is not included in the specific model. Moreover, the basic relations of the model have not been empirically determined.

Second, our model does not explicitly include the relationship between regional and national growth. This problem may be approached from two different sides. Either we start out from a national growth model and then break it down into regional components, or we begin with a regional model and integrate the growth models of regions into a national system. The first approach has been taken by the shift analysis.[35] The second approach understands national growth as the outcome of the interaction of regional growth determinants. This second approach seems to be more promising for the regional approach, as it implies an analysis of interregional interaction. It is followed in the next chapter.

Third, our model is aggregated, and additional insight into the problem of regional economic growth can be expected if the model is disaggregated into different sectors. This requires an integration of sectoral-growth theory with regional analysis. Input-output models may be useful from the sectoral aspect, but an interregional input-output model does not include such important growth determinants as the interregional movement of factors of production, reductions in interregional trade barriers, and changes in the terms of trade. More-

---

[34] *Ibid.*
[35] Perloff *et al., op. cit.,* p. 70.

over, technical change and relations on the internal increase in labor and capital cannot be easily introduced into this type of analysis.

Fourth, an important unsolved problem is the interdependence of the process of economic growth and the spatial structure. The solution of this question lies in the integration of growth theory and a dynamic theory of location—which, however, does not yet exist. A nearly unsurmountable impediment to the successful analysis of this problem is that location theory is basically oriented toward the firm, thus being even more disaggregated than sectoral models, whereas growth theory is formulated on a highly aggregated level.

Finally, our model neglects changes in the social system as a growth determinant. With respect to this variable, regional growth theory faces the same problem as the development analysis of national economies—a widening gap between abstract models and sociological or institutional studies. So far, only a few attempts[36] have been made to integrate these different approaches of economic theory. Bridging the gap remains a task for the future. It presupposes the mastering of formal models and the domination of sociological analysis. It is a job for sages. Using Domar's expression, we have only "plucked at the sage's sleeve."[37]

APPENDIX A
CONDITION FOR REGIONAL GROWTH DIFFERENCES

Simplify Eqs. 6-48 and 6-49. Define

$$U = {}_{II}j_I K_{II} + {}_{II}j_I' \dot{K}_{II}^i \tag{A-1}$$

$$V = {}_Ij_{II} K_I + {}_Ij_{II}' \dot{K}_I^i \tag{A-2}$$

Then Eq. 6-48 becomes

$$\dot{K}_I = (r_I - r_{II}) \left(\frac{U}{r_I} + \frac{V}{r_{II}} \right) + \dot{K}_I^i \tag{A-3}$$

Equation 6-49 becomes

$$\dot{K}_{II} = - (r_I - r_{II}) \left(\frac{U}{r_I} + \frac{V}{r_{II}} \right) + \dot{K}_{II}^i \tag{A-4}$$

Define

$$T = {}_{II}\epsilon_I \cdot L_{II} + {}_{II}\epsilon_I' \cdot \dot{L}_{II} \tag{A-5}$$

$$Z = {}_I\epsilon_{II} \cdot L_I + {}_I\epsilon_{II}' \cdot \dot{L}_I^i \tag{A-6}$$

Then Eqs. 6-52 and 6-53 become

$$\dot{L}_I = (w_I - w_{II}) \left(\frac{T}{w_I} + \frac{Z}{w_{II}} \right) + \dot{L}_I^i \tag{A-7}$$

[36]H. J. Bruton, "Contemporary Theorizing on Economic Growth," in B. F. Hoselitz (ed.), *Theories of Economic Growth,* Free Press, New York, 1960, pp. 293-298.

[37]E. D. Domar, *Essays in the Theory of Economic Growth,* Oxford U. P., New York, 1957, p. 12.

$$\dot{L}_{\text{II}} = -(w_{\text{I}} - w_{\text{II}}) \left(\frac{T}{w_{\text{I}}} + \frac{Z}{w_{\text{II}}} \right)^{\cdot} + \dot{L}_{\text{II}}^{i} \tag{A-8}$$

From Eqs. 6-36 and 6-37 the difference in the rates of growth between the two regions is

$$\frac{\dot{O}_{\text{I}}}{O_{\text{I}}} - \frac{\dot{O}_{\text{II}}}{O_{\text{II}}} = \frac{\dot{\alpha}_{\text{I}}}{\alpha_{\text{I}}} - \frac{\dot{\alpha}_{\text{II}}}{\alpha_{\text{II}}} + a_{\text{I}} \frac{\dot{K}_{\text{I}}}{K_{\text{I}}} - a_{\text{II}} \frac{\dot{K}_{\text{II}}}{K_{\text{II}}} + (1 - a_{\text{I}}) \frac{\dot{L}_{\text{I}}}{L_{\text{I}}} - (1 - a_{\text{II}}) \frac{\dot{L}_{\text{II}}}{L_{\text{II}}} \tag{A-9}$$

Introducing expressions A-3, A-4, A-7, and A-8 into A-9, we have

$$\frac{\dot{O}_{\text{I}}}{O_{\text{I}}} - \frac{\dot{O}_{\text{II}}}{O_{\text{II}}} = \frac{\dot{\alpha}_{\text{I}}}{\alpha_{\text{I}}} - \frac{\dot{\alpha}_{\text{II}}}{\alpha_{\text{II}}} + \frac{a_{\text{I}}}{K_{\text{I}}} \left[(r_{\text{I}} - r_{\text{II}}) \left(\frac{U}{r_{\text{I}}} + \frac{V}{r_{\text{II}}} \right) + \dot{K}_{\text{I}}^{i} \right]$$

$$+ \frac{a_{\text{II}}}{K_{\text{II}}} \left[(r_{\text{I}} - r_{\text{II}}) \left(\frac{U}{r_{\text{I}}} + \frac{V}{r_{\text{II}}} \right) - \dot{K}_{\text{II}}^{i} \right]$$

$$+ \frac{(1 - a_{\text{I}})}{L_{\text{I}}} \left[(w_{\text{I}} - w_{\text{II}}) \left(\frac{T}{w_{\text{I}}} + \frac{Z}{w_{\text{II}}} \right) + \dot{L}_{\text{I}}^{i} \right]$$

$$+ \frac{(1 - a_{\text{II}})}{L_{\text{II}}} \left[(w_{\text{I}} - w_{\text{II}}) \left(\frac{T}{w_{\text{I}}} + \frac{Z}{w_{\text{II}}} \right) - \dot{L}_{\text{II}}^{i} \right] \tag{A-10}$$

Rearranging terms,

$$\frac{\dot{O}_{\text{I}}}{O_{\text{I}}} - \frac{\dot{O}_{\text{II}}}{O_{\text{II}}} = \frac{\dot{\alpha}_{\text{I}}}{\alpha_{\text{I}}} - \frac{\dot{\alpha}_{\text{II}}}{\alpha_{\text{II}}} + (r_{\text{I}} - r_{\text{II}}) \left(\frac{U}{r_{\text{I}}} + \frac{V}{r_{\text{II}}} \right) \left[\frac{a_{\text{I}}}{K_{\text{I}}} + \frac{a_{\text{II}}}{K_{\text{II}}} \right]$$

$$+ \frac{a_{\text{I}}}{K_{\text{I}}} \dot{K}_{\text{I}}^{i} - \frac{a_{\text{II}}}{K_{\text{II}}} \dot{K}_{\text{II}}^{i} + (w_{\text{I}} - w_{\text{II}}) \left(\frac{T}{w_{\text{I}}} + \frac{Z}{w_{\text{II}}} \right) \left[\frac{1 - a_{\text{I}}}{L_{\text{I}}} + \frac{1 - a_{\text{II}}}{L_{\text{II}}} \right]$$

$$+ \frac{1 - a_{\text{I}}}{L_{\text{I}}} \cdot \dot{L}_{\text{I}}^{i} - \frac{(1 - a_{\text{II}})}{L_{\text{II}}} \dot{L}_{\text{II}}^{i} \tag{A-11}$$

Define the growth rates of output, the internal capital, and labor stocks by small letters and let

$$G = \frac{a_{\text{I}}}{K_{\text{I}}} + \frac{a_{\text{II}}}{K_{\text{II}}} \tag{A-12}$$

and

$$E = \frac{(1 - a_{\text{I}})}{L_{\text{I}}} + \frac{(1 - a_{\text{II}})}{L_{\text{II}}} \tag{A-13}$$

Then for region I to have a higher growth rate than that of region II,

$$\frac{\dot{O}_{\text{I}}}{O_{\text{I}}} > \frac{\dot{O}_{\text{II}}}{O_{\text{II}}} : \frac{\dot{\alpha}_{\text{I}}}{\alpha_{\text{I}}} + (r_{\text{I}} - r_{\text{II}}) \left(\frac{U}{r_{\text{I}}} + \frac{V}{r_{\text{II}}} \right) G + a_{\text{I}} k_{\text{I}} + (1 - a_{\text{I}}) l_{\text{I}}$$

$$> \frac{\dot{\alpha}_{\text{II}}}{\alpha_{\text{II}}} - (w_{\text{I}} - w_{\text{II}}) \left(\frac{T}{w_{\text{I}}} + \frac{Z}{w_{\text{II}}} \right) E + a_{\text{II}} k_{\text{II}} + (1 - a_{\text{II}}) l_{\text{II}} \tag{A-14}$$

APPENDIX B
CONDITION FOR COMPENSATION OF GROWTH DIFFERENCES

Assume the multiplier is the only form of interregional exchange. Then we can derive a condition for region II to have a greater induced increase in income than region I where an autonomous increase occurs. The derivation follows Vanek's procedure.[38]

Assume an autonomous increase in investment demand in region I by A. We have

$$Y_I = C_I(Y_I) + X_I(Y_{II}) - M_I(Y_I) + A \qquad \text{(B-1)}$$

$$Y_{II} = C_{II}(Y_{II}) + X_{II}(Y_{II}) - M_{II}(Y_{II}) \qquad \text{(B-2)}$$

$$Y_I = c_I Y_I + m_{II} Y_{II} - m_I Y_I + A \qquad \text{(B-3)}$$

$$Y_{II} = c_{II} Y_{II} + m_I Y_I - m_{II} Y_{II} \qquad \text{(B-4)}$$

Solving Eq. B-4 for Y_{II} and introducing the result into Eq. B-3,

$$Y_I = c_I Y_I + \frac{m_{II} \cdot m_I}{1 - c_{II} + m_{II}} Y_I - m_I Y_I + A \qquad \text{(B-5)}$$

Solving for Y_I,

$$Y_I = \frac{1 - c_{II} + m_{II}}{(1 - c_I + m_I)(1 - c_{II} + m_{II}) - m_I m_{II}} \qquad \text{(B-6)}$$

Differentiating Eq. B-6 with respect to A and denoting the numerator of Eq. B-6 as N, we have

$$\frac{dY_I}{dA} = \frac{1 - c_{II} + m_{II}}{N} \qquad \text{(B-7)}$$

Solving Eq. B-3 for Y_I and substituting the result into Eq. B-4,

$$Y_{II} = c_{II} Y_{II} + \frac{m_I \cdot m_{II}}{1 - c_I + m_I} Y_{II} \frac{m_I A}{1 - c_I + m_I} - m_{II} Y_{II} \qquad \text{(B-8)}$$

Solving for Y_{II},

$$Y_{II} = \frac{m_I}{(1 - c_{II} + m_{II})(1 - c_I + m_I) - m_I m_{II}} \cdot A \qquad \text{(B-9)}$$

The denominator in Eq. B-9 is identical to the one in Eq. B-6. Differentiating Eq. B-9 with respect to A yields

$$\frac{dY_{II}}{dA} = \frac{m_I}{N} \qquad \text{(B-10)}$$

From Eq. B-7 and Eq. B-10 it follows that

$$\frac{dY_{II}}{dA} \overset{>}{<} \frac{dY_I}{dA} : m_I \overset{>}{<} 1 - c_{II} + m_{II} \qquad \text{(B-11)}$$

[38] J. Vanek, *International Trade—Theory and Economic Policy*, Irwin, Homewood, Ill., 1962, p. 106.

or, from the definition of the propensity to save,

$$\frac{dY_{II}}{dA} > \frac{dY_I}{dA} : m_I > s_{II} + m_{II} \tag{B-12}$$

PROBLEMS

1. The more immobile an internal growth determinant, the greater the growth differential. Comment.

2. How does the interregional immobility of external effects influence growth differentials?

3. Assume region I realizes a stronger expansion than region II. Which mechanisms reinforce this original growth differential. Which mechanisms reduce it?

4. Assume the increase in technical knowledge in a region is labor-using. The new technical knowledge is immobile. Discuss the reinforcing effect.

5. Draw conclusions from the mobility theorems for regional growth policy.

6. To what extent are growth differentials affected by the movement of commodities?

7. Discuss the relationship between regional and national growth. Explain national development as the result of interacting regional growth determinants.

part IV

REGIONAL GROWTH POLICY

chapter **8**

Goal Relations of Regional and National Growth Policy

In the first three parts we have set forth a general framework of regional economic growth analyzing the most important determinants of development and their interrelations. Chapters 1-7 are centered around regional theory which we defined as the study of economic behavior in space. The following two chapters are concerned with regional policy—those activities that try to influence economic behavior in space. Accordingly we have to introduce an actor exercising such an influence. Although large firms do represent one important actor in the above sense, normally the government is regarded as the relevant policy maker. In the following chapters we therefore have to explicitly allow for government activity and we have to study the way in which the behavior of governments affects the process of regional economic growth.

A. THE DECISION STRUCTURE OF A POLICY PROBLEM

Each policy problem consists of three basic elements:[1] the goals the policy maker desires to attain, the actual situation, and the set of instruments used to transform the actual situation into the desired one. Each of these elements requires comment.

1. For any policy decision the goals to be attained must be known. Since the time of Max Weber[2] it has been agreed upon that it is not a function of the scientist to establish these goals. According to Popper[3] the distinguishing crite-

---

[1] On the theory of economic policy, compare: E. S. Kirschen *et al.*, "Economic Policy in Our Time," Vol I.—*General Theory*, Amsterdam, 1954; J. Tinbergen, *Economic Policy— Principles and Design*, North Holland, Amsterdam, 1956; J. Tinbergen, *On the Theory of Economic Policy*, North Holland, Amsterdam, 1952; H. Giersch, *Allgemeine Wirtschaftspolitik,* Gabler, Wiesbaden, Germany, 1960. On the distinction of means and ends, compare G. Myrdal, "Value in Social Theory," in P. Streeten, *A Selection of Essays on Methodology,* Routledge & Kegan Paul, London, 1958.

[2] M. Weber, *The Methodology of the Social Sciences*, trans. and edited by E. A. Shils and H. A. Finch, Free Press, New York, 1949, p. 1.

[3] K. R. Popper, *The Logic of Scientific Discovery*, Basic, New York, 1959, p. 41.

rion between a scientific and a nonscientific statement is that a scientific statement can be refuted by empirical evidence. Value judgments by scientists, such as stressing the importance of certain targets or establishing hierarchies of objectives, do not satisfy this condition. From this methodological position it follows that only two ways exist to introduce a statement on the objectives of regional policy—as a personal conviction or in a hypothetical fashion. As the personal convictions of the writer certainly do not interest the reader, we can only introduce hypothetical goals and then discuss what measures have to be taken *if* a specific goal is accepted. This will be the course followed in Chapter 9. The positive scientist may, however, study two important questions relating to the goals of regional policy without engaging in any value judgment.

First, we can study the social and political process by which goals are established. We may, for instance, analyze the different levels of policy makers influencing regional processes, such as the federal government, the states, and subunits of the states, and we can study how the regionally relevant goals come into existence at these separate levels and in which way the goal establishment of these actors is interrelated. We can analyze the effect of different political organizations—such as centralized governments or the French planification—on regional policy. And we may try to explain the existing mechanisms which lead to the formulation of regional goals, such as the voting process and the influence of pressure groups.[4] Finally, we can study the behavior of the political actor. Does he have clear-cut, long-run targets at the start, with a definite hierarchy of goals, or are the objectives only formulated in a loose fashion as attainment levels,[5] and does the actor possibly use a piecemeal approach[6] to regional policy, shifting his goals from time to time?

Second, we can analyze the relation between the goals the policy maker wants to reach. We can disclose, without any value judgment, whether the achievement of goal A conflicts with goal B, helps to reach the other objective, or is neutral to it. Our answers to the aforementioned questions are open to empirical refutation.

2. The second element of any policy problem is the analysis of a given situation. The study of a situation not only consists of the observation of reality and the systematic gathering of information, but also implies an explanation of the actual world in terms of hypotheses. The policy maker must know why a specific situation has developed before he starts influencing it. Moreover, he also needs information on the probable development of the situation under the assumption that the policy variables are not changed. Will the situation improve or worsen without government interference? Such a status quo forecast and the

[4]R. A. Dahl and C. E. Lindblom, *Politics, Economics, and Welfare*, Harper & Row, New York, 1953.

[5]H. A. Simon, "Theories of Decision-Making in Economics and Behavorial Science," *American Economic Review*, Vol. 49 (1949), p. 263.

[6]H. Zimmermann, "The Treatment of Imprecise Goals; The Case of Regional Science," *Regional Research Institute Discussion Paper Series*, No. 9, Philadelphia, Pa. 1966.

explanation of a given situation rely heavily on model building and represent the link between regional theory and regional policy.

3. Finally, if the actual situation is not consistent with the objectives and if the status quo forecast shows that the system will not reach the goals by itself, a change in government activity becomes necessary. This statement implies a value judgment—that once the desired goal and the actual goal differ by some specified degree, government interference is desirable.

Let z^* represent the objective, for instance, the growth rate of a region, and let z stand for the realized target value. Let AB indicate the permissible deviation from the target without government interference becoming necessary. Then point C denotes the situation when policy measures have to be used to transform the actual situation into the desired one. (See Fig. 8-1.)

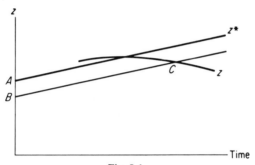

Fig. 8-1

In this context the following three problems arise. First, we need information on all existing and politically feasible means. Second, we must know the effects of these policy measures on the relevant variables, i.e., our targets. In contrast to a status quo forecast, we must now engage in an impact analysis which also uses hypotheses and represents another link to regional theory. Third, we must choose the instrument or the set of measures which are best suited to the attainment of the desired situation. Here decision models and decision criteria become important.

Figure 8-2 summarizes the basic structure of a policy problem in a flow chart.

B. POSSIBLE RELATIONS BETWEEN GOALS

The relation between goals of economic policy[7] may be harmonious, conflicting, or neutral.

1. An harmonious goal relation exists if the realization of goal A leads to a better realization of another goal B. If we plot the two goals on the axes of a

---

[7]On the goals of regional policy and their interrelation compare W. R. Thompson, *A Preface to Urban Economics*, Johns Hopkins Press, Baltimore, Md., 1967, Chap. 5.

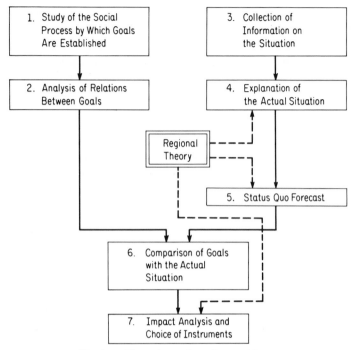

Fig. 8-2. Flow chart of a policy problem.

diagram, with goal realization increasing from the origin, we obtain the relationship shown in Fig. 8-3a. The curve indicating the realization of one goal for alternative values of the other target is called the goal-relation curve.

2. Goals may be independent of each other. This relation of neutrality implies that the application of policy measures which lead to the realization of goal A does not affect the target value of B. The realized value of B will be the same before and after the application of the policy instruments. The instruments will move the economy from Z to T (Fig. 8-3b.) Strict neutrality between goals may not be found too often in practical policy problems, but some cases where the effects on the realization of another objective are not too strong may be treated as neutral relationships.

3. Finally, goals may conflict with each other. The realization of goal A results in a worse realization of B.[8] The case of conflicting goals can be represented by a trade-off curve of the form in Fig. 8-3c.

Information on the slope and the shape of the goal-relation curve is an important prerequisite for the analysis of economic policy and the solution of

[8]Examples are the relation between price stability as described by the Philipps curve and internal and external equilibrium. On the Philipps curve, compare P. A. Samuelson and R. M. Solow, "Analytical Aspects of Anti-Inflation Policy," *American Economic Review, Papers and Proceedings*, Vol. L (1960), pp. 182–194.

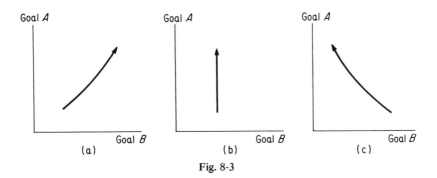

Fig. 8-3

policy problems. If goals conflict, we may search for policy instruments which possibly can reduce the conflict between different objectives. Or the policy maker may have to reconsider his priorities and may have to subordinate one goal under the other by means of a value judgment. In the following we analyze the goal-relation curves (1) in the case of growth policies of different regions, and (2) in the case of regional and national growth policies.

C. GOAL RELATIONS BETWEEN THE GROWTH POLICIES OF DIFFERENT REGIONS

1. Let us suppose each of our two regions, I and II, tries to maximize its output. Output in region I (O_I) is a function of resources available in that region. These resources R_I may be internal factors of production originating in the region, or they may be external factors of production being attracted from region II. The amount of factors of production available in the region including those attracted, will determine regional output:

$$O_I = f(R_I) \qquad (8\text{-}1)$$

Output of region II depends on the amount of factors of production available there:

$$O_{II} = f(R_{II}) \qquad (8\text{-}2)$$

Total supply of factors of production in both regions is fixed at $\overline{R}$. Thus we have

$$\overline{R} = R_I + R_{II} \qquad (8\text{-}3)$$

Let us assume that technical knowledge is given and that both production functions are of the form

$$f(0) = 0 \qquad f' > 0 \qquad f'' < 0 \qquad (8\text{-}4)$$

representing declining marginal productivities.

Starting with these rather simplified assumptions, we can derive the trade-off curve between output in both regions by making use of a four-quadrant diagram. On the north axis of Fig. 8-4 we plot output in region I, O_I. The east axis mea-

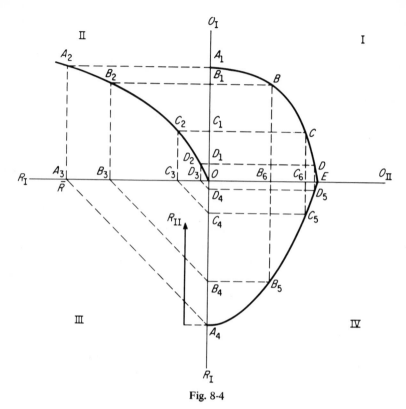

Fig. 8-4

sures output in II (O_{II}). The west and the south axis show resources in region I, namely, R_I. Since

$$R_{II} = \overline{R} - R_I, \tag{8-5}$$

the south axis also shows resources available in region II, measured from $\overline{A}_4$ and increasing toward the origin.

In the second quadrant $O_I = f(R_I)$ represents output as a function of resources in region I, the curve indicating a given state of technical knowledge. Quadrant III is used to transfer R_I values from the west to the south axis. From Eq. 8-5 these values can also be reinterpreted as R_{II}. Quadrant IV shows the production function in region II. The curve in IV, as the one in quadrant II, reflects diminishing marginal returns.[9]

Total resources $\overline{R}$ can be used either in one of the two regions alone or partly in both regions. If all of $\overline{R}$ is used in region I, OA_3 represents R_I, R_{II} is zero. A_2 is the corresponding point on the production function, and A_1 is the first point on our goal-relation curve, with OA_1 output in region I and no output

[9]Due to the assumption of having only one factor of production marginal returns and returns to scale are identical.

in region II. If all the resources are used in region II, then $R_I = 0$ and R_{II} is represented by A_4O. Output in II is OE; there is no output in region I.

Normally, resources will be partly used in I and partly in II. These situations are represented by points B, C, and D. Point B is constructed by starting from point B_3. Using OB_3 of all available resources in I, we get an output of $B_3B_2 = OB_1$ in I. Using $OB_3 = OB_4$ of $\overline{R}$ in I means that of the given amount of resources only $A_3B_3 = A_4B_4$ remains for production in II. This leads to an output of $B_4B_5 = OB_6$ in II. Points C, D, and all other points of the curve in quadrant I are constructed similarly.

The curve A_1BCDE represents the relation between the goals of increasing regional outputs. The slope of the curve depends on the form of the production functions in quadrants II and IV. Under the assumption of diminishing marginal productivity, the curve will be concave to the origin. The goal-relation curve shows a trade-off case between the two regional goals. An increase in output in region I may only be reached by reducing output in II.

A shift of functions 8-1 and 8-2 may be thought of as representing a change in the regional state of technical knowledge. If region I is in a higher stage of development, its production function would be represented by a higher slope, whereas the slope of the curve of region II, measured from the origin of its production function, would be lower. The trade-off curve will be biased toward region I, showing a large output in I and a rather low output in region II. Consequently an increase in technical knowledge in region I which is not communicated to region II shifts the goal-relation curve in favor of region I.

2. Figure 8-4 is based on the assumption of perfect interregional mobility of the resource R. Figure 8-5 illustrates the goal-relation curve for a partly immobile resource. It is assumed that each region has a completely immobile stock of resource R. Quantity OX_3 cannot leave region I; A_4Y_4 is the immobile resource of region II. Under these assumptions each region has a guaranteed level of output. The output of region I cannot fall short of X_1O; the minimum output of region II is given by OB. A conflicting relationship between the growth objectives of the two regions does not exist for these minimum points of regional production. A conflict only arises for the mobility range Y_3X_3. Assume region I employs the immobile resources OX_3. Then region II can produce output X_4X_5. As a point of the goal-relation curve in quadrant I, Z results. If region I attracts all mobile resources and uses the quantity OY_3, its output is given by OY_1. The corresponding point in the first quadrant is Y. For alternative combinations of the mobile part of the resource, the points of the goal-relation curve are found similarly.

From the construction of the goal-relation curve it follows that point Y cannot lie to the left of B. Point Z cannot be below X_1. With immobility of the resource R, the goal-relation curve reduces to a section of the original curve in Fig. 8-4. If the mobility range denoted by Y_3X_3 is decreased further, the guaranteed production points of both regions move away from the origin and

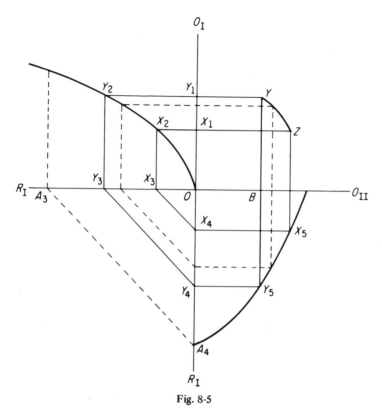

Fig. 8-5

the trade-off curve shrinks into a smaller section. In the extreme case, the goal-relation curve melts into a single point which indicates the output levels of both regions under the assumption of complete immobility. A goal conflict does not exist any longer and the two goals are neutral to each other. On the other hand, the conflict range increases if the resource becomes more mobile. In this case the guaranteed production points move toward the origin which is reached if perfect mobility prevails.

3. If two kinds of resources are introduced into the analysis, the goal-relation curve has to be derived with the help of the Edgeworth box. Assume the capital and labor supplies are completely mobile. The production isoquants indicate the output levels that can be reached with alternative combinations of output. Curve O_1ABSO_2 is the contract curve with mobility of both factors (Fig. 8-6).

From the contract curve, the goal-relation curve between the two regional outputs can be derived by transferring the output levels of the production isoquants from Fig. 8-6 to Fig. 8-7. The curve $O_1' A' S' O_2'$ is the goal-relation curve, if both factors are mobile.

Assume now that capital is immobile and that the immobile capital stocks

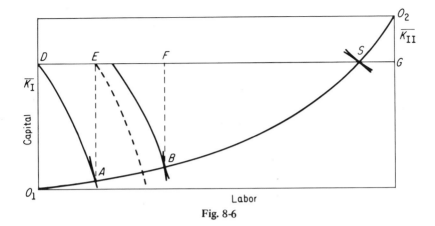

Fig. 8-6

in the two regions are given by $\overline{K_I}$ and $\overline{K_{II}}$. Then a different goal-relation curve results. For instance, if the total labor supply is employed in region II, this area can maximally reach point D in Fig. 8-6, since all points below line DA are excluded due to the immobility of capital. Compare point D with the solution in case of the perfect mobility of capital. With perfect mobility of capital, region II can reach a higher output level denoted by O_1. Or, with region II having the same output level (point A), region I can have a positive output which is not possible at D. Consequently with immobile capital, the goal-relation curve of Fig. 8-7 shifts to the left. The point corresponding to D is D'. A', E', and S' are points corresponding to A, E, and S in Fig. 8-6.

Moving from O_1 to S in Fig. 8-6, the optimal production points are not found on the contract curve O_1O_2 but on the line DS. Moving from O_2 toward S, the optimal production points lie on the line GS. Optimality is here defined

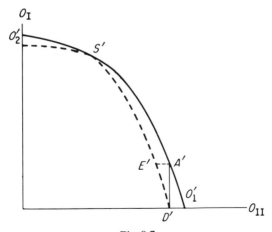

Fig. 8-7

for a complete immobility of one factor. Only point S denotes a situation where the contract curve $O_1 B_2$ is identical to the contract curve with immobile capital DG. It follows that all points of the goal-relation curve in Fig. 8-7 are shifted to the left except point S. The intensity of the shift declines while approaching point S.

With Figs. 8-5 through 8-7 we have discussed the changes in the trade-off curve that result from the immobility of factors of production. Additional problems can be analyzed. Thus we can discuss the question of how the goal-relation curve is affected if labor is also partly immobile or if the immobility of capital is reduced. This additional analysis confirms our conclusion that the conflicting relationship between regional growth policy is a function of inter-regional factor mobility and that the conflict increases with an increase in mobility.

4. The trade-off relation between the growth policies of different regions rests on the assumption that the two regions are competing for a limited amount of resources and that region I can only attract these resources by withdrawing them from region II. There may, however, be cases when the withdrawal effect is insignificant. In a more than two-region case, for instance, resources needed in region I may be withdrawn not only from region II but also from all other regions, thus lessening the withdrawal effect on region II.

At the same time the expanding region may induce development in the other regions through the leveling effects discussed in Chapter 7. The expanding region may demand more imports, thus initiating a multiplier process in the stagnant area. Changes in the terms of trade may also improve the situation of the region which has to give up resources. We may think of these factors as shifting the goal-relation curve in favor of the originally nonexpanding region.

5. Algebraically the trade-off curve is determined by calculating the solution set for the two regional production functions for alternative interregional distributions of the given amount of resources. The function that relates the corresponding elements of these two solution sets is the goal-relation curve. Assuming simplified production functions we have

$$O_I = \alpha R_I^a \tag{8-6}$$

where α is an efficiency coefficient representing a given state of technical knowledge[10] and a is the elasticity of production with respect to resources in region I. For region II,

$$O_{II} = \beta R_{II}^b \tag{8-7}$$

Substituting Eq. 8-5 into Eq. 8-7,

$$O_{II} = \beta (\bar{R} - R_I)^b \tag{8-8}$$

---

[10]The coefficient α can also be interpreted as including a constant set of resources, compare G. C. Archibald and R. G. Lipsey, *An Introduction to a Mathematical Treatment of Economics*, Weidenfeld and Nicolson, London, 1967, p. 217.

From Eq. 8-6,

$$R_I = \frac{1}{\alpha^{1/a}} \, O_I^{1/a} \qquad (8\text{-}9)$$

Substituting Eq. 8-9 in Eq. 8-8,

$$y = O_{II} = \beta \left(\bar{R} - \frac{1}{\alpha^{1/a}} \cdot O_I^{1/a} \right)^b \qquad (8\text{-}10)$$

6. Equation 8-10 is the goal-relation curve relating output of regions I and II. The curve depends on the efficiency coefficients, the elasticity of production in the two regions, and the amount of total resources. The first derivative $y' = dO_{II}/dO_I$ is the rate of transformation between the two goals. If $y' > 0$, the goal-relation curve has a positive slope. The two goals are in harmony. If $y' = 0$, the two goals are completely independent of each other. If $y' < 0$, a trade-off situation prevails.

The first derivative is negative.[11] Consequently a conflicting relationship exists between the growth goals of the two regions. Region I can only increase its output at the expense of region II, and vice versa.

7. The second derivative y'' indicates the shape of the trade-off curve for positive O_I and O_{II}.

(a) If $y'' < 0$, y' has a negative slope. As $y' < 0$, y also has a negative slope. Because of the negative slope of y', the negative slope of y must decrease. The trade-off curve is concave to the origin.

(b) If $y'' = 0$, y' has a slope of zero. As $y' < 0$, y must be a straight line with a negative slope.

(c) If $y'' > 0$, y' has a positive slope. As $y' < 0$, y has a negative slope. Be-

---

[11] The first derivative is:

$$y' = \frac{dO_{II}}{dO_I} = \beta \left(\bar{R} - \frac{1}{\alpha^{1/a}} O_I^{1/a} \right)^{b-1} \frac{-1}{\alpha^{1/a}} \frac{1}{a} O_I^{1/a-1} \qquad (1)$$

For all $\alpha, \beta > 1$ and a, b > 0 and $O_I, O_{II} > 0$:

$$y' < 0$$

Proof: The right-hand term of (1) is negative. $y' < 0$, if the left-hand term is positive. The left-hand term is negative, if

$$\bar{R} < \frac{1}{\alpha^{1/a}} \cdot O_I^{1/a} \qquad (2)$$

From Eq. 8-6, writing the production function as an inequality:

$$O_I \leqslant \alpha \bar{R}^a \qquad (3)$$

Solving Eq. (3) for $\bar{R}$, we have

$$\bar{R} \geqslant \frac{1}{\alpha^{1/a}} O_I^{1/a} \qquad (4)$$

Equation (4) excludes Eq. (3). Thus the first term cannot become negative. A conflicting relationship between the growth policies of the two regions exists.

cause of the positive slope of y', the negative slope of y increases. The curve is convex to the origin.

For the second derivative y'' we have [12]

$$y'' \gtreqless 0 : (b-1)\, T - \left(\frac{1}{a} - 1\right) S \gtreqless 0 \tag{8-11}$$

where T and S are positive.

We have the following results:

(a) For increasing marginal productivities in the production activities, namely, $a > 1$ and $b > 1$:

$$(b-1)\, T - \left(\frac{1}{a} - 1\right) S > 0 \tag{8-12}$$

Thus

$$y'' > 0 \tag{8-13}$$

This implies a convex trade-off curve.

(b) For constant marginal productivities, $a = 1$ and $b = 1$, we have

$$y'' = 0 \tag{8-14}$$

The trade-off curve is a straight line.

(c) For decreasing marginal productivities $a < 1$ and $b < 1$,

$$(b-1)\, T - \left(\frac{1}{a} - 1\right) S < 0 \tag{8-15}$$

Then

$$y'' > 0 \tag{8-16}$$

The trade-off curve is concave.

The algebraic derivation confirms our geometric analysis. The growth goals of regions are in conflict with one another and, under the simplified assumptions of one factor of production and declining marginal productivities, the goal-relation curve is convex to the origin.

---

[12] The second derivative is:

$$y'' = (b-1)\,\beta \left(\bar{R} - \frac{1}{\alpha^{1/a}} \cdot O_I^{1/a}\right)^{b-2} \cdot \left(\frac{1}{\alpha^{1/a}} \cdot \frac{1}{a}\, O_I^{1/a - 1}\right)^2$$
$$- (1/a - 1)\,\beta \left(\bar{R} - \frac{1}{\alpha^{1/a}} \cdot O_I^{1/a}\right)^{b-1} \cdot \frac{1/a\,O_I^{1/a - 2}}{\alpha^{1/a}} \tag{1}$$

Rewriting Eq. (1) by introducing T and S,

$$y'' = (b-1)\, T - (1/a - 1)\, S \tag{2}$$

where S and T are positive.

D. COMPATIBILITY AND CONFLICT BETWEEN REGIONAL AND NATIONAL GROWTH POLICIES

1. There is the possibility of a goal conflict not only between growth policies of different regions but also between regional and national growth goals. Using Fig. 8-4 to determine maximum output in the system of both regions, it can be shown that there is a goal conflict between maximizing output in a single region and maximizing output in a system of regions. Total output of the two regions O_T is the sum of the two regional outputs. O_T can be derived from Fig. 8-4 by adding up the vertical and the horizontal distance of a point on the trade-off curve from the north and the east axis. This method is used to construct curve ETA_1 in Fig. 8-8. Total output is plotted on the vertical axis, output of region I

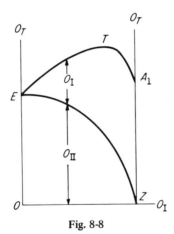

Fig. 8-8

is shown on the x-axis. Curve ETA_1 shows total output O_T as a function of output in region I. Curve EZ denotes the goal-relation curve between the two regional outputs.

Point A_1 in Fig. 8-8 represents a situation in which all factors of production are used in region I. A_1 in Fig. 8-8 corresponds to A_1 in Fig. 8-4. For A_1 total output of the system as a whole is identical to output in region I, output of II being zero. Therefore section ZA_1 is equal to section OZ. Point E in Fig. 8-8 represents a situation where all resources are used in II. It corresponds to point E in Fig. 8-4. For E, O_T is identical with O_{II}, as $O_I = 0$. Other points of the curve ETA_1 are constructed by adding up O_I and O_{II} from Fig. 8-4.

Figure 8-5 illustrates the relations between regional and national growth policy. Both relations of harmony and of conflict are shown. Starting at point E an increasing output of region I will lead to an increase in total output. Thus there is a harmonious relation between the two goals moving from E to T. The same is true if we try to increase output in region II starting from A_1. Moving from A_1 to T, both output of region II and of the two regions as a whole, can be increased.

The relation of goals changes into one of conflict if we want to increase output of region I by moving beyond T toward A_1. This, however, is normally the goal of the planner in region I who wants to increase regional product in I, not taking into consideration the situation in the other region and in the system as a whole. The same reasoning applies if the planner of region II wants to move beyond T toward E. By such a policy output in region II will be increased, but total output will fall. In these cases the goals of regional and national growth policy are conflicting.

Algebraically total output O_T is equal to the sum of the two regional outputs:

$$O_T = O_I + O_{II} = \alpha R_I^a + \beta R_{II}^b \qquad (8\text{-}17)$$

Using Eq. 8-5 we have

$$O_T = \alpha R_I^a + \beta (\overline{R} - R_I)^b \qquad (8\text{-}18)$$

If R_I is substituted by O_I according to Eq. 8-9, Eq. 8-18 represents the goal-relation curve between total output of the two regions and output in region I. Differentiating Eq. 8-18 with respect to R_I yields as a condition for maximum output of the two-region system:

$$\frac{dO_T}{dR_I} = 0: \; \alpha a R_I^{a-1} = \beta b (\overline{R} - R_I)^{b-1} \qquad (8\text{-}19)$$

Condition 8-19 specifies that the maximum of total output is reached where the marginal productivities of resources are equal in both regions.

Marginal productivities can be represented by a tangent to the production functions. Equality of marginal productivities will be reached when the tangents to the corresponding points of the two production functions in Fig. 8-4 are vertical to each other. In Fig. 8-4 there is only one point on the trade-off curve which allows the marginal productivities of additional resources in both regions to become equal, the point being situated between B and C. All other points on the trade-off curve involve situations in which the marginal productivities in both regions differ.

If the trade-off curve between regional growth policies is a straight line with a negative 45-degree slope, total output of both regions will be the same for all alternative allocations of resources in both regions. The marginal productivities are identical for all points of the goal-relation curve and no single solution exists.[13]

In the case of a convex trade-off curve, total output will be greatest if the region with the highest marginal productivity gets all the resources. Such a

---

[13]If the trade-off curve between regional growth policies is a straight line and has a slope m with $0 < m < 1$ or $1 < m < \infty$, a corner solution will result as in the case of a convex trade-off curve.

policy may, of course, conflict with other goals such as reducing interregional income differences.

2. The discussion of the goal relations of regional growth policy yields to the following results. (a) Growth policies of different regions are not compatible with each other if the spillover effect of the expanding region is negligible and the withdrawal effect caused by the expanding region is important. (b) Growth policies at the regional and the national level may be in harmony or in conflict. A harmonious relation prevails if regional growth policy tries to increase regional output—and if the marginal productivity is still below the marginal productivity in the other region. A conflicting relation prevails if regional planners try to push regional output to a point where the marginal productivity in the region will be lower than in other regions.

The construction of the trade-off curve suggests a possible solution for conflicting-goal relationships—namely, to influence the underlying factors that cause the conflicting situation. A very unfavorable trade-off curve for a region may be changed by increasing the coefficients of efficiency and the production elasticities of resources through an increase in the state of technical knowledge and an improvement in organizational efficiency. If this approach is not possible, only a value judgment can "solve" the conflict by establishing the priority of one objective over the other.

E. PREVENTING WIDELY DIVERGENT INTERREGIONAL INCOME DIFFERENCES

The goal system of regional growth policy includes more objectives than those mentioned so far and thus is much more complicated in reality. Only one of the many goals relevant for regional growth policy (including the noneconomic objectives of a society) will be mentioned here—the goal of preventing too extreme differences in income between regions. If this restriction is not introduced, the objective of a maximum output in the total economy may require in an extreme solution, that all activities are concentrated in region I and that the regional output of II becomes zero. A restraint may be introduced to prevent such an outcome. Normally this restriction is expressed in per capita units. If both regions have the same population, and if the distinction between regional income and output is negligible,[14] the above condition may be expressed as

$$O_I - O_{II} \geqslant v_0 \qquad (8\text{-}20)$$

with an output difference greater than v_0 not being tolerated. This restriction of regional growth policy may also be stated in such a way that a minimum relation of regional outputs must be reached.[15]

---

[14]On the distinction between regional income and regional output compare p. 69.
[15]A. Rahman, "Regional Allocation of Investment—An Aggregative Study in the Theory of Development Programming," *Quarterly Journal of Economics*, Vol. 77 (1963), pp. 26–39.

$$\frac{O_I}{O_{II}} \geqslant v_1 \quad \frac{O_{II}}{O_I} \geqslant v_2 \qquad (8\text{-}21)$$

These restrictions are shown in Fig. 8-9 as two straight lines, v_1 and v_2.

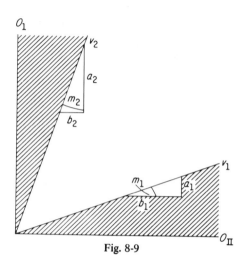

Fig. 8-9

The first restraint $O_I/O_{II} \geqslant v_1$ excludes all solutions on and below the line v_1 because only points above line v_1 satisfy condition 8-21. This restraint is measured by tangent $m_1 = a_1/b_1$. It protects region I from a relatively low income compared to region II.

The second condition specifies that the relation between O_{II} and O_I must surpass a minimum value v_2. This restraint is measured by tangent $m_2 = b_2/a_2$ because in this case the relation between O_{II} and O_I is relevant. This constraint excludes all combinations of O_{II} and O_I which are below line v_2. Thus it protects region II against a too low income in comparison with region I.

The restraints specified in condition 8-21 conflict with the goal of a maximum total output in the two-region system if they become effective. Suppose that the optimum solution for the national economy consisting of two regions is represented by a point on the transformation curve which lies below v_1. If this restraint is realized through the use of policy instruments, the maximum total output cannot be reached. The opportunity cost of preventing too high differences in regional income can then be measured by the loss of total output O_T caused by the restraint.

Figure 8-9 restricts the permissible solutions of Fig. 8-4 and it can be easily integrated in this diagram. Then Figs. 8-4, 8-8, and 8-9 represent a geometrical picture of a simplified goal system of regional growth policy. In the next chapter we analyze how the available policy instruments have to be used in order to reach these goals.

PROBLEMS

1. Introduce the objective of regional stability expressed in terms of regional income or employment. Discuss the relation with other goals of regional policy.

2. Derive the goal-relation curve of Fig. 8-4 if the production functions in both regions are characterized (a) by increasing marginal productivities, and (b) by constant marginal productivities.

3. State how the goal-relation curve between the output of two regions is affected (1) if the total amount of resources increases over time, and (2) if technical progress occurs in both regions. Show the implications for the goal-relation curve between total output and the output of region I (Fig. 8-8).

4. Assume an unequal distribution of technical knowledge in favor of region I. How does this influence the goal-relation curves in Figs. 8-4 and 8-8?

5. Assume the resource is only partly mobile. Derive Fig. 8-8. How is the goal-relation curve of Fig. 8-8 affected if two factors of production are introduced as in Figs. 8-6 and 8-7?

6. Assume the production functions in both regions are of the Leontief type (constant input-output coefficients). Derive the goal-relation curve of Fig. 8-4.

chapter 9

Instruments for Regional Growth Policy

Government interference with the process of economic growth becomes necessary if discrepancies between the actual and the desired situation arise. Assume, for instance, that market forces fail to achieve the target growth rate for a two-region system. This may necessitate an attempt by the policy maker to increase the actual rate of growth. Then a set of decisions has to be made in order to determine those instrument variables which are best suited to transform the actual situation into the desired one.

Policy measures relating to regional growth problems control and influence a long-run phenomenon. Having an impact on the location of private activities, they represent an important determinant of the economic landscape and obtain effects which are usually irreversible in the short run. These decisions on instrument variables for regional growth policy therefore require careful analysis. Methods are needed which allow the optimal selection of instrument variables with respect to given targets. These methods have been developed by economic theory in the form of explication models, decision models, and decision criteria.

A. EXPLICATION MODELS AND DECISION MODELS FOR INSTRUMENT SELECTION

1. *Instrument choice with explication models.* Explication models[1] are defined as a set of functional relationships explaining phenomena of reality, but usually[2] do not include targets and optimizing procedures. An example is

---

[1] On the difference between explication models and decision models, compare H. K. Schneider, "Modelle für die Regionalpolitik," in H. K. Schneider (ed.), *Beiträge zur Regionalpolitik,* Schriften des Vereins für Sozialpolitik, Vol. 41, Duncker & Humblot, Berlin, Germany, 1968.

[2] An exception are those models which explain the optimizing behavior of economic units such as households. These models are explication models in the form of decision models.

the regional growth model presented in Chapter 6. Models of this type generally do not include policy variables, i.e., those variables which are easily changed by government (tax rates, expenditures) and the monetary authority. The typical explication model takes into account only those functional relationships which exist between the central variable (z_1) and the explanatory variables (x_i) as indicated by relation (1) in Fig. 9-1. Thus the model of Chapter 6 concentrates

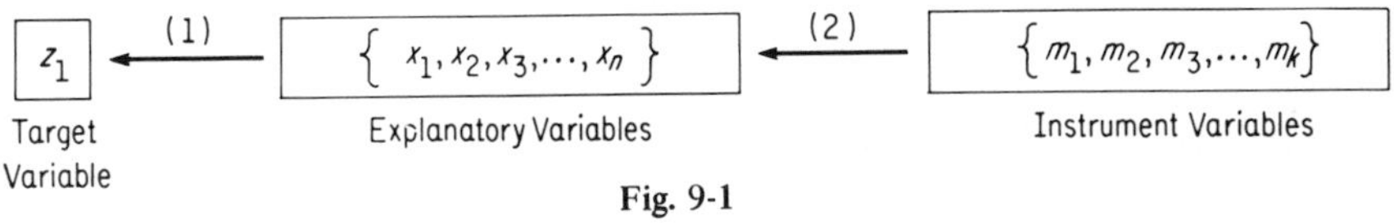

$$\boxed{z_1} \xleftarrow{\quad(1)\quad} \boxed{\{\, x_1, x_2, x_3, \ldots, x_n \,\}} \xleftarrow{\quad(2)\quad} \boxed{\{\, m_1, m_2, m_3, \ldots, m_k \}}$$

Target   Explanatory Variables   Instrument Variables
Variable

Fig. 9-1

on the determinants of regional income, but such factors as regional capital, labor, and technical knowledge, do not represent the policy variables which the regional planner can easily change.

Note that the set of the explanatory variables (x_i) can be understood as a system of endogenous and exogenous variables being interdependent of each other. Some of the explanatory variables are "farther away" from the central variable than others. Thus x_n may not directly influence z, but z may be a function of x_{10} which in turn may depend on x_n.

Relation (2) denotes the functional relationship between the set of instrument variables $\{m_1, m_2, \ldots, m_k\}$ and the explanatory variables $\{x_1, x_2, \ldots, x_n\}$. Conceivably, the m-set may influence the target directly, but normal expectation is an indirect relationship between the instrument variables and the target variable. Thus the policy variables represent the last element in a chain of functional relationships.

Information on relation (2), what is often called the impact analysis of instrument variables, is a prerequisite for decision making. If information of this type is included in an explication model, the theoretical framework may be used to analyze the effects of changes in the instrument variables on the target variable.

An example of such an impact analysis of instrument variables would be to extend our regional growth model of Chapter 6 and to explicitly introduce the instrument variables which influence the target variable, namely, regional income, via the growth determinants. The formal framework would comprise all policy means which influence growth determinants. Those measures include steps which improve the quality of the regional labor force, stimulate internal capital accumulation, induce research expenditures, attract factors of production, and increase internal and external demand. These instrument variables of an aggregated growth model will not formally be introduced into the model but will be discussed in a general fashion in a survey of the available instruments.

Another example of using explication models for decision making in regional growth policy is input-output models.[3]   Input-output models explain interactions between different sectors in the economy. Let a region have three sectors and assume that the government intends to attract additional industries to the region. Assume also that a location study has shown that the region can possibly attract three different activities with a given sum of government expenditure. Given a target of income maximization, the policy maker will choose that sector which will have the strongest impact on regional income. This impact not only exists in the value added of the new sector, but it also includes the repercussions of the new sector on the already existing activities. The impact of the new sector is measured by the change in the value added of all sectors in the region. This change in regional income can be calculated by the following procedure.

The original matrix of production coefficients (at moment t) is given by

$$A_t = \begin{bmatrix} a_{11} & a_{12} & a_{13} \\ a_{21} & a_{22} & a_{23} \\ a_{31} & a_{32} & a_{33} \end{bmatrix}$$

(9-1)

where a_{12} denotes the input requirement per unit of output of sector 2 from sector 1.

Let X_1 indicate the output of sector 1 and F_1 the final demand for commodity 1.   Assume a closed-region with neither imports nor exports. The system of equations for the region is

$$\begin{bmatrix} X_1 \\ X_2 \\ X_3 \end{bmatrix} - \begin{bmatrix} a_{11} & a_{12} & a_{13} \\ a_{21} & a_{22} & a_{23} \\ a_{31} & a_{32} & a_{33} \end{bmatrix} \cdot \begin{bmatrix} X_1 \\ X_2 \\ X_3 \end{bmatrix} = \begin{bmatrix} F_1 \\ F_2 \\ F_3 \end{bmatrix}$$

(9-2)

Equation 9-2 describes the row balance of an input-output system. It states that the total output of a sector minus intermediate demand equals final demand.   Intermediate demand is calculated by multiplying the matrix of production coefficients with the output vector.

Expressing Eq. 9-2 in matrix form and indicating that the vectors and the matrix of production coefficients relate to the original time period t, we have

$$X_t - A_t X_t = F_t$$

(9-3)

Introducing the identity matrix I, we get

$$(I - A_t) X_t = F_t$$

(9-4)

[3] On input-output models compare W. Miernyk, *The Elements of Input-Output Analysis*, Random House, New York, 1967; W. Isard, *Methods of Regional Analysis: An Introduction to Regional Science*, M.I.T. Press, Cambridge, Mass., Chap. 8; H. B. Chenery and P. G. Clark, *Interindustry Economics*, Wiley, New York, 1959; W. Leontief, *Studies in the Structure of the American Economy*, Oxford U.P., New York, 1964; R. F. Kuenne, *The Theory of General Economic Equilibrium*, Princeton U.P., Princeton, N.J., 1963. On the estimation of the coefficients compare L. N. Moses, "The Stability of Interregional Trading Patterns and Input-Output Analysis," *American Economic Review*, Vol. 45, 1955, pp. 803–832; W. Isard, T. W. Langford, and E. Romanoff, *Philadelphia Region Input-Output Study*, Preliminary Working Papers, 1968.

Solving for the output level of the different sectors

$$X_t = (I - A_t)^{-1} F_t \qquad (9\text{-}5)$$

where $(I - A)^{-1}$ denotes the inverted Leontief matrix.

If final demand F_t and the matrix of production coefficients A_t, are known, the output level for the different sectors X_t can be determined. Assume a given ratio of value added per unit of output of each sector c_i. Then regional income Y_t is the total value added in each sector, times the output level, summed over all sectors.

$$Y_t = \sum_{i=1}^{3} c_i X_i \qquad (9\text{-}6)$$

Now assume that a fourth sector is attracted to the area. Then an additional row and an additional column have to be introduced into the matrix of production coefficients. The additional column indicates the input requirement of the new sector with respect to the outputs of the other sectors. The additional row denotes the input requirements of the already existing activities from the new sector. The new sector in period $t + 1$ may provide some of the inputs which had been produced by other sectors in period t. In this case the input coefficients of the original matrix A_t change. The new matrix is given by

$$A_{t+1} = \begin{bmatrix} a_{11} & a_{12} & a_{13} & a_{14} \\ a_{21} & a_{22} & a_{23} & a_{24} \\ a_{31} & a_{32} & a_{33} & a_{34} \\ a_{41} & a_{42} & a_{43} & a_{44} \end{bmatrix} \qquad (9\text{-}7)$$

In addition to the elements of matrix A, the final demand and the output vector change, since an additional commodity has been introduced. F_4, the final demand for the output of sector 4, is zero if the new product is only used as an intermediate input.

The system of equation now reads

$$\begin{bmatrix} X_1 \\ X_2 \\ X_3 \\ X_4 \end{bmatrix} - \begin{bmatrix} a_{11} & a_{12} & a_{13} & a_{14} \\ a_{21} & a_{22} & a_{23} & a_{24} \\ a_{31} & a_{32} & a_{33} & a_{34} \\ a_{41} & a_{42} & a_{43} & a_{44} \end{bmatrix} \cdot \begin{bmatrix} X_1 \\ X_2 \\ X_3 \\ X_4 \end{bmatrix} = \begin{bmatrix} F_1 \\ F_2 \\ F_3 \\ F_4 \end{bmatrix} \qquad (9\text{-}8)$$

In matrix form Eq. 9-8 becomes

$$X_{t+1} - A_{t+1} \cdot X_{t+1} = F_{t+1} \qquad (9\text{-}9)$$

The new sector will demand inputs from the other sectors and may therefore lead to an expansion in the other industries. Conversely, its output may compete with the products of other sectors and lead to a reduction of their output level. The overall effect on the output level X_{t+1} is given by

$$X_{t+1} = (I - A_{t+1})^{-1} F_{t+1} \qquad (9\text{-}10)$$

Multiplying the output vector of the different sectors with value added, we get the new regional income Y_{t+1}:

$$Y_{t+1} = \sum_{i=1}^{4} c_i X_{i\,(t+1)} \qquad (9\text{-}11)$$

The new regional income results in a change in final demand which has additional repercussions and may lead to a new increase in income. This effect and any subsequent effects of the same type are ignored here.

The change in regional income caused by the introduction of sector 4 is given by

$$\triangle Y_4 = Y_{t+1} - Y_t = \sum_{i=1}^{4} c_i X_{i\,(t+1)} - \sum_{i=1}^{3} c_i X_{i\,(t)} \qquad (9\text{-}12)$$

The same procedure is repeated for sectors 5 and 6. If the costs of attracting these sectors are identical, the sector with the highest change in regional income will be located in the area. In this case an explication model has been used to decide a policy problem.

Other uses of an input-output model include an impact analysis of increased government expenditures on the output level of the different sectors. An increase in government expenditures will change the elements of the final-demand vector since government demand is included in final demand. The new final-demand vector can be used to calculate the change in regional income. Letting the region be an open system, part of the increased government demand may leak out of the region through an increase in imports from other regions. In this case the other region experiences an increase in its income. This result may be desirable if the policy maker intends to establish a growth pole which is to induce economic development in other areas. On the other hand, this spillover effect may be undesirable if the government plans to stimulate development in a depressed area through its increase in demand. Information on the effects of an increase in government demand on regional income can be obtained by the following procedure.

Let superscripts denote regions and let subscripts indicate sectors. Then a two-region system with three sectors is given by

$$
\begin{bmatrix} X_1^1 \\ X_2^1 \\ X_3^1 \\ ---- \\ X_1^2 \\ X_2^2 \\ X_3^2 \end{bmatrix}
-
\begin{bmatrix}
a_{11}^{11} & a_{12}^{11} & a_{13}^{11} & a_{11}^{12} & a_{12}^{12} & a_{13}^{12} \\
a_{21}^{11} & a_{22}^{11} & a_{23}^{11} & a_{21}^{12} & a_{22}^{12} & a_{23}^{12} \\
a_{31}^{11} & a_{32}^{11} & a_{33}^{11} & a_{31}^{12} & a_{32}^{12} & a_{33}^{12} \\
\hline
a_{11}^{21} & a_{12}^{21} & a_{13}^{21} & a_{11}^{22} & a_{12}^{22} & a_{13}^{22} \\
a_{21}^{21} & a_{22}^{21} & a_{23}^{21} & a_{21}^{22} & a_{22}^{22} & a_{23}^{22} \\
a_{31}^{21} & a_{32}^{21} & a_{33}^{21} & a_{31}^{22} & a_{32}^{22} & a_{33}^{22}
\end{bmatrix}
\cdot
\begin{bmatrix} X_1^1 \\ X_2^1 \\ X_3^1 \\ ---- \\ X_1^2 \\ X_2^2 \\ X_3^2 \end{bmatrix}
=
\begin{bmatrix} F_1^1 \\ F_2^1 \\ F_3^1 \\ ----- \\ F_1^2 \\ F_2^2 \\ F_3^2 \end{bmatrix}
\qquad (9\text{-}13)
$$

or in matrix form with partitioned matrices and vectors:

$$\begin{bmatrix} X^1 \\ \hline X^2 \end{bmatrix} - \begin{bmatrix} A^{11} & A^{12} \\ \hline A^{21} & A^{22} \end{bmatrix} \cdot \begin{bmatrix} X^1 \\ \hline X^2 \end{bmatrix} = \begin{bmatrix} F^1 \\ \hline F^2 \end{bmatrix} \tag{9-14}$$

A^{11}, A^{22} denote the intraregional and A^{12}, A^{21} indicate the interregional coefficients.

With given intraregional and interregional coefficients and with given final-demand vectors F^1 and F^2 for the two regions, the output level of the three sectors can be determined.

$$\begin{bmatrix} X^1 \\ \hline X^2 \end{bmatrix} = \begin{bmatrix} I - \begin{bmatrix} A^{11} & A^{12} \\ \hline A^{21} & A^{22} \end{bmatrix} \end{bmatrix}^{-1} \cdot \begin{bmatrix} F^1 \\ \hline F_2 \end{bmatrix} \tag{9-15}$$

Assume that the government increases its expenditures in region I. Then region I has a new final-demand vector $F^1_{(t+1)}$. The final-demand vector of region 2 remains the same. This system with the new final-demand vector determines the new output levels in the two regions, $X^1_{(t+1)}$ and $X^2_{(t+1)}$. Multiplying the new output vector of region II with the value added of each sector gives the new income of region II, $Y^2_{(t+1)}$.

The change in the income in region II is given by $Y^2_{(t+1)} - Y^2_{(t)} = \Delta Y^2$

or

$$\Delta Y^2 = \sum_{i=1}^{3} c_i X^2_{i(t+1)} - \sum_{i=1}^{3} c_i X^2_{i(t)} \tag{9-16}$$

This change in income of region II is caused by a change in government expenditures in the region. With a similar procedure the income change in region I may be calculated.[4]

Another application of input-output analysis to a decision problem is to determine the reliance on imports and the export surplus or deficit[5] of the new industries that are to be attracted to the region. This approach has been used in the construction of self-sufficiency charts. Finally, input-output models can be used to decide which of the new industries have the potential to use the outputs which are already provided by the regional sectors (backward linkages), and to determine which products can be supplied by the new sector for the already existing activities (forward linkages). This problem is easily solved if a triangularized matrix can be developed. A triangularized matrix reorders the different industries according to their dominance. Ideally, only the elements below the

---

[4] The change in income in region II leads to a new final demand vector which in turn has feedbacks on intermediate demand. These repercussions are ignored.

[5] Miernyk, *op. cit.*, p. 99.

diagonal from the left top to the right bottom are filled. The rows then indicate the backward linkages and the columns the forward linkages.[6]

The example of using input-output models for decision making in regional policy points out the aforementioned problem of the absences of instrument variables in explication models. Ideally, explication models should include specific instrument variables, such as tax rates, subsidies, and infrastructure outlays. These models comprise, however, only rather general instrument variables, such as the activity level of a sector in an input-output framework but not the policy variables determining the output level. Nevertheless an explication model can be used as a decision technique, as has been shown. This approach, however, has the disadvantage of involving a trial-and-error procedure of obtaining the best solution. Suppose, for instance, that the choice is to be determined not between three single different industries but between different combinations of industries. Then the approach using explication models for decision making becomes rather troublesome. In this case decision models may be more convenient.

2. *Instrument choice with decision models.* A decision model cast in the form of the programming approach is a system of relationships which includes (1) an objective function to be maximized or minimized, and (2) a set of restraints which restrict the solution of the objective function. The important difference from an explication model is that a decision model explicitly introduces goals.[7] These are included in the objective function; they also appear as institutional or political restraints. Thus the objective function may prescribe the maximization of total output for a two-region system, with the political restraint that the difference in regional outputs cannot surpass a given ratio (compare Eq. 8-21). The decision model includes both targets and functional relationships which describe the structure of reality. It must contain information on the interrelation between the outputs of the regions, their determinants, and the interactions of these determinants. Ideally, it would also comprise relations between instrument variables, the explanatory variables, and the target variable. These relations are introduced in the form of technological and behavioral restraints.

To rewrite the problem of selecting different industries in the form of a decision model, let activities $X_1, \ldots, X_n$ already be represented in the region

[6]Miernyk, *op. cit.*, p. 92; H. Aujac, "La hierarchie des industries dans un tableau des échanges interindustrielles," *Revue Economique*, Vol. 11 (1960), pp. 169–238.

[7]On the formulation of a goal system in terms of a linear program compare C. Leven, "Establishing Goals for Regional Economic Development," *Journal of the American Institute of Planners*, Vol. 30 (1964), pp. 100–110. On linear programming, compare R. G. Spiegelman, "Activity Analysis Models in Regional Development Planning," *Papers and Proceedings of the Regional Science Association*, Vol. 17 (1966), pp. 143–159; W. Isard, *Methods of Regional Analysis: An Introduction to Regional Science*, Chap. 10; W. Isard, "Interregional Linear Programming," *Journal of Regional Science*, Vol. 1 (1958), pp. 1–59; B. Stevens, "An Interregional Linear Programming Model," *Journal of Regional Science*, Vol. 1 (1958), pp. 60–98.

and let the potentially feasible activities be $X_{n+1}, X_{n+2}, X_{n+3}$. These three activities represent instrument variables, the object being to determine at which level these instrument variables should be operated. The net value added per unit of output of the different activities is denoted by c_i. Then regional income is defined as

$$Y = c_1 X_1 + c_2 X_2, \ldots, c_n X_n + c_{n+1} X_{n+1} + c_{n+2} X_{n+2} + c_{n+3} X_{n+3}$$

$$(9\text{-}17)$$

Equation 9-17 is the objective function which may be rewritten by summing up the net value added of the already existing activities $i = (1, \ldots, n)$ and the potential activities $i = (n+1, \ldots, n+3)$:

$$Y = \sum_{i=1}^{n} c_i X_i + \sum_{i=n+1}^{n+3} c_i X_i \quad \max \qquad (9\text{-}18)$$

The objective function is subject to the following restraints. Each activity may be limited by a capacity restraint T which indicates the maximum possible output of that activity:

$$X_i \leqslant T_i \, (i = 1, \ldots, n+3) \qquad (9\text{-}19)$$

All activities cannot use more of the primary resources than is available. For convenience it is assumed that labor is the only primary factor:

$$\sum_{i=1}^{n+3} a_{Li} X_i \leqslant \overline{L} \qquad (9\text{-}20)$$

where $\overline{L}$ indicates the total labor supply and a_{Li} is the labor input coefficient.

A final-demand vector F_i is given. Final demand has to be satisfied. Consequently the residual of total output after the satisfaction of intermediate demand must be greater than or equal to final demand:

$$X_i - \sum_{n=1}^{n+3} a_{ik} X_k \leqslant F_i \qquad (i = 1, \ldots, n+3) \qquad (9\text{-}21)$$

Note that these restraints are not included in an explication model but that the expressions on the left-hand side of restraints 9-20 and 9-21 contain the same functional relationships as an explication model.

The model described by Eq. 9-18 through 9-21 determines the output of activities $i = (1, \ldots, n+3)$ which yield maximum regional income. Contrary to an explication model, the solution gives the optimum output level for all activities. No trial-and-error process is necessary. Conceivably all three potential activities $n+1 \ldots n+3$ will be added to the regional activities. With constant primary resources and with constant input requirements, the older activities have to be reduced. It is even possible that an old activity has to be given up in favor of a new one.

Equations 9-18 through 9-21 represent the primal of a linear program. The solution of this program involves three different steps.[8]

First, we have to find a feasible solution. A feasible solution is defined as a solution which satisfies the restraints. The first feasible solution to be included in the solution procedure is the one in which only disposal activities[9] (slack variables) are operated.

Second, the shadow prices associated with the feasible solution are calculated. These shadow prices associated with the activity levels of a given program indicate the opportunity costs of that program. They denote the relative scarcity of each resource with respect to an improvement in the value of the objective function.[10]

Third, the shadow prices are used to determine whether any increase in the value of the objective function is possible by introducing a new activity into the initial program. This is determined by the simplex criterion. The procedure is repeated until the value of the objective function can no longer be increased by changing a given program. Associated with the activity levels of the choice variables which maximize the objective function are the shadow prices corresponding to the equilibrium condition in which the price of each commodity is equal to its cost of production.[11] These shadow prices are the result of the dual.[12] Information on these shadow or scarcity prices is helpful for the allocation decisions of the policy maker.

The above model is a rather simple framework of the variables entering a decision process. A much more complex regional development model has been presented by Spiegelman, Baum, and Talbert.[13] They construct a planning framework for a five-county area in central Kentucky. The objective function is to minimize the external capital needed for the development of the region. This criterion was chosen because capital can be regarded to be the scarcest factor of production in the region. A similar objective function is chosen by Chenery and Kretschmer[14] and—with respect to labor—by Moses.[15] Other targets are intro-

---

[8]H. B. Chenery, "Comparative Advantage and Development Policy," *Surveys of Economic Theory*, Vol. II—*Growth and Development*, prepared for the American Economic Association and the Royal Economic Society, St. Martin's, New York, 1965, p. 142.

[9]W. Isard, *Methods of Regional Analysis: An Introduction to Regional Science*, p. 421.

[10]Spiegelman, *op, cit.*, p. 144.

[11]Chenery, *op, cit.*, p. 138

[12]On the interpretation of the dual, compare W. Isard, *Methods of Regional Analysis: An Introduction to Regional Science*, W. Isard, "Interregional Linear Programming," *Journal Regional Science*; Stevens, *op. cit.*

[13]R. G. Spiegelman, E. L. Baum, and L. E. Talbert, "Application of Activity Analysis to Regional Development Planning," U.S. Department of Agriculture, Technical Bulletin No. 1339, Washington, D.C., 1965.

[14]H. B. Chenery and K. S. Kretschmer, "Resource Allocation for Economic Development," *Econometrica*, Vol. 24 (1956), pp. 365–399.

[15]L. N. Moses, "A General Equilibrium Model of Production, Interregional Trade, and the Location of Industry," *Review of Economics and Statistics*, Vol. 42 (1960), pp. 373–399.

duced in the form of restraints. Thus income and consumption targets, the availability of labor, and export chances limit the minimization of the objective function.

The activity matrix of the Spiegelman-Baum-Talbert model includes some 339 economic activities, namely, all activities peculiar to the region, actual and potential. The potential sectors have been selected in separate studies, and it is generally feasible to locate them in the area.[16] The model rejects all those industries which do not satisfy the objective function and selects those activities which minimize external investment. In addition to the selection of these activities, the model determines the income generated by the newly attracted industries, the net foreign balance both on current and capital account, and the labor surplus or deficit. Such a disaggregated theoretical framework represents a powerful tool of decision making which is directly relevant for empirical policy problems.

For illustration, four other policy questions for which decision models have application are presented. (1) Given a set of resources $R_1, \ldots, R_m$ and a set of activities $X_1, \ldots, X_n$, at which level should these activities be undertaken in order to reach a maximum of regional income?[17] (2) Given the same assumptions for a multiregion system, what are the activities that maximize the total output of all regions?[18] (3) Given an investment sum, how can this sum be allocated among different regions, among different sectors in one region, and among different sectors in different regions?[19] (4) How can social overhead capital be used as a policy variable in order to produce a maximum output of a two-region system?[20]

B. DECISION CRITERIA AND STRATEGIES

Very often the regional planner is not able to construct a formal decision model because of a lack of data or the impossibility to express a complex policy problem in terms of a decision model. Then decision criteria may be used if instrument variables are to be selected. The following criteria are relevant for regional growth policy.

[16]The prechoice of industries only eliminates those activities which cannot be expected to locate in the area at all. Thus a heavy capital good industry is unlikely to move to an agricultural region.

[17]W. Isard, *Methods of Regional Analysis: An Introduction to Regional Science,* Chap. 10.

[18]W. Isard, "Interregional Linear Programming," *Journal of Regional Science;* Stevens, *op. cit.*

[19]A. P. Hurter and L. N. Moses, "Regional Investment and Interregional Programming," *Papers and Proceedings of the Regional Science Association,* Vol. 13 (1964), pp. 105–119.

[20]A. Rahman, "Regional Allocation of Investment—An Aggregative Study in the Theory of Development Programming," *Quarterly Journal of Economics,* Vol. 77 (1963), pp. 428–438; N. Sakashita, "Regional Allocation of Public Investment," *Papers and Proceedings of the Regional Science Association,* Vol. 19 (1967), pp. 161–182.

1. *Comparative-cost criterion.* One aspect of regional growth policy is to influence the location of private industry. If, for instance, the planner desires to attract industries to a depressed region, he has to make a choice among different possible activities. As previously mentioned, this problem can be studied with the help of an input-output model which determines the regional income generated by a new industry. This approach, however, presupposes that the industries in question can feasibly be located in the region. The prechoice of these activities may be undertaken with the comparative-cost criterion.[21] In order to preselect the principally possible activities, the regional planner has to determine the location advantage of the region by comparing the production and transportation costs of different activities. The activities with low costs will be the select set of activities which then, in a second step, will be tested for their impact on regional income.

The comparative-cost criterion may also analyze the production and transportation costs of one activity at alternative locations.[22] This study may not only be undertaken for one single activity but for a set of interrelated firms. In this case the policy maker is interested in the location advantage of industrial complexes.[23] Industrial-complex analysis may lead to a different location policy than isolated location studies for single activities, since external economies between the different activities are taken into consideration. Thus a spatial point may not have a comparative advantage for isolated activities, but it may have an advantage if these activities are combined.

2. *Benefit-cost criterion.* In contrast to comparative-cost analysis which usually only refers to private costs, the benefit-cost criterion requires the estimation of both social costs and social benefits of a policy measure.[24] External economies are explicitly taken into consideration. This procedure has so far been used as an allocation criterion for specific types of social wants, i.e., for those goods that are not subject to the exclusion principle.[25] Assume that with

[21]W. Isard, *Methods of Regional Analysis: An Introduction to Regional Science,* p. 233; W. Isard and T. Reiner, "Regional and National Economic Planning and Analytical Techniques for Implementation," in W. Isard and J. H. Cumberland (eds.), *Regional Economic Planning—Techniques of Analysis for Less Developed Areas,* OECD, Paris, 1960. On decision criteria, compare T. A. Reiner, "Sub-National and National Planning: Decision Criteria," *Papers and Proceedings of the Regional Science Association,* Vol. 14 (1965), pp. 107–136.
[22]Note that the comparative cost criterion is based on the Weberian framework of location analysis.
[23]W. Isard, *Methods of Regional Analysis: An Introduction to Regional Science,* Chap. 9; W. Isard, E. W. Schooler, and T. Vietorisz, *Industrial Complex Analysis and Regional Development,* M.I.T. Press, Cambridge, Mass., 1960.
[24]On benefit cost analysis compare A. R. Prest and R. Turvey, "Cost-Benefit Analysis: A Survey," *Economic Journal,* Vol. 75 (1965), pp. 683–735, O. Eckstein, *Water-Resource Development: The Economics of Project Evaluation,* Harvard U. P., Cambridge, Mass., 1958; O. Eckstein, "Benefit-Cost Analysis and Regional Development," in W. Isard and J. H. Cumberland (eds.), *Regional Economic Planning—Techniques of Analysis for Less Developed Areas,* OECD, Paris, 1960.
[25]R. A. Musgrave, *The Theory of Public Finance,* McGraw-Hill, New York, 1959, p. 9.

a given sum of investment funds alternative projects within a region or in a system of regions are considered. Then, according to the benefit-cost approach, those projects should be undertaken which have the highest benefit-cost ratio. If comparable projects are technically feasible in different regions, the region with the highest benefit-cost ratio should receive the investment funds. This approach arrives at an optimal allocation of resources in those sectors of the economy where the market mechanism does not operate effectively.

The benefit-cost criterion may be interpreted not only in terms of the optimal allocation of resources, but in terms of other targets as well. For regional growth policy the benefits caused by an instrument variable may be measured in terms of the contribution of a policy measure to the growth target. Let the objective be to increase the growth rate of a two-region system given some amount of investment. If investment is undertaken in region I, the growth rate of region I will rise and, through the spillover effect, the growth rate of region II may also increase. The overall effect on the growth rate of the two-region system represents the benefit of investing in region I. The costs can be interpreted as the loss in the potential growth rate which occurred by not investing in region II. A comparison of the realized growth rate and the rate forgone yields the benefit-cost ratio.

3. *Productivity criterion and development potential.* The previous example estimates benefits and costs in terms of the contribution or forgone contribution to the growth rate. A similar approach is taken when the marginal-productivity criterion[26] is used. According to this guideline investment should be undertaken in that region in which it yields the highest long-run productivity. Assume the government can spend a given sum of investment $\bar{J}$ in either of two regions. Then the increase in potential output in each region is given by

$$dO_\mathrm{I} = \left(\frac{dO}{J}\right)_\mathrm{I} \bar{J}$$

$$dO_\mathrm{II} = \left(\frac{dO}{J}\right)_\mathrm{II} \bar{J} \qquad (9\text{-}22)$$

where dO/J denotes the marginal productivity of investment. Sum $\bar{J}$ should be invested in that area in which the increase in potential output is the greatest, the criterion being $dO_\mathrm{I} \gtrless dO_\mathrm{II}$. The productivity criterion may be applied both to

---

[26] It can be shown that the productivity criterion is logically equivalent to the simplex criterion used in linear programming. Compare H. B. Chenery, "Comparative Advantage and Development Policy," p. 143/4. The productivity criterion is discussed at length in the German regional science literature: H. Jürgensen and H. G. Voigt, *Produktivitätsorientierte Regionalpolitik als Wachstumsstrategie Hamburgs,* Vandenhoek & Ruprecht, Göttingen, Germany, 1965; D. Marx, *Wachstumsorientierte Regionalpolitik,* Vandenhoek & Ruprecht, Göttingen, Germany, 1966. On the concept of the development potential, compare H. Giersch, "Das ökonomische Grundproblem in der Regionalpolitik," in H. Jürgensen (ed.), *Gestaltungsprobleme der Weltwirtschaft,* Göttingen, 1964, pp. 386–400.

public and private investment. In the case of private investment, however, we usually assume that the market mechanism allocates the investment funds according to perceived opportunities, thus reflecting the differences in factor rewards and in marginal productivities. Here government interference may become necessary (1) if factor prices in the market economy reflect only short-run productivities, (2) if the long-run productivity is different from the short-run productivity, and (3) if the allocation of resources is inflexible with changes in the factor rewards. Under these conditions the optimal allocation of resources in a static sense does not represent a dynamic or long-run optimum. One cause for the difference between short-run and long-run factor rewards is the existence of pecuniary external economies which are only revealed in the process of economic development and are not anticipated by the allocation of the market mechanism.

The criterion of the long-run productivity of investment is one approach to measure the development potential of a region. According to this interpretation, the development potential changes with net investment and with variations in the marginal productivity of capital. A rise in the productivity of investment reflects such phenomena as improvements in the technological structure, progress in organizational efficiency, and changes in the social system. An increase in the labor force is not explicitly taken into consideration.

Another approach to estimate the growth potential is to start from a production function and interpret the development potential as the total differential of output with respect to time. From

$$O = f(t, K, L) \tag{9-23}$$

we have [27]

$$\dot{O} = \frac{\partial f}{\partial t} + \frac{\partial f}{\partial k} \cdot \dot{K} + \frac{\partial f}{\partial L} \cdot \dot{L} \tag{9-24}$$

The potential increase of output depends on the increase of technical knowledge, capital, and labor, and on the marginal productivities of these factors. The development potential is also affected by the withdrawal or the attraction of factors of production. It should be remembered from Chapter 5 that the interregional exchange of commodities influences the realization of the development potential.

4. *Strategies.* In a multiregion system the regional planner will compare the development potential of different regions. If the overall objective is to maximize output of the multiarea system, the region with the greatest contribution to that target, i.e., with the highest growth potential, will be developed first. However three different concepts of the development potential have to be distinguished:

(1) The free-market development potential which is defined for situations without any government interference.

[27] On the derivation, compare Footnote 12, Chap. 6.

(2) The status quo development potential which is defined for a given level or a status quo of government activity.

(3) The policy-influenced development potential which explicitly takes into account the impact of policy measures on growth potential. In addition to the increase in output from the market forces, this concept also includes the increments of income being induced by changes in the level of government activity.

The development potential of a region may differ depending on which type of definition is used. Assume the regions of a nation are ordered according to their free-market development potential. Then it is conceivable that the ranking of these regions changes if the influence of government activity on the growth potential is taken into account. For instance, let the government spend a fixed sum alternatively in each region and ignore the revenue aspect of public activity. If the same sum of expenditures has different effects in the different areas, the original ordering of development potentials may be changed.

The choice of one of the concepts as a guideline for regional growth policy depends to some extent on the type of economic system and thus on the value judgments concerning government interference. Let us assume that the policy maker decides in favor of the third definition. Then he will use his instrument variables in that region which has the highest policy-influenced development potential. Since growth is a long-run problem, the policy-influenced development potential of a region does not only depend on the instrument variables used in the initial situation, but it is also a function of the policy measures of subsequent periods. The development potential of a region therefore depends on the sequence of policy means. A coordinated sequence of policy instruments is called a strategy.

Two different strategies for the growth policy of a two-region system[28] are described in Fig. 9-2. The goal-relation curve between the output of different regions as derived in Fig. 8-4 of Chapter 8 is denoted by TT. Over time, the total amount of resources and technical knowledge in the two-region system will increase, and in each period the goal-relation curve is shifted outward. The increase in resources and technical knowledge and the interregional distribution of these growth determinants depend on the policy instruments used. Assume that point A represents the situation in which a maximum total output of the two-region system is reached initially with total output being defined as the sum

---

[28] Strategies may not only be developed for a multiregion system but also for a single region. Two possible strategies which have been widely discussed in the literature are the development via an excess of social overhead capital or via a shortage of social overhead capital. The first approach holds that infrastructure outlays lead to pecuniary external economies which in turn will stimulate private activity. The second approach would first establish directly productive activities, which then would be followed by social overhead outlays. Compare A. O. Hirschman, *The Strategy of Economic Development,* Yale U. P., New Haven, Conn.; N. M. Hansen, "Unbalanced Growth and Regional Development," *Western Economic Journal,* Vol. 4 (1965), pp. 3–14; P. Streeten, "Unbalanced Growth," *Oxford Economic Papers,* Vol. 11 (1959), pp. 167–191.

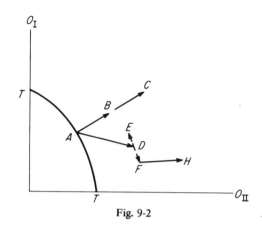

Fig. 9-2

of the distances of point A from the two axes. Assume the policy maker wants to reach a higher total output in the future. He then may choose either of the two following strategies:

First, the total output can be increased by raising output in the two regions simultaneously. This would require a similar increase of growth determinants in both regions and/or a distribution of policy variables over the two-region system in such a way that a similar expansion of both regions results. This strategy is represented by line ABC, where B and C indicate the situations realized at the end of different planning periods.

The second approach would increase total income by developing one region first. For instance, instrument variables are used to promote economic growth in region II. O_{II} is increased from A to D. At point D the following effects may be induced by the increased economic activity of region II. Firms realize economies of scale and agglomeration economies arise. Factor rewards in II are higher than in I because new technical knowledge is created which is not communicated to I. In this case factors will be withdrawn from region I and output in II will increase (effect DF). On the other hand, region I may experience a leveling effect (effect DE). In Fig. 9-2 it has been assumed that once point D is reached, growth in region II is reinforced, partly at the expense of area II, by section DF. In the next planning period the application of policy instruments leads to point H.

Strategy $ADFH$ is preferred to strategy ABC if it finally results in a higher output of the two-region system. The outcome will depend on differences in the development potential of regions for given planning periods. Regional growth pole theory[29] has taken a strong stand on the strategy to be followed, " . . .

[29] On growth-pole theory, compare F. Perroux, *L'économie du XXème siecle*, Presses Universitaires de France, Paris, 1964; F. Perroux, "La Firme Motrice dans la Région et la Région Motrice," *Théorie et Politique de l'Expansion Régionale*, Actes du Colloque International de l' Institut de Science Economique de l'Université de Liége, Brussels, Belgium, 1961, pp. 257–305; J. Paelinck, "La Théorie du Développement Régional Polarisé, *Cahiers*

Growth does not appear everywhere and all at once; it appears in points or growth poles, with variable intensities; it spreads along diverse channels and with varying terminal effects for the whole of the economy."[30]   A *regional growth pole* is defined as a set of interdependent expanding industries of an area.[31]   The complex of industries is viewed as consisting of a key industry and a set of activities which are linked to the key sector. The key industry is by definition expanding at a high rate, has a high level of output, and has strong linkages with the other activities of the region.[32]   The backward or forward linkages refer to the input and output side of an input-output matrix.

The direct diffusion effects of an expansion in the key industry on the input side can be calculated by using the input-output coefficients in the column of the key sector. The key industry increases its demand for the outputs of other activities in the region. It may also attract those sectors to the area from which it imported its input in an earlier stage of development. On the output side, the key industry provides inputs for other sectors of the economy. It may also release spending power of the household sector by lowering the price for its products. The overall effects on regional income via the forward and backward linkages can be calculated by similar procedures as used in Eqs. 9-1 through 9-16.

The network of economic interdependence is not only viewed in a static fashion, but is also interpreted dynamically. The key sector realizes internal economies by producing larger quantities. Economies of scale and innovations reduce the output price of the key industry, creating pecuniary external economies for the other activities. The key activity also sets the pace for other firms in realizing new technical knowledge. Immobile external economies—i.e., agglomeration economies,—arise. The reinforcing effects discussed in Chapter 7 come into play and internal and external variables are polarized. The withdrawal effect increases the relative growth differential. Eventually a psychological climate is established which induces further growth. Changes in the social system accompany, reinforce, or may even cause the original polarization.[33]

One of the basic reasons for a growth pole to arise is the immobility of at least one growth determinant. Initially, when the process of polarization is started, the potential growth-pole region must have immobile resources, im-

de l'Institut de Science Economique Appliquée, Série L, No. 15 (1965); F. Perroux, *Economic Space—Theory and Applications*, in J. Friedman and W. Alonso (eds.), *Regional Development and Planning—A Reader*, M.I.T. Press, Cambridge, Mass., 1966, pp. 173–186; J. Friedmann, "A General Theory of Polarized Development," The Ford Foundation, Urban and Regional Advisory Program in Chile, Santiago, Chile, 1967 (mimeo), p. 11; J. Friedmann, *Regional Development Policy—A Case Study of Venezuela*, M.I.T. Press, Cambridge, Mass., 1966, Chap. 2; Hirschman, *op. cit.*; N. M. Hansen, *op. cit.*; N. M. Hansen, "Development Pole Theory in a Regional Context," *Kyklos*, Vol. 20 (1967), pp. 709–727.
[30] F. Perroux, *L'économie du XXème siecle*, p. 143.
[31] Compare J. R. Boudeville, *Problems of Regional Economic Planning*, Edinburgh U. P., Edinburgh, Scotland, 1966, p. 11.
[32] N. M. Hansen, "Development Pole Theory in a Regional Context," p. 717.
[33] Compare J. Friedmann, "A General Theory of Polarized Development," Part I.

mobile factors of production, immobile natural resources, or other determinants which are not available in other areas, such as specific location factors or a larger amount of infrastructure capital. Only these immobilities can explain the location of the key industry and its development. Also, the growth pole will only persist if the immobilities are upheld or if additional immobilities—such as immobile external economies and immobile new technical knowledge—arise.

If the basic proposition of growth-pole theory is correct—and our experience in different countries provides quite a few examples—then the growth-pole region has the higher development potential. In this case the planner may develop region II before he tries to stimulate growth in region I.

Two problems associated with regional development policy are (1) that the growth-pole strategy may aggravate interregional income differentials, and (2) that different strategies may lead to different final results

The policy maker may intend to reach national development via a regional growth pole (or a set of growth poles) with the expectation that in later planning periods the leveling effects for the slowly growing or stagnating regions and the autonomous changes in these areas become strong enough to reduce the interregional income differential. This outcome, however, is questionable, and the growth pole may reinforce its own expansion by inducing internal and external growth determinants. The growth-pole strategy may therefore require a spatial distribution of economic activities which conflicts with other goals. In this case a restraint as discussed in Eq. 8-21 of Chapter 8 may limit the applicability of the growth pole strategy.

Strategies for growth policy relate to a series of planning periods. If the development potential is used as a guidepost for regional policy, a situation may arise where region I has a higher long-run development potential than region II, but where region II has a higher growth potential in the short run. For instance, region II may have the advantage of an early start. If the development strategy first develops region II, the long-run optimum may never be reached—economies of scale, external economies, and the reinforcement of internal and external growth determinants in region II may prevent region I from fully realizing its long-run growth potential.

Let line AF in Fig. 9-3 represent the optimal strategy to reach a long-run maximum output of the two-region system and divide the time period necessary for the movement from A to F into several planning periods. Arrows indicate the development potential of each planning period. With strategy AF the highest increase is achieved in the third period. Assume that the regional planner only has sufficient information for each planning period. Then the planning horizon at situation A does not surpass B or comparable points. Also assume that with this limited information the best strategy to maximize the output level of the two-region system is to reach B. At B induced effects occur (BC). The next policy action is also only formulated for a given planning horizon. The new maximum output is at D. The resulting sequence $ABCDEG$ may not reach the

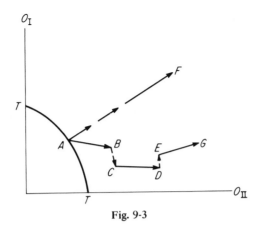

Fig. 9-3

long-run optimum as denoted by F if the early start of region I is not compensated by the process of development. The larger the information horizon of the regional planner, the easier it will be to maximize total income in the long run. If in the above example the planning horizon is enlarged, it may be necessary from the target of a long-run maximum national output to protect the region with a late start (I) against the withdrawal effect from the region with the higher short-run development potential (II). Analogous arguments, as in the case of infant industries in international trade, may be used to justify some type of protective policy for infant regions with a high long-run development potential.

C. A SURVEY OF THE INSTRUMENT VARIABLES

The instruments of regional growth policy may be classified according to three different criteria: (1) the determinants of regional growth which they influence, (2) the size of the area which they are basically supposed to affect and (3) the intensity of interference with the market economy.[34]

1. If instruments are classified according to the growth determinants which they influence the following categories are obtained.

(a) *Labor-supply measures.* Under this heading all policy variables are included which influence the regional labor supply. These instruments may be directed toward an internal or an external increase in the labor supply. They comprise efforts to influence birth and death rates, the decision of the individual worker between labor and leisure, measures to increase the quality of the labor force, and also policy variables which can attract needed workers to the area.

(b) *Capital-supply measures.* This is the set of instruments which affect the availability of investment funds in an area and which increase the investment

[34] Another criterion would be to classify instruments according to the economic systems in which they are used.

opportunities in a region. The instruments included are those which increase intraregional savings, attract capital from outside, and increase the quality of the existing capital stock. One important aspect is the supply of social infrastructure capital.

(c) *Technical progress instruments.* These are instruments that relate to all those variables which enlarge the technical horizon of a regional system. All measures which speed up the rate of inventions and innovations are considered in this context. One important set of means are those instruments which intensify the embodiment effect of technical knowledge in capital and labor. All measures, for instance, which reduce the average age of the capital stock are relevant to this group.

(d) *Demand-influencing instruments.* Under this heading all means are summarized which increase internal or external demand for the products of an area. These measures include government spending and those policy variables which influence private consumption and investment demand.

(e) *Location policy.* Regional growth policy may also be viewed as location policy with the basic aim to influence the distribution of economic activities in space. Location policy includes the first three types of policy measures, but may contain other instruments as well. Thus location policy[35] also includes subsidies to attract industries and efforts of the government to increase the information horizon of the individual firm regarding the locational characteristics of spatial points.

(f) *Mobility policy.* The instruments included in this set either increase the mobility of commodities or the mobility of factors of production. We have seen that an increase in the mobility of commodities leads to allocation gains which represent a higher output of a two-region system. An increase in the interregional mobility of factors ensures a greater efficiency in the allocation of resources by letting factors move to the place of their optimal use. However, it should be remembered from Chapter 7 that varying factor mobilities are a precondition for interregional growth differentials. Note that the mobility policy with regard to factors overlaps with the first three policies.

2. A second criterion for the classification of policy instruments is the size of the area which they are intended to affect. For a nation, defined as a multiregion system, regional and national instrument variables can be distinguished.

(a) *Regional instruments.* These include those policy variables that are intended to influence the economic activity of a region. These measures will mostly affect the internal variables of our model, such as the intraregional capital formation, the intraregional labor supply, the intraregional increases in technical knowledge, and the location of industries within regions. The definition of

---

[35] On location policy, compare E. M. Hoover, *The Location of Economic Activity,* McGraw-Hill, New York, Chaps. 14–16; K. Töpfer, *Die Beeinflussbärkeit privater Pläne,* Bertelsmann, Gütersloh, Germany, 1969.

these policy measures requires that their effects can be limited to a specific area. Examples are the means operated by regional policy makers, such as local expenditures and tax rates, and those instruments controlled by the central government that can be defined for subunits of the nation.

Regional policy instruments are characterized by the fact that they can, and normally do, discriminate between different types of regions.[36] The direction of the discrimination depends on the policy targets and the situations in the regions. Two situations have attracted considerable interest so far; the case of depressed areas and the case of overagglomerated regions.[37] Another distinction is that between strategic and nonstrategic areas.

(b) *National instruments.* These have as a frame of reference the national economy. Here an additional distinction may be introduced depending on whether the nation is viewed as a system of regions or as a "one-point" economy. Instruments applied to a system of regions (interregional instruments) are intended to influence phenomena of interregional interaction, the most important example being the mobility policy for goods and factors. Purely national instruments view the nation as a "one-point" economy and include such variables as defense spending, import duties, and interest rates. Although these measures are defined for the area of a nation, they may affect different subunits of the nation in a different way. Similarly, as purely regional and interregional measures have an impact on the national economy, the national-policy measures affect the economic processes in different subunits.

Very little information is available on the regional incidence of national-policy variables. Take for example a tariff increase,[38] which is usually regarded as a national-policy instrument. Then regions in which the protected industry is located may experience an increase in activity since world competition is no longer felt. On the other hand, areas in which industries use the output of the protected industry as an input, may feel a decline in their economic activity since the input costs have risen. Another example which has been studied by economists is the spatial impact of defense expenditures.[39] A change in defense expenditures has strong impacts for those regions in which the defense industry is located. Similar problems arise for such policy measures as farm-price

---

[36]Note that the concept of the planning region implies that policy instruments with a spatially limited impact exist.

[37]These two cases are discussed by G. H. Borts and J. L. Stein, *Economic Growth in a Free Market*, Columbia U. P., New York, Chap. 9; also compare H. O. Nourse, *Regional Economics*, McGraw-Hill, New York, Chap. 8.

[38]Nourse, *op. cit.*, p. 230.

[39]M. L. Weidenbaum, "Shifting the Composition of Government Spending: Implications for the Regional Distribution of Income," *Papers and Proceedings of the Regional Science Association*, Vol. 17 (1966), pp. 163–167; R. E. Bolton, "Defense Purchases and Regional Growth," The Brookings Institution, Washington, D. C., 1966; R. S. Peterson and C. M. Tiebout, "Measuring the Impact of Regional Defense-Space Expenditures," *Review of Economics and Statistics*, Vol. 46 (1964), pp. 421–428.

supports[40] and federal taxes. Information on the regional impact of national instruments is a prerequisite for consistent regional and national policies.

3. The third criterion for the classification of policy variables is to rank them according to their interference with private activity. The following catalogue of instruments implies a declining interference with private activity.

(a) *Activities undertaken by the government.* The strongest interference with private activities occurs if the government operates the activities itself. In a market economy this may be limited to the satisfaction of social wants to which, by definition, the exclusion principle does not apply. Conceivably the government may also take over activities other than the satisfaction of social wants, if a value judgment comes to this conclusion.

(b) *Direct controls.* The government may principally decide in favor of private activities, but it may control these activities very strictly by prescribing values for the most important variables of private activity. The policy of direct control, which has been operated in war situations, uses price and wage stops, and may go as far as to dictate output and employment levels for different activities. All these instruments could be used in a regionally discriminatory fashion.

(c) *Indirect controls.* Measures of indirect control do not fix some central variable like output levels, prices, and wages, but try to influence these variables by changing their determinants and by controlling some of the conditions under which private activities operate. Instruments of indirect control include all measures of monetary and budget policy. Since the applicability of monetary policy for regional problems has not been analyzed, the analysis concentrates on those instruments which appear in the public budget.

(1) On the expenditure side there may be distinguished three important measures—social-overhead outlays, transfers, and subsidies. Social-overhead outlays[41] cause both an income effect and a capacity effect. In the period in which the additional infrastructure capital is created, costs are incurred and income is generated in the region. Depending on the marginal propensities to import, some of this additional income leaks out of the region and an income effect arises in other areas.

The income effect represents only one aspect of the impact of infrastructure investment. The other aspect is a capacity effect. This capacity effect does not imply a direct increase in the production potential of a region, as in the case of directly productive investment, but causes external economies which in turn will induce private activity.

---

[40] Weidenbaum, *op. cit.*, p. 171, On the regional impact of sectoral policies, compare P. Bauchet, "Die regionalen Auswirkungen der in Frankreich in bestimmten Sektoren angewandten Wirtschaftspolitik," Eine Studie für die Kommission des Europäischen Wirtschaftsgemeinschaft, Brussels, Belgium, 1961.

[41] On the role of infrastructure investments for regional economic growth compare Rahman, *op. cit.*, Sakashita, *op. cit.*; P. G. Jansen, *Infrastruktur-Investitionen als Mittel der Regionalpolitik*, Bertelsmann, Gütersloh, Germany, 1968.

Assume for example that infrastructure investment relates to the transportation sector. Let there be two producers, I and II, along a distance axis (Fig. 9-4).[42] Let each producer be characterized by constant production costs,

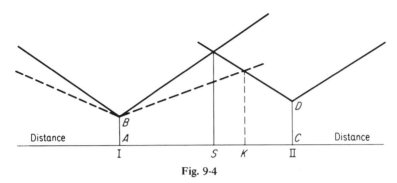

Fig. 9-4

with mill price AB for producer I and mill price CD for producer II. The transport costs per unit of commodity increase with distance. Point S characterizes the partitioning of the market between the two producers I and II. Assume infrastructure investment is undertaken, and that as a consequence the transport rate of producer I is reduced while the transport rate of II remains constant. Then the market area of II will widen. The increase in the market area is denoted by SK. If U-shaped cost curves are assumed, a widening of the market leads to a fuller utilization of economies of scale and to increased efficiency in the economic system.

Another policy instrument which has been used in the context of regional growth policy is the transfer of income to individuals. This measure is proposed to correct the interregional distribution of income. Funds are withdrawn from persons in high-income regions and are paid to persons in low-income areas. This interregional transfer of funds places members of the low-income region on a higher level of total utility, whereas the total utility of members of the high-income group is reduced. Let region I and II be represented by a single taxpayer I and II. Assume that both regions (taxpayers) have different utility schedules with marginal utility declining for both, and that taxation is undertaken according to the principle of equal marginal sacrifice.[43] In Fig. 9-5 income of region I is given by OA and income of II is denoted by $O'H$. Assume the total tax yield needed for government activity is LH. Then, according to the principle of equal marginal sacrifice, region II will pay the tax. But even after II has paid the tax of LH equal sacrifice is not yet reached. A consequent extension of the principle of

---

[42] Compare E. M. Hoover's margin lines, *Location Theory and the Shoe and Leather Industries,* Harvard U. P., Cambridge, Mass, 1937; W. Isard, *Location and Space Economy,* M. I. T. Press, Cambridge, Mass., Chap. 6; M. L. Greenhut, *Microeconomics and the Space Economy,* Scott, Foresman, Chicago, 1963, p. 147, Jansen, *op. cit.,* p. 40.
[43] Musgrave, *op. cit.,* p. 97.

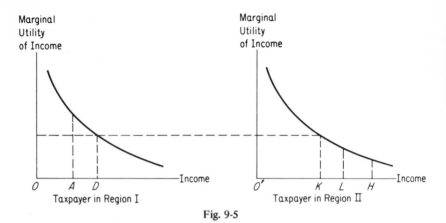

Fig. 9-5

equal marginal sacrifice will require that marginal utility of both regions is equal after taxation. This can be reached if region II pays an additional tax of KL, thereby increasing its marginal utility. This tax yield is used as a transfer to region I, leading to an increase of income in region I by AD, thus reducing marginal utility there.

Figure 9-5 illustrates the argument in favor of a negative interregional income tax. In addition to the usual criticism of this approach, which stresses the impossibility of comparisons of interpersonal utility schedules, we should also point out some of the consequences for regional growth. A transfer of income from one region to the other will lead to adjustments in both regions with respect to all aspects of private activity. The high-income region may reduce consumption, saving, investment, and the supply of labor. Conceivably the production potential of the region may be reduced. Thus an interregional distribution policy may impede growth in the advanced area. The area receiving the transfer is likely to increase demand, but the increase in demand is not a sufficient condition for development. The decisive question is how the determinants of the supply side will be affected by the interregional shift of income. The transfer in income through a tax-transfer mechanism may, for instance, lead to a greater reduction of output in one region than it leads to an increase of output in the other region. The policy maker may be willing to regard the loss of potential output as an opportunity cost for reaching a more equal interregional distribution of income. Of course this statement represents a value judgment which is not for the scientist to make.

Besides income transfers to individuals, the government may pay subsidies to specific industries in specific areas. Subsidies have mainly been used to influence the location decisions of private activities. They may be freight subsidies for regions with a comparative location disadvantage[44] or they may include

[44]Thus the West German government pays transport subsidies to firms which are located near the eastern border. The argument is that these firms have been cut off from their former markets by the division of Germany.

interest subsidies, tax reductions, grants, and loans for those firms which decide in favor of depressed areas. Also, subsidies can be used that increase the mobility of industrial plants, thus reducing the costs of relocation. This measure has been applied where overagglomerated areas exist and where industry is reluctant to leave these regions.[45] A survey of the different measures is given in the literature.[46]

(2) On the revenue side, taxes and bond revenues are the two instruments which can be used as regional policy variables. Lower tax rates for depressed areas represent one way to attract industry. Here the question arises: To what extent do regionally differentiated tax structures influence private location decisions? The first available empirical investigations of this question came to inconclusive results.[47] It may also be asked whether a given national tax structure has different effects on regional activities. Assume the national tax system is regressive and that regions are in different stages of development. Possibly a regressive tax rate may restrict activities in the low-income regions relatively more than in a high-income area. Or suppose that the national tax system is progressive. Will this system affect economic activities in the different regions in a different way and be an impediment to a growth pole? The questions we have raised so far relate to the effects of taxation (ignoring the expenditure side) and to different types of expenditures with a *ceteris paribus* of the revenue side. But in addition to these problems, we have to study the combined effects of expenditures and taxation. To what extent is the rate of growth of a multi-region system influenced if the taxes raised in region I are spent in another area? How are the growth rates of different regions affected? All these questions point out the relevance of a new field, regional public finance,[48] which would attempt

---

[45]This instrument has been relied upon in the French planification in order to move firms away from Paris.

[46]The policy variables of location policy can be studied with respect to the French planification and the Mezzogiorno in Italy. Compare *Government Measures for the Promotion of Regional Economic Development—Results of a Study Carried Out in Different Countries by the International Information Centre for Local Credit,* Martinus Nijhoff, The Hague, Netherlands, 1964; J. and A. M. Hackett, *Economic Planning in France,* Harvard U. P., Cambridge, Mass., 1963, Chap. 13. On the different instruments, compare J. E. Moes, *Local Subsidies for Industry,* U. of North Carolina Press, Chapel Hill, 1962; M. D. Bryce, *Policies and Methods for Industrial Development,* McGraw-Hill, New York, 1965, E. M. Hoover, *The Location of Economic Activity,* Chap. 15, L. H. Klaassen, *Area Economic and Social Redevelopment,* OECD, Paris 1965; T. Wilson, *Policies for Regional Development,* University of Glasgow Social and Economic Studies, Edinburgh, 1964.

[47]Compare W. V. Williams, "A Measure of the Impact of State and Local Taxes on Industry Location," *Journal of Regional Science,* Vol. 7 (1967), pp. 49–59, R. J. Struyk, "An Analysis of Tax Structure, Public Service Levels and Regional Economic Growth," *Journal of Regional Science,* Vol. 7 (1967), pp. 175–183; J. F. Due, "Studies of State-Local Tax Influences on Location of Industry," *National Tax Journal,* Vol. 14 (1961), pp. 169–173.

[48]Another field of study which is connected with regional policy is the analysis of the institutional setting of regional planning. Here the following problems arise: By which procedures is a national plan regionalized? Which processes must be followed to establish consistency between regional and national planning? Which institutional settings for regional planning have been established in different countries? How do the institutional set-

to analyze the effects of government activity in a spatial setting. Only some first steps have been undertaken in the direction of this new area of economic research.[49]

(d) *Moral suasion*. Moving down the scale of intensity of government interference, the government can try to influence the attainment levels of private individuals by reasoning in terms of the public interest. Assume a region is depressed. Then the government may try to convince private firms that a location in an area is beneficial to the country. Very often this policy of moral suasion is the only weapon the government has at its hand and, used in an efficient way, it may be a successful tool.[50]

(e) *Information policy*. Finally, information policy represents that set of measures which interferes the least with private activities. Information policy attempts only to increase the information horizon of the individual decision maker. The government does not intervene with the attainment level of the individual, nor does it influence such variables as income, profits, wages, and prices through its budget policy. Information policy involves efforts to increase the knowledge of the locational characteristics of different spatial points, but it may be conceived as being broader than a pure location policy. It may attempt to increase the mobility of knowledge on economic opportunities of capital and labor. Also it may include all those efforts which reduce interregional differences in the distribution of technical knowledge. In this case, however, the negative feedback on the incentives for inventions has to be taken into consideration.

PROBLEMS

1. For the impact analysis of alternative activities on regional income, discussed in Eqs. 9-1 through 9-7, assume that the region imports intermediate and

---

tings of regional planning in different countries and different economic systems compare? What are the advantages of centralized and decentralized government? Can an optimal distribution of political power be established? On this emerging field of study, compare Boudeville, *op. cit.;* J. and A. M. Hackett, *op. cit.,* Chap. 13; J. Friedmann, *Regional Development Policy—A Case Study of Venezuela,* p. 7; N. M. Hansen, "Regional Planning in a Mixed Economy," *Southern Economic Journal,* Vol. 32 (1965), pp. 176–90; J. Tinbergen, *Centralization and Decentralization in Economic Policy,* North Holland, Amsterdam, 1954.

[49] For contributions to regional public finance, compare A. T. Peacock, "Towards a Theory of Interregional Fiscal Policy," *Public Finance,* Vol. 20 (1965), pp. 7–17; J. Airov, "Fiscal-Policy Theory in an Interregional Economy—General Interregional Multipliers and Their Application," *Papers and Proceedings of the Regional Science Association,* Vol. 19 (1967), pp. 83–108; C. M. Tiebout, "A Pure Theory of Local Expenditures," *Journal of Political Economy,* Vol. 64 (1956), pp. 416–424. For an historical analysis, compare J. B. Legler, "Regional Distribution of Federal Receipts and Expenditures in the 19th Century," *Papers and Proceedings of the Regional Science Association,* Vol. 19 (1967), pp. 141–159.

[50] The policy of moral suasion has been discussed at length for monetary policy. Compare, for instance, J. W. Hanks and R. Stucki, *Money, Banking and National Income,* Knopf, New York, 1956, p. 282.

final commodities before the new sector is located in the area. The original matrix A_t of Eq. 9–1 then has a fourth row and a fourth column. Row 4 indicates the input requirements of the regional sectors in terms of imports. Column 4 denotes the input requirements of the importing activity of region I, which is the export activity of region II. For convenience it is assumed that the export sector of II does not need inputs from region I. The system of equation then reads:

$$
\begin{bmatrix} X_1 \\ X_2 \\ X_3 \\ M \end{bmatrix} - \begin{bmatrix} a_{11} & a_{12} & a_{13} & 0 \\ a_{21} & a_{22} & a_{23} & 0 \\ a_{31} & a_{32} & a_{33} & 0 \\ a_{M1} & a_{M2} & a_{M3} & 0 \end{bmatrix} \cdot \begin{bmatrix} X_1 \\ X_2 \\ X_3 \\ M \end{bmatrix} = \begin{bmatrix} F_1 \\ F_2 \\ F_3 \\ F_4 \end{bmatrix}
$$

where M indicates total imports and F_4 stands for imports of final commodities. Assume that the new sector which is introduced produces substitutes for imports. Calculate its impact on regional income.

2. Assume the regional planner wants to increase regional employment. Also assume that each sector has a fixed labor requirement per unit of output. Calculate the effects of a change in final demand in region I on employment in regions I and II. Follow a similar procedure as in Eqs. 9-13 through 9-16.

3. Discuss the factors which make for a change in the intraregional and interregional coefficients.

4. Formulate the dual of the primal presented in Eqs. 9-18 through 9-21.[51]

5. Discuss the formal structure of the Spiegelman-Baum-Talbert model.

6. Explain the diffusion effects of a growth pole with an input-output framework. Try to get a systematic survey of all the diffusion effects involved.

7. Discuss the impact of a national policy variable (subsidies to the x-industry, defense expenditures) for regional growth.

8. Explain the role of infrastructure investment as an instrument variable for location and regional growth policy.

9. Discuss the policy instrument used in French regional growth policy.

10. Compare the institutional setting of regional policy in different countries. Evaluate advantages and disadvantages of alternative institutional procedures.

11. Assume n policy makers at the regional level and one national policy maker. By which methods can their plans be made consistent? How can these methods be institutionalized? Discuss the problem of consistent planning if sector plans are also made (compare the role of the sector commissions in the French planification).

[51] Compare Hurter and Moses, *op. cit.*

Selected Bibliography*

BOOKS

Alonso, W., and J. Friedmann (eds.). *Regional Development and Planning–A Reader*, M.I.T. Press, Cambridge, Mass., 1964.

Bolton, R. E. *Defense Purchases and Regional Growth*, The Brookings Institution, Washington, D.C., 1966.

Borts, G. H., and J. L. Stein. *Economic Growth in a Free Market*, Columbia U. P., New York, 1964.

Boudeville, J. R. *Problems of Regional Economic Planning*, Edinburgh U. P., Edinburgh, Scotland, 1966.

Davin, L. E. *Economie régionale et croissance*, Éditions Génin, Paris, 1964.

Friedmann, J. *Regional Development Policy: A Case Study of Venezuela*, M.I.T. Press, Cambridge, Mass., 1966.

Government Measures for the Promotion of Regional Economic Development. Results of a Study carried out in Different Countries by the International Information Center for Local Credit, Martinus Nijhoff, The Hague, Netherlands, 1964.

Greenhut, M. L., and W. T. Whitman (eds.). *Essays in Southern Economic Development*, U. of North Carolina Press, Chapel Hill, 1964.

Hoover, E. M. *The Location of Economic Activity*, McGraw-Hill, New York, 1963.

Isard, W. *Methods of Regional Analysis: An Introduction to Regional Science*, M.I.T. Press, Cambridge, Mass., 1960.

———, E. W. Schooler, and T. Vietorisz. *Industrial Complex Analysis and Regional Development*, Wiley, New York, 1959.

Jürgensen, H., and H. G. Voigt, *Produktivitätsorientierte Regionalpolitik als Wachstumsstrategie Hamburgs*, Vandenhoek & Ruprecht, Göttingen, Germany, 1965.

*The bibliography includes only publications that deal with the problem of regional economic growth.

203

Klaassen, L. H. *Area Economic and Social Redevelopment,* OECD, Paris, 1965.

Marx, D. *Wachstumsorientierte Regionalpolitik,* Vandenhoek & Ruprecht, Göttingen, Germany, 1966.

Mattila, J. M., and W. R. Thompson. *An Econometric Model of Postwar State Industrial Development,* Wayne State U. Press, Detroit, Mich., 1959.

Nourse, H. O. *Regional Economics,* McGraw-Hill, New York, 1968.

Ohlin, B. *Interregional and International Trade,* Harvard Economic Studies, Harvard U.P., Cambridge, Mass., 1954.

Perloff, H. S., *et al. Regions, Resources and Economic Growth,* Johns Hopkins Press, Baltimore, Md., 1960.

Romans, J. T. *Capital Exports and Growth Among U.S. Regions,* Wesleyan U. P., Middletown, Conn., 1965.

Schneider, H. K. (ed.). *Beiträge zur Regionalpolitik, Schriften des Vereins fur Sozialpolitik,* Vol. 41, Duncker & Humblot, Berlin, Germany, 1968.

Siebert, H. *Zur Theorie des regionalen Wirtschaftswachstums,* Mohr, Tübingen, Germany, 1967.

Théorie et Politique de l'Expansion Régionale. Actes du Colloque International de l'Institut de Science Economique de l'Université de Liége, Brussels, Belgium, 1961.

Thompson, W. R. *A Preface to Urban Economics,* Johns Hopkins Press, Baltimore, Md., 1967.

Tiebout, C. M. *The Community Economic Base Study, Supplementing Paper No. 16,* Committee for Economic Development, 1962.

Wilson, T. *Policies for Regional Development,* University of Glasgow Social and Economic Studies, Edinburgh, Scotland, 1964.

ARTICLES

Airov, J. "Fiscal-Policy Theory in an Interregional Economy: General Interregional Multipliers and Their Application," *Papers and Proceedings of the Regional Science Association,* Vol. 19 (1967), pp. 83-108.

———. "Some Regional Aspects of Accelerated National Growth," *Journal of Farm Economics,* Vol. 45 (1963), pp. 1061-1072.

———. "The Construction of Interregional Business Cycle Models," *Journal of Regional Science,* Vol. 5 (1963), pp. 1-20.

Andrews, R. B. "Mechanics of the Urban Base," *Land Economics,* Vol. 29 (1953), pp. 161-167, 263-268, 343-350; Vol. 30 (1954), pp. 52-60, 164-172, 260-269, 309-319; Vol. 31 (1955), pp. 47-53, 144-155, 245-256, 361-371; Vol. 32 (1956), pp. 69-84.

Borts, G. H. "An Approach to Measuring Regional Growth Differentials," *Papers and Proceedings of the Regional Science Association,* Vol. 4 (1958), pp. 207-220.

————. "The Equalization of Returns and Regional Economic Growth," *American Economic Review*, Vol. 50 (1960), pp. 319-347.

————, and J. L. Stein. "Regional Growth and Maturity in the United States —A Study of Regional Structural Change," *Schweizerische Zeitschrift für Volkswirtschaft and Statistik*, Vol. 98 (1962), pp. 290-321.

Chenery, C. H. "Development Policies for Southern Italy," *Quarterly Journal of Economics*, Vol. 76 (1962), pp. 515-547.

Fahri, L. (ed.). "Mise en valeur des ressources régionales" in *Cahiers de l'Institut de Science Economique Appliquée*, Serie L 13, No. 142 (1963).

Friedmann, J. "A General Theory of Polarized Development," The Ford Foundation, Urban and Regional Advisory Program in Chile, Santiago, Chile, 1967 (mimeo).

————. "Locational Aspects of Economic Development," *Land Economics*, Vol. 32 (1956), pp. 213-227.

————. "Regional Economic Policy for Developing Areas," *Papers and Proceedings of the Regional Science Association*, Vol. 11 (1963), pp. 41-61.

Giersch, H. "Das ökonomische Grundproblem in der Regionalpolitik," in H. Jürgensen (ed.), *Gestaltungsprobleme der Weltwirtschaft*, Vandenhoek & Ruprecht, Göttingen, Germany, 1964.

Greenhut, M. L. "Needed—A Return to Classics in Regional Economic Development," *Kyklos*, Vol. 19 (1966), pp. 461-480.

Hansen, N. M. "Development Pole Theory in a Regional Context," *Kyklos*, Vol. 20 (1967), pp. 709-727.

————. "Regional Planning in a Mixed Economy," *Southern Economic Journal*, Vol. 32 (1965), pp. 176-190.

————. "Unbalanced Growth and Regional Development," *Western Economic Journal*, Vol. 4 (1965), pp. 3-14.

Hill, F. G. "Regional Aspects of Economic Development," *Land Economics*, Vol. 38 (1962), pp. 85-98.

Hughes, R. B. "Interregional Income Differences: Self Perpetuation," *Southern Economic Journal*, Vol. 28 (1961), pp. 41-45.

Leven, C. L. "Establishing Goals for Regional Economic Development," *Journal of the American Institute of Planners*, Vol. 30 (1964), pp. 100-110.

Melamid, A. "Regional Analysis of Resources and Growth," *Social Research*, Vol. 29 (1963), pp. 495-498.

Metzler, L. A. "A Multiple Region Theory of Income and Trade," *Econometrica*, Vol. 18 (1950), pp. 329-354.

Milhau, J. "La théorie de la croissance et l'expansion régionale," *Economie Appliquée*, Vol. 9 (1956), pp. 349-366.

Moroney, J. R., and J. M. Walker. "A Regional Test of the Hekscher-Ohlin Hypothesis," *Journal of Political Economy*, Vol. 74 (1966).

Nelson, P. "Migration, Real Income and Information," *Journal of Regional Science*, Vol. 1 (1959), pp. 43–74.

North, D. C. "Location Theory and Regional Economic Growth," *Journal of Political Economy*, Vol. 53 (1955), pp. 243–258.

Parenteau, R. "Les problèmes du développment régional dans un état fédératif," *Revue d'Economie Politique*, Vol. 73 (1963), pp. 161–222.

Perroux, F. "Note sur la notion de pôle de croissance," *Economie Appliquée*, Vol. 8 (1955), pp. 307–320.

Pfister, R. L. "The Terms of Trade as a Tool of Regional Analysis," *Journal of Regional Science*, Vol. 3 (1961), pp. 57–65.

Rahman, A. "Regional Allocation of Investment, An Aggregative Study in the Theory of Development Programming," *Quarterly Journal of Economics*, Vol. 77 (1963), pp. 57–64.

Sakashita, N. "Regional Allocation of Public Investment," *Papers and Proceedings of the Regional Science Association*, Vol. 19 (1967), pp. 161–182.

Siebert, H. "Die Anwendung der Mengentheorie für die Abgrenzung von Regionen," *Jahrbuch für Sozialwissenschaft*, Vol. 18 (1967), pp. 215–222.

———. "Goal Conflicts in Regional Growth Policy," *Zeitschrift für Nationalökonomie*, April 1969.

———. "Zur interregionalen Verteilung neuen technischen Wissens," *Zeitschrift für die Gesamte Staatswissenschaft*, Vol. 123 (1967), pp. 231–263.

Spiegelman, R. G. "Activity Analysis Models in Regional Development Planning," *Papers and Proceedings of the Regional Science Association*, Vol. 17 (1966), pp. 143–159.

———, E. L. Baum, and L. E. Talbert. "Application of Activity Analysis to Regional Development Planning," U. S. Department of Agriculture, Technical Bulletin No. 1339, Washington, D.C., 1965.

Stein, J. R. "A Theory of Interstate Differences in the Rates of Growth of Manufacturing Employment in a Free Market Area," *International Economic Review*, Vol. 1 (1960), pp. 112–128.

Thomas, M. D. "The Export-Base and Development Stages Theories of Regional Economic Growth: An Appraisal," *Land Economics*, Vol. 40 (1964), pp. 421–432.

Tinbergen, J. "Regional Planning: Some Principles," *Netherlands Economic Institute*, Publication No. 21/60, Rotterdam, 1960 (mimeo).

Wolpert, J. "Behavioral Aspects of the Decision to Migrate," *Papers and Proceedings of the Regional Science Association*, Vol. 15 (1965), pp. 159–169.

Glossary of Most Frequently Used Symbols

a_I	production elasticity of capital in region I
a_{ik}	input output coefficient
α	efficiency parameter
$\dot{\alpha}$	neutral technical change
C	consumption demand
dC	change in consumption demand
dD	change in demand
E	invention
$_I\in_{II}$	mobility coefficient of the labor stock in region I
$_I\in'_{II}$	mobility coefficient of the additional labor stock in region I
J	investment demand
dJ	change in investment demand
$_Ij_{II}$	mobility coefficient of the capital stock in region I
$_Ij'_{II}$	mobility coefficient of additional capital in region I
K	capital stock
dK	change in capital stock
$\dot{K}$	change in capital stock
dK^I	total change in the capital stock of region I
$^IdK^I$	internal change in the capital stock of region I
$^IdK^{II}$	capital moved from region I to II
$\cdot k$	rate of growth of capital
L	labor supply
dL	change in the labor supply
$\dot{L}$	change in the labor supply
dL^I	total change in the labor supply of region I

$^{I}dL^{I}$	internal change in the labor supply of region I
$^{I}dL^{II}$	labor moved from region I to II
l	rate of growth of labor
M	imports
dM	change in imports
m	propensity to import
O	potential output
dO	change in potential output
$\dot{O}$	change in potential output
P	terms of trade
dP	change in the terms of trade
$\dot{P}$	change in the terms of trade
P_X	price of exports
P_M	price of imports
p	price of a commodity
q	quantity of a commodity
r	rate of return
S	savings
s	savings propensity
T	technical knowledge
dT	change in technical knowledge
t	time point (as subscript)
w	wage rate
X	exports
dX	change in exports
X	output level of a sector (with subscripts)
Y	income
dY	change in income
$d^{a}Y$	change in income in real terms

Indexes

NAME INDEX

Abramovitz, M., 4, 124
Adelman, I., 25
Airov, J., 97, 200
Alonso, W., 14, 22, 64, 191
Andrews, R. B., 95
Archibald, G. C., 45, 127, 168
Asimakopulos, A., 99
Aujac, H., 182
Avondo-Bodino, G., 20

Balassa, B., 85
Bauchet, P., 196
Baum, E. L., 184, 201
Berelson, B., 55
Berge, C., 20
Berry, B. J. L., 16, 34
Bhagwati, J., 104, 105
Binswanger, H. C., 19
Black, J., 105
Boeventer, E. von, 15, 31
Bohm, P., 124
Bolton, R. E., 195
Borts, G. H., 70, 133, 139, 140, 195
Bössmann, E., 57
Boudeville, J. R., 18, 19, 23, 50, 191, 200
Brackett, C. A., 23
Bruton, H. J., 153
Bryce, M. D., 199

Cani, J. S. de, 59
Cartwright, D., 59
Charnes, A., 59
Chenery, H. B., 124, 178, 184, 187
Cherry, C., 55, 56
Clark, P. G., 178

Clarkson, G. P. E., 14
Cooper, W. W., 59
Cootner, P. H., 125
Cumberland, J. H., 186

Dahl, R. A., 160
Deane, Phyllis M., 85
Domar, E. D., 153
Due, J. F., 199
Duesenberry, J. S., 24, 29
Duncan, O. D., 35
Dunn, E. S., 15, 94

Eckstein, O., 186
Enke, S., 35

Feinstein, A., 55
Ferguson, C. E., 29
Festinger, L., 58
Finch, H. A., 159
Fouraker, L., 94
Friedmann, J., 14, 22, 37, 64, 69, 73, 151, 191, 200

Giersch, H., 159, 133, 187
Gilbert, E. N., 59
Greenhut, M. L., 1, 16, 31, 84, 134, 197
Griffiths, J. C., 59
Griliches, Z., 74
Guenin, J. de, 59, 60, 61

Haberler, G. von, 92
Hackett, A. M., 199
Hackett, J., 199
Hahn, F. H., 142
Haire, M., 59

Hanks, J. W., 200
Hanna, F. A., 133
Hansen, A. H., 28
Hansen, N. M., 133, 189, 191, 200
Hauser, P. M., 35
Henderson, J. F., 125
Hicks, J. R., 99
Hirsch, W. Z., 2
Hirschman, A. O., 45, 126, 142, 147, 189, 191
Hochwald, W., 2, 4, 94
Hoffmann, W. G., 133
Holland, E. P., 14
Hoover, E. M., 1, 31, 39, 194, 197, 199
Hurter, A. P., 185, 201

Isard, W., 1, 6, 16, 18, 124, 126, 134, 141, 178, 182, 184, 185, 186, 197

Janowitz, M., 55
Jansen, P. G., 196, 197
Jaszi, G., 4
Johnson, H. G., 99, 102, 110
Johnson, R. A., 55
Johnston, R. D., 72
Jürgensen, H., 31, 187

Kaldor, N., 24, 41
Kast, F. W., 55
Katz, E., 59
Kemp, M. C., 85, 99
Keynes, J. M., 24, 97
Kindleberger, C. P., 95
Kirschen, E. S., 159
Klaassen, L. H., 199
Klove, R. C., 18
Kneebone, B. T., 13
König, D., 20
Koopman, B. O., 59
Kravis, I., 96
Kretschmer, K. S., 184
Kuenne, R. F., 178
Kuznets, S., 3

Lampard, E. F., 94
Lancaster, K., 144
Langford, T. W., 178
Lazarsfield, P. F., 59
Lefeber, L., 3
Legler, J. B., 200
Leontief, W., 178
Leven, C., 182
Lindblom, C. E., 160
Lindner, S. B., 92, 93, 96

Lipsey, R. G., 45, 127, 144, 168
Lösch, A., 19

Machlup, F., 26, 55
MacQueen, J., 61
Mansfield, E., 75
Marshak, J., 57
Marx, D., 187
Matthews, R. C. O., 142
McDonough, A. M., 55
Meade, J. E., 24, 125
Meier, G. M., 94, 97
Meier, R. L., 55
Merton, R. K., 54
Meyer, J. R., 18
Miernyk, W., 178, 181, 182
Miller, R. G., 61
Moes, J. E., 199, 201
Morill, R. L., 14
Morrison, C. C., 145
Moses, L. N., 3, 178, 184, 185
Mundell, R. A., 76
Musgrave, R. A., 186, 197
Muth, R. F., 94
Myrdal, G., 142, 147, 159

Nelson, P., 58, 59
Nelson, R. B., 6, 41
North, D. C., 94, 95, 132
Nourse, H. O., 1, 18, 95, 195
Nutter, G. W., 4

Ohlin, B., 76, 83
Okun, B., 64
Orcutt, G. H., 14

Paelinck, J., 190
Parsons, T., 46, 53
Peacock, A. T., 200
Perloff, H. S., 63, 94, 98, 132, 133, 152
Perroux, F., 45, 143, 151, 190, 191
Peterson, R. S., 195
Pfister, R. L., 98
Philipps, A. W., 162
Popper, K. R., 123, 159
Pred, A., 16, 34
Predöhl, A., 140
Prest, A. R., 186

Quandt, R. E., 125

Rahman, A., 173, 185, 196
Reiner, T., 186
Reza, F. M., 55

Richardson, G. B., 73
Richardson, R. W., 64
Robinson, E. A. G., 140
Rogers, E. M., 75
Romanoff, E., 178
Romans, J. T., 66
Rosenzweig, J. E., 55
Rostow, W. W., 125, 133
Rotman, B., 13
Ruggles, N. D., 4
Ruggles, R., 4
Ruttan, V. W., 37

Sakashita, N., 185, 196
Salter, W., 41
Samuelson, P. A., 25, 162
Schneider, H. K., 13, 176
Schooler, E. W., 186
Schramm, W., 55, 56
Schumpeter, J. A., 37
Scitovsky, T., 124, 125
Shannon, C., 55
Shils, E. A., 53, 159
Siebert, H., 13, 78
Simon, H. A., 14, 53, 54, 83, 160
Södersten, B., 102, 105, 109
Solow, R. M., 24, 41, 45, 162
Sombart, W., 94
Spiegelman, R. G., 182, 184, 201
Stein, J. L., 70, 139, 195
Stevens, B. H., 15, 23, 182, 184, 185
Stigler, G., 59, 83

Stouffer, S. A., 62
Streeten, P., 85, 98, 105, 159, 189
Struyk, R. J., 199
Stucki, R., 200
Suppes, P., 13, 17
Sutherland, A., 75

Talbert, L. E., 184, 201
Thompson, W. R., 161, 133, 148
Thünen, J. H. von, 15
Tiebout, C. M., 94, 95, 96, 97, 115, 195, 200
Tinbergen, J., 97, 159, 200
Tolley, G. S., 62
Töpfer, K., 194
Turvey, R., 186

Ullmann, M. B., 18
Usher, A. P., 37

Vanek, J., 64, 95, 155
Vietorisz, T., 186
Voigt, H. G., 187

Weaver, W., 55
Weber, A., 141
Weber, M., 159
Weidenbaum, M. L., 195, 196
Williams, W. V., 199
Wilson, T., 199
Wolpert, J., 53, 54, 58

Zimmermann, H., 160

SUBJECT INDEX

Adoption, 74, 75, 80, 82
Adoption coefficient, 75
Agglomeration, 2, 5
Agglomeration economies, 40, 130, 141, 190, 191
Allocation gains, 85, 86–94, 98, 99, 102, 106, 109, 111, 114, 115, 146, 194
Allocation of resources, 90–94, 187, 188
Amenity factor, 63
Area concept, 4, 69, 133
Aspiration level, 53–55, 57, 61, 62, 64, 160, 200
Availability hypothesis, 96
Axiom scheme of separation, 17, 18, 19, 22

Balance of payment, 66, 104
Balance of trade, 99, 107

Basis multiplier, 97
Belgium, 50
Benefit-cost criterion, 186–187
Bit, 56, 57
Bounded rationality; see Limited rationality
Budget policy, 196

Capacity, 4, 5, 24, 42, 66, 96, 97, 114, 130
Capital, 11, 25, 26, 28–31, 34, 35, 40, 41, 64, 66–68, 72, 74, 75, 83, 100, 111, 113, 120, 121, 127–130, 135–140, 142–145, 166, 167, 184, 188
    intensity, 143
    -supply measures, 193
    transfer, 67, 68, 113
Carryover, 97

Causal therapy, 148
Central place, 19, 34
Ceteris paribus, 28, 35, 36, 41, 42, 109,
    110, 126, 131, 135, 138, 140
Cobb-Douglas function, 45, 127
Cognitive dissonance, 58
Commodity exchange; *see* Exchange of
    commodities
Communication, 39, 57–59, 61, 70, 71,
    74, 77, 78–81, 83, 111, 112, 142
  channel, 57, 58, 59, 69, 79
  obstacle; *see* Information obstacle
Comparative advantage, 51, 90, 91, 145,
    186
Comparative cost criterion, 186
Competing migrants, 62
Competition, 73, 87
Competitive range, 87, 88
Concentration curve, 133
Consistency of a model, 123
Consistency between regional and national
    planning, 199
Consumption goods, 53, 66, 67, 74, 76,
    78, 84, 97
Contract curve, 65, 83, 100, 166, 167,
    168
Contraction effect, 143
Customs union, 85

Decision criterion, 161, 185–188
Decision model, 2, 161, 182, 185
Defense expenditures, 195
Delineation of regions, 2, 5, 16–23
Delivered price, 85, 87
Demand, 24, 42–45, 84, 85, 89, 94,
    95–98, 104–109, 111, 112, 114,
    122, 126, 130, 134, 145, 149, 177
  -influencing instruments, 194
  shift, 98
Depreciation, 38, 41, 67, 68, 72, 73, 113,
    121
Development potential, 28, 45, 66, 132,
    187–189, 192, 193
Diffusion, 75, 80
Diffusion effect of growth poles, 191; *see
    also* Leveling effect
Direct control, 196
Disaggregation, 131
Diseconomies, 125, 147
Disposal activity, 184
Distance, 1, 12, 18, 59, 62, 63, 141, 197
Dual effect of factor movement, 64–66,
    143
Dynamic analysis, 6, 26, 35, 133
Dynamic theory of location, 31, 153

Economic landscape, 1, 3, 5, 11, 13, 14,
    16, 34, 46, 176
Economies of scale, 146, 192
Edgeworth box, 64, 68, 76, 100, 166
Employment, 175
Entropy, 56
Equilibrium analysis, 3
Excess-demand (supply) function, 86–87
Exchange of commodities, 2, 3, 4, 5, 49,
    50, 51, 52, 53, 68, 76–78, 84–115,
    126, 141, 145–146, 150, 188
Exchange rate, 91
Exclusion principle, 186, 196
Expansion, 4, 24, 94, 100, 104, 110, 115
Expansion effect, 28, 29, 42, 49, 64–66,
    68, 75–77, 83, 84, 90–92, 94, 97,
    98, 99, 106, 110–111, 113
Expectation, 29
Explanation, 119
Explanatory variable, 177
Explication model, 176, 177, 180, 182,
    183
Export, 66, 87, 89, 90, 92, 94, 95, 97, 99,
    100–110, 111, 112, 113, 145, 148,
    150, 178
Export-base theory, 94–98, 111, 115, 145
Export demand; *see* Interregional demand
Export deficit (surplus), 181
External economies, 124–126, 130, 131,
    140–141, 146, 186, 188, 190–192,
    196, 197
  pecuniary, 124–126, 141, 146, 147
  technological, 124–125, 141, 147

Factor mobility; *see* Mobility
Factor endowment, 91
Farm-price support, 195, 196
Feasible solution, 184
Feedback effect, 14, 15, 149, 181
Final demand, 178, 179, 180, 181, 183
Firm, 34, 39, 44, 45, 71, 72, 73, 96, 115,
    159
First-best solution, 144
Flow of funds, 66
Flow variable, 26, 38, 127
Foreign currency, 91
Foreign investment, 66
French planification, 160
Friction of space, 1, 39, 51, 87

Gains from trade; *see* Allocation gains
Goal, 3, 5, 7, 53, 54, 57, 61, 159, 160,
    161, 172, 174, 175, 177, 182, 184,
    187, 188, 192, 193, 195
  conflict, 161, 162, 166, 169, 171, 172

Goal (*continued*)
-finding process, 160
harmony, 161, 169, 171
neutrality, 161, 162
-relation curve, 162-172, 175, 189
relations, 159-175
of regional growth policies, 163-170
of regional and national growth policies, 171-172
Government activity, 6, 159, 160, 161, 176, 188, 189
Government expenditures, 177, 180, 181
Graph theory, 20, 21, 22, 32, 59, 79, 80, 81
Grid system, 12
Group membership, 58
Growth determinant, 5, 6, 24, 45, 49, 119, 132, 137-145, 151, 159, 163, 177, 190, 191, 193, 198
external, 7, 49, 51, 53-78, 84-114, 137-145
internal, 24-45, 51, 84, 94, 98, 99, 100, 102, 104
Growth differential; *see* Interregional growth differential
Growth pole, 19, 44, 151, 180, 190-193, 199
Growth potential; *see* Development potential
Growth rate, 31, 127, 135-146, 176, 187, 199
Guaranteed production points, 165

Hierarchy of goals, 160
Holland, 50
Homogeneity, 18, 22
Household sector, 11

Identification, 109
Imitation, 72, 73, 80
Immiserizing growth, 104
Immobility; *see* Mobility
Impact analysis, 161, 177, 180
Implications of the model, 126, 132-152
Import, 66, 86, 87, 90, 92, 94, 95, 97, 99, 100-110, 111, 112, 145, 149-150, 168, 178, 180
level, 103
substitute, 104, 105, 108, 110
Incidence, 32-35, 36, 39-41, 44-45
Income; *see* Regional income
effect, 106
produced, 69
received, 69
Indifference curve, 90, 92, 107
Indirect control, 196
Indivisibilities, 40

Industrial-complex analysis, 126
Infant region, 193
Information, 29, 38-40, 54-59, 61, 62, 67, 69-75, 78-82, 121, 135, 142
content, 55
flow, 57, 58, 59, 62, 70, 79, 80, 81, 85, 135
informal, 57, 58, 59, 62, 71
impulse, 57, 71
lag, 40
obstacle, 40, 60, 81, 85
policy, 200
theory, 54-57, 61, 83
Infrastructure, 25, 63, 66, 68, 79, 126, 185, 189, 192, 194, 196, 197
Infrastructure outlays, 182
Innovation, 36-40, 72, 79, 81
partial, 72
total, 72
Input, 25, 26, 27, 53, 66, 69, 125, 126
coefficient, 178, 179
-output model, 2, 97, 126, 131, 152, 178-182, 186, 191
-output table, 23
price, 147
requirements, 178, 179
Institutional setting of regional planning, 198
Instrument variable; *see* Policy instruments
Integration, 85, 114
Intermediate demand, 178, 183
Internal economies, 40, 126, 191
International trade theory, 49-51, 91-92, 95, 96, 193
Interregional
commodity, 51-52, 88
demand, 94, 95-98, 109, 111, 148
exchange of commodities; *see* Exchange of commodities
growth differential, 7, 119, 131, 132-156, 191
income differences, 133-134, 173, 192
interaction, 2, 3, 5, 6, 49, 50, 52, 53, 76-78, 84-115, 126-131, 141; *see also* Mobility of factors and Exchange of commodities
mobility of labor; *see* Mobility
multiplier; *see* Multiplier
optimum, 3
price difference, 88, 91, 92
specialization, 89, 91
trade; *see* Exchange of commodities
Intervening opportunities, 62
Invention, 36-40, 69, 71, 72, 78-80, 121
Investment, 28-29, 31, 34, 38, 41, 43, 45, 66-67, 72, 74, 97, 113-114, 120, 122, 185, 187

Key industry, 191, 192

Labor, 26, 35, 36, 41, 53–66, 72, 75, 83,
    120, 121, 125, 127, 130, 135–143,
    166, 180
Labor-supply measures, 193
Land, 11, 25, 26, 28, 77, 147
    demand for, 147
Leading region, 132
Leading sector, 133
Leakage, 149
Leontief matrix, 179
Leveling effect, 146–151, 168, 190, 192
Limited rationality, 53, 54, 61, 83
Linear programming, 182–185, 187
Linkage, 20, 21, 45, 126, 141, 181, 182,
    191
Location, 1, 3, 5, 11, 13, 14, 15, 16, 40,
    55, 61, 63, 64, 72, 73, 134, 153,
    176, 186, 192, 198, 199, 200
    of agricultural activities, 1, 11, 13,
        15, 16, 19
    of consumption activities, 12
    of industries, 1, 11, 13, 15, 16, 19
    policy, 194
    of production activities, 12, 19
    of residential activities, 1, 11, 13, 15,
        16, 34
    study, 178
    of tertiary activities, 1, 11, 13, 15, 16
    theory, 153
    unit, 11, 12
Locational
    advantage, 36, 134, 186
    characteristics, 13, 14
    point, 13
    requirement, 13, 14, 79

Macroconcept of the static structure, 6
Marginal man, 54
Marginal productivity, 30, 36, 65, 92, 136,
    140, 163, 164, 165, 170, 172, 175,
    188, 189
Marginal productivity criterion, 187
Marginal-value product, 30, 136
Market economy, 193, 196
Market mechanism, 125, 187, 188
Mass media, 57, 58, 59
Message, 55
Migration; see Mobility of labor
Mill price, 88, 89, 197
Minimum output levels; see Guaranteed
    production points
Mobility
    of capital, 61, 66–68, 120, 127–129,
        137–139, 167
    coefficient, 128–131, 137–138
    of commodities, 76–78, 84, 85–89,
        110–115, 126, 145, 151; see also
        Exchange of commodities

Mobility (continued)
    of factors, 2, 5, 35, 36, 39–41, 49, 51–
        83, 84, 96, 110–115, 126–131,
        165–168
    differing degrees, 136–146
    international, 62
    interregional, 62
    intraregional, 32, 62
    of labor, 36, 53–66, 77, 111, 130, 137–
        143, 166
    policy, 194, 195
    range, 165
    of technical knowledge, 69–76, 78–83,
        135, 137, 139
Monetary policy, 196
Moral suasion, 200
Movement of factors; see Mobility of
    factors
Multiple-group membership, 58
Multiplier, 95, 96, 114, 115, 148–150,
    155, 168
Multiplier-accelerator model, 24
Multiregion system, 185

National development and relation to
    regional growth, 5, 152, 171–173,
    192
National economy, 3, 22, 45, 50, 52, 69,
    173, 174, 195
National growth policy, 171–173
National-policy instrument, 195
Negative interregional income tax, 198
Network study, 59
Neutralization policy, 148

Objective function, 182–185
Offer curve, 106
Opportunities, 55, 57, 58, 59, 60, 62, 63,
    77, 188, 194
Opportunity costs of goals, 174, 184
Optimality with immobility of one re-
    source, 167
Optimizing behavior, 176; see also Limited
    rationality
Optimum analysis, 5
Organizational innovations, 39
Origin, 34, 120
Output, 24–26, 30, 31, 36–39, 42, 43, 53,
    66, 69, 77, 78, 83, 88, 89, 94, 96,
    119, 125, 126, 127, 135, 138,
    163–167, 171, 173, 174, 179, 180,
    181, 185, 188, 190, 193
Output vector, 179, 180

Pareto optimum, 5, 125
Partial location theory, 1, 15, 23
Patent system, 40, 73, 81

Pattern of persistence, 77
Philipps curve, 162
Physical capital, 67
Piecemeal policy, 160
Place utility, 54, 61, 62
Planning period, 190, 192, 193
Polarization, 32-33, 34-36, 39-41, 45, 191
Policy instruments, 3, 5, 7, 159, 161-163, 176, 177, 182, 183, 185, 187, 189, 190, 193-200
Policy maker, 154-160, 163, 176, 178, 180, 186, 189, 190, 192, 193
Population, 35, 36, 120, 147
Possibility analysis, 6, 109, 132, 152
Predisposition of receiver, 54, 57, 59, 70, 79
Pressure groups, 160
Price effect, 107
Price structure of production functions, 125
Principle of equal marginal sacrifice, 197-198
Priorities, 163, 173
Private costs, 186
Probability theory, 59
Process innovations, 39
Product innovations, 39
Production
    advantage, 52, 85, 91, 92, 136
    conditions, 52, 84, 89, 98
    elasticities, 127, 135, 136
    function, 24, 25, 28, 39, 41, 65, 66, 89, 125, 127, 132, 136, 164, 165, 168, 172, 175, 188
    -possibility frontier; see Transformation curve
    potential; see Capacity
Productivity criterion, 187
Profit, 29, 34, 40, 43, 73, 76
Profit rate; see Rate of return
Propensity to import, 148-150
Protection, 87
Public investment; see Infrastructure

Ratchet effect, 34, 77
Rate
    of return, 29, 30, 31, 34, 67, 68, 120, 127-129, 136-140, 143
    of transformation between goals, 169
    of transformation between outputs, 90
Raw-material innovations, 39
Reallocation of resources, 90, 92, 106, 115, 125, 145
Receiver, 57, 59, 70, 71, 79, 81
Redundancy, 56

Reference-group behavior, 53, 54, 55, 59
Region, 2, 5, 6, 16, 21
    agglomerated, 195, 199
    closed, 6, 24, 69, 85
    contracting, 152
    core, 151
    delineation of, 2, 5, 16-23
    depressed area, 180, 186, 195, 199
    exchange, 19
    nodal, 19
    open, 49, 51, 53, 68, 69, 85, 94, 180
    planning, 22, 23
    size of, 22, 50, 149
    stagnant, 152, 168
    trade, 19
    types of, 151-152
    underdeveloped, 5, 149
Regional
    commodity, 51-52, 88-89, 96
    -demand pattern, 52
    growth, 3, 4, 6, 11
        closed region, 24-46
        open region, 49-115
        two-region-system, 126-130
    growth policy, 144, 148, 159-174, 176, 178, 185, 187, 189, 193
    incidence of national policy instruments, 196
    income, 28, 29, 42, 43, 49, 50, 69, 83, 84, 93, 94, 95, 98, 102, 103, 109, 111, 112, 119, 133, 148, 149, 173, 177-181, 183, 185, 186, 190
    policy, 3, 5, 71, 145, 148, 159, 160, 161, 168, 174
    policy instruments, 194, 195
    product; see Output
    public finance, 198
Regionally balanced growth, 133
Regressive tax rate, 199
Reinforcing effect, 142-144, 145, 151, 191
Research, 38, 39, 70, 71, 78, 121
Residents concept, 4, 69, 133
Restraints, 182, 183, 185
Retained earnings, 29, 34, 72
Returns to scale, 164
Robertson lag, 28

Savings, 28, 29, 43, 68, 72, 73, 120
Saving function, 43
Search behavior, 38, 54, 59-62, 69, 70
Search costs, 61-62
Search theory, 59-61, 83
Second-best solution, 145
Sector, 178, 179, 180, 185
Sectoral-growth theory, 152
Sectoral policy, 196
Self-fulfilling prophecy, 58
Self-sufficiency chart, 181

Sender, 56, 57, 58, 59, 70, 80, 81
Sequential-information gathering, 61
Set theory, 12–22, 78–82
Shadow price, 184
Shift analysis, 152
Signal, 55, 56, 57, 71
Simplex criterion, 184, 187
Simulation model, 14, 16, 23, 59
Size of market area, 197
Slack variable, 184
Social
  action, 53
  benefit, 130, 186, 187
  cost, 130, 186, 187
  overhead capital; see Infrastructure
  structure, 57
  system, 19, 25, 28, 42, 46, 54, 62, 85,
    141, 153, 188, 189
  wants, 186, 196
Space, 1, 5, 11, 12, 13, 22, 36, 51, 54, 62,
    71, 83, 159
Spatial
  effects of growth determinants, 31–35,
    36, 39–41, 44–45, 51
  effects of national instruments, 195
  incidence, 32–36, 39–40, 44–45
  origin, 32–36, 39–40, 44–45
  point, 11, 12, 13, 14, 16, 17, 18, 21,
    32, 33, 34, 39, 44, 45, 55, 56,
    61, 66, 76, 78–82, 186, 194
  structure, 6, 28, 31, 34, 35, 41, 44, 51,
    71, 72, 153
Spillover effect, 148, 180, 187
Stability, 175
Stage theory of regional development, 132
Stationary state, 31
Status-quo forecast, 160
Stimulus-response, 53
Stock variable, 26, 28, 127
Strategy, 5, 7, 188–193
System, 19
Subsidy, 182, 196, 198
Supply, 24, 42, 44, 85–88, 103–108, 119,
    126
  deficit, 109
  place, 34
  surplus, 109
Surprise value, 55

Target; see Goal
Tariff, 85, 195
Tax, 196, 199
  rate, 177, 182
  -transfer mechanism, 198
  yield, 198
Technical knowledge, 25, 26, 27, 35, 36–
    41, 46, 64, 69–76, 78–83, 111,

Technical knowledge (continued)
    112, 121, 135–136, 139, 143, 146,
    163, 165, 168, 173, 175, 188
Technical progress, 36–42, 46, 83, 87, 93,
    101, 102, 110, 115, 135
  export-biased, 101
  factor neutral, 101, 142
  import-biased, 101
Technical-progress function, 42
Technical-progress instruments, 194
Terms of trade, 90, 92, 93, 98–110, 111–
    115, 122, 168
  definition, 101
  deterioration of, 104, 109, 115, 145,
    150
  improvement in, 103, 108, 111, 115,
    145
Thünen rings, 15
Time, 5, 11, 26, 62
Trade; see Exchange of commodities and
    International trade theory
Trade barriers, 50, 51, 84–89, 90, 92, 93,
    94, 95, 98, 99, 106, 111, 114, 122,
    146
Trade-off curve, 162, 163, 165, 166, 168–
    173
Trade surplus, 113
Transfer of capital goods, 66–68, 111
Transfer of technical knowledge; see Mo-
    bility of technical knowledge
Transfer payment, 196, 197, 198
Transformation curve, 65, 66, 68, 75, 76,
    83, 90, 91, 92, 100, 101, 102, 106,
    114, 174
Transmission interval, 73
Transmission of growth impulses, 94–104,
    114
Transportation, 3, 11, 25–27, 52, 87, 93,
    102, 126
Transportation cost, 1, 16, 39, 40, 41, 51,
    52, 62, 64, 65, 76, 77, 85–89, 114,
    115, 186, 197
Transport innovations, 39, 40
Transport input, 25
Transport resources, 25, 26
Triangularized matrix, 181
Two-region model, 51–52, 62, 126–130,
    134–152, 168, 174, 176, 180, 182,
    185, 187, 189, 190, 192

Uncertainty, 55, 56, 57
Urban area, 98
Use place, 32

Value added, 178, 179, 180, 183
Value judgment, 160, 161, 163, 198

Volume structure of production functions, 125

Voting process, 160

Wage rate, 29, 34, 35, 36, 40, 43, 55, 57, 59, 63, 65, 76, 120, 137–140, 143

Welfare, 4, 99
    effects, 99, 102, 103, 109, 114, 122
    gains, 102, 109, 111, 115
    losses, 102, 103, 109, 111
Withdrawal effect, 64, 76, 97, 111, 143, 151, 152, 168, 173, 191, 193